Saints and she-devils

Uoluptas.   Uirtus.

Saints
and
she-devils

Images of women
in the 15th and 16th centuries

2/91

The Rubicon Press

The Rubicon Press Ltd.
57 Cornwall Gardens
London SW7 4BE

© 1987 Foundation Werkplaats Wetenschap en Maatschappij
Prins Hendriklaan 19A te Zeist (NL)

© 1987 Translations:
C.M.H. Sion, MA: pp. 59–82 and 101–127
R.M.J. van der Wilden, MA: 7–58, 83–100
and 129–159

British Library Cataloguing in Publication Data

Saints and she-devils : images of women in
the 15th and 16th centuries
1. Women in art — History
I. Dresen-Coenders, Lène
II. Bange, Petty
III. Tussen heks & heilige. *English.*
704.9'424 N7630

ISBN 0-948695-06-4

The original Dutch edition was published in 1985 by SUN, Nijmegen (NL) under the title *Tussen heks en heilige* (ISBN 90 6168 250 9) for the exhibition of the same name held in the Nijmeegs Museum 'Commanderie van Sint-Jan'.

This book was compiled by a study group consisting of Lène Dresen-Coenders (editor), Petty Bange, Ton Brandenbarg, Grietje Dresen, Ellen Muller, Jeanne Marie Noël and Renée Pigeaud.

Layout and cover design: Leo de Bruin, Utrecht
Front cover: Arnt van Tricht (Kalkar, from c. 1530 onwards)
Towel rail, c. 1540, oak, polychrome high relief
Städtisches Museum Haus Koekoek, Cleves.
p. 2: *Hercules at the crossroads* from: Sebastian Brant, *Stultifer Navis,*
Latin translation of the *Narrenschiff* by Jacobus Locher Philomusus
Paris, Geoffroy de Marnef, 1498. 4° Illustration fol. 129 v: p.2
Rijksmuseum
Meermanno-Westreenianum, The Hague.
p. 6: Follower of the Master of Koudwater ('s-Hertogenbosch, c. 1470–1480) *St Anne with Virgin and Child* Walnut with original polychrome (damaged), Museum voor Religieuze Kunst, Uden.

Printed and bound by Biddles Ltd. of Guildford and King's Lynn

Contents

Introduction   7

Petty Bange, Grietje Dresen, Jeanne Marie Noël,
*'Who can find a virtuous woman?' Married and
unmarried women at the beginning of the modern time*   9

Renée Pigeaud, *Woman as temptress. Urban morality
in the 15th century*   39

Lène Dresen-Coenders, *Witches as devils'
concubines. On the origin of fear of witches and
protection against witchcraft*   59

Ellen Muller, *Saintly virgins. The veneration of
virgin saints in religious women's communities*   83

Ton Brandenbarg, *St Anne and her family. The
veneration of St Anne in connection with concepts
of marriage and the family in the early-modern period*   101

Ellen Muller, Jeanne Marie Noël, *Humanist views
on art and morality. Theory and image*   129

Introduction

The present-day changes in the division of roles between man and woman, and the resistance they engender in 'traditional' circles, give rise to a number of questions. Where are the roots of the so-called traditional distribution of roles, in which the husband is allocated the part of the master and bread-winner of the household and his wife's role is to care for the home and behave with modesty, chastity and obedience? How old is this tradition and to what extent does it apply to all sections of the population? To find an answer to these questions requires the co-operation of people from numerous disciplines. Historians, art historians, theologians, philosophers and social scientists have to consult the sources at their disposal and collectively endeavour to achieve as well-founded an interpretation as possible.

There are indications that during the transition from the Middle Ages to the modern era (1400–1600) people were just as preoccupied with the role of woman as they are at the present day. It was the period of growing persecution of witches on the one hand and of new idealised images on the other. The theme of 'woman' was treated in numerous learned tracts. Literature and the visual arts vied with one another to present examples of the good woman, but more especially of the bad, who were lecherous, domineering or crafty.

An interdisciplinary study group chose this period for in-depth research. Separate studies have been published by members of the study group on subjects including: the rise of the persecution of witches and its socio-psychological background; the excessive veneration of St Anne – the grandmother of Jesus – and the motives

of her propagandists; the shift from chivalrous to bourgeois motifs in prints portraying the man-woman relationship; and a new type of education for girls from the bourgeoisie, the so-called 'French' schools.

From the very beginning the study group also set itself the objective of carrying out preparatory work with a view to a presentation of art-historical material. This material is to be found in European and American museums in great quantity and variety. The contributions, which are published here with the title *Saints and She-Devils*, discuss these works of art from the point of view of the process of social change, to which the man-woman relationship was subject. They formed the basis for an exhibition of the same name (Dutch title: *Tussen heks en heilige*), which was held in Nijmegen in the museum 'De Commanderie van St Jan' from November 1985 to January 1986 with the backing of the Ministry of Welfare, Health and Culture. They also form the basis for a new exhibition entitled 'Helse en hemelse vrouwen' (Diabolic and Saintly Women) to be held in the Rijksmuseum Catharijneconvent in Utrecht from March to June 1988. Other variants may well be conceivable.

The translation of this collection of articles was made possible thanks to a subsidy from the Emancipation Research Stimulation Group of the Ministry of Social Affairs. The study group hopes that this book will make a contribution to the international discussion on the development of the Western image of woman.

The authors of *Saints and She-Devils* have tried to show the extent to which our 'traditional' image of woman bears the stamp of the transition period from the

Middle Ages to the modern era. Now that we have for centuries been accustomed to the idealised picture of the masterful husband and the sweet, submissive and solicitous wife, we find it hard to imagine how great the fear of woman's power was at that time and how many means were employed to keep it in check. Our surprise about this situation can perhaps help us to be more open-minded about the way in which we view the present shifts in the balance of power between man and woman in their social context. Those who fear, for instance, that the emancipation of women is a question of an extremely slow ongoing process, may be encouraged by the fact that there was a time when women had a more influential voice. Those who believe that the so-called traditional role of woman is determined by religious principles or biological facts, will discover that the image of woman is also subject to change and is a product of its time. Those who are afraid that an 'elite' may take no account of the situation of the 'ordinary' woman, will be reassured to know that it was precisely amongst the 'ordinary' women that a qualified balance of power lasted longest in the old situation. Fear is a bad counsellor. That is something else which we can learn from the period around 1500, when the fear of woman's power led to belittlement, ridicule, persecution and ultimately to a restriction of her role, which still affects us today.

Lène Dresen-Coenders

PETTY BANGE, GRIETJE DRESEN, JEANNE MARIE NOËL

'Who can find a virtuous woman?' Married and unmarried women at the beginning of the modern time

I. HISTORICAL BACKGROUND

The period from 1300 to 1500, thus the 14th and 15th centuries, are known as the Late Middle Ages. This indicates that though this period still belongs to the Middle Ages, a number of impulses had already been generated for the major changes, as a result of which the centuries thereafter were no longer counted as part of the medieval period. These changes took place in the social, economic, political, religious and cultural fields. A short elucidation will be given below. From 1500 onwards – there is, of course, no question of a clearly defined boundary – we refer to the New Age, which begins with the Renaissance and Humanism, when we are talking about art or scholarship. Of course terms such as Late Middle Ages and New Age were applied by historians to this period at a much later date, but that does not alter the fact that during this time people themselves did sometimes realise that changes were taking place.

During the 14th century, Europe was ravaged by various disasters, both natural and of man's making. Already by the beginning of the century the population explosion of the previous period had led to food shortages, which became even more serious on account of the crop failures resulting from climatological deterioration when it became wetter and colder. In 1347 the plague germ was carried from China via the Eastern Mediterranean and the Italian cities. In a few years this was to wipe out about a quarter to a third of the population. After this great epidemic the plague, the 'Black Death', remained endemic, which meant that from time to time there were fresh outbreaks here and there. In the 17th century it returned with even greater intensity and in 1635 in Nijmegen, for instance, there was a severe outbreak, which resulted in the death of some 6000 people in the course of one year.

From 1337 to 1453 the Hundred Years' War was fought out on French territory with the English fiefs in France as the stakes. The English were ultimately forced to withdraw from all the areas they had held with the exception of Calais, which remained in their hands until 1558, when it was captured by the French. For the population, particularly in the country areas, the progress of the often badly paid English and French armies, though for the farmer their 'nationality' made no real difference, meant repeated plundering and ruined harvests.

It was at this period that the first mass peasant revolts took place: in 1326 in Flanders, in 1358 in the Paris area and in 1381 in the neighbourhood of London. The position of the peasants, which had gradually been improving with fewer burdens and obligations, was threatened by the factors mentioned above and this lead to a number of outbreaks of rebellion. It is noticeable that in all three of these revolts the leader did not come from the peasant class and that the neighbouring town or towns backed the rebellion. At the end of the 14th century a similar type of revolt took place in the north of Holland against price increases and heavier burdens which was also supported by the townspeople: the so-called Cheese and Bread Rebellion. Just like the other three, this was soon crushed. However, the most notorious were the peasant revolts in the German Empire, also called peasant wars, which had already begun by the end of the 14th century and continued through to the beginning of the 16th century. Here again, the peasants opposed the nobility and the clergy as they wanted to impose heavy burdens on them. The years 1524–1525 formed the climax of the struggle, when the peasants ultimately suffered a crushing defeat.

During this time the Low Countries were also affected by most of the disasters mentioned above, which resulted in a higher death rate than in the preceding period. It is impossible to give an accurate figure for the total population, but it seems likely that it was in the neighbourhood of 2.5 million. The greatest concentration of population was along the coast and the estuaries with only about a third of the population living in the towns.

Up to ±1450 agricultural productivity was on the increase, which did not however mean that the value of the products was increasing.Indeed, at the beginning of the 15th century there can even be said to have been a grain crisis during some of the years in various areas; that is to say that the grain prices were unfavourable in relation to other products and to wages. Through intensification of arable farming the Low Countries managed to survive this crisis reasonably well, although the great grain crisis of the Eighties had disastrous consequences. The failure of the harvest led to a great deal of malnutrition, which made people very susceptible to all kinds of disease, including comparatively harmless illnesses.

In the social field the Late Middle Ages were a time of change. The idea of the division of mankind into three classes – clergy, nobles and peasants, those who pray, those who fight and those who work – which was of real significance in the Early Middle Ages and still remained so in the main medieval period, did not suddenly disappear, but was opened up by the advent of a new class, the bourgeoisie, which came to play an increasingly large part in society. The bourgeoisie, who like the peasants had to work hard to provide for its keep, was therefore regarded with disdain by the nobility, though with a certain degree of envy at the same time, on account of the amount of money that was sometimes earned. It was thus more or less in spite of themselves that noble families sometimes allied themselves with rich merchants. The towns, where the powerful bourgeois class grew up, also had another group within its walls: the day labourers, the very poorest section, who, attracted by urban prosperity, had exchanged their miserable existence in the country for life in the town, which in many cases was even more wretched. In the Netherlands the towns played an important part in the economic and cultural field, although the population in the country continued to form the majority. In the province of Holland in particular there were a number of towns which were large for that period (i.e. 10,000–20,000 inhabitants), such as the trading town of Amsterdam or the industrial town of Leiden. Although there were also towns of importance in the East of The Netherlands (Nijmegen, Deventer) comparatively more people in this area lived in the country.

From the political point of view The Netherlands were far from being a unified entity. Officially the greatest part still belonged to the German Empire, but in practice most of the feudal lords went their own way. A good example of this are the Counts of Holland, who were very independent and frequently took no notice of the German Emperor.

In the 15th century the Dukes of Burgundy managed, by means of conquests and marriages, to unite a number of the Netherlandish territories under them. Their policy of centralisation led, amongst other things, to the establishment of an auditing chamber to supervise the collection of taxes and of the Court of Malines as the highest judicial body. In each territory a Stadholder was appointed as the representative of the duke. However, after the death of Charles the Bold in 1477, the new Duchess, his daughter Mary, who was married to the late Emperor Maximilian, was obliged to concede a number of privileges, so that the centralisation was to some extent reversed. When she died, in 1482, her husband became regent for their son, who was still a minor.

The course of events altered rapidly when this boy, Duke Philip the Fair, came to power in 1494, and entered into matrimony with a Spanish Crown Princess in 1496, later enabling his son Charles to unite the German Empire and the Kingdom of Spain under his leadership. It lasted only a few decades before The Netherlands rose in rebellion against their overlord (then Philip II). This revolt was to last eighty years resulting in the independence of the Northern Netherlands, in 1648.

After a period of comparative prosperity and calm at the beginning of the 16th century, the political situation in the Northern Netherlands again became unstable from about 1530 onwards and the economic situation deteriorated. The rural industries proved dangerous competitors for the towns, which then tried to introduce a number of restrictive measures with varying degrees of success. The situation in the towns themselves was not always favourable either at this period: the majority of the inhabitants had a very low standard of living, wealth being in the hands of a very small minority. The 16th century too had its share of crop failures with resultant famine. The unstable political situation led to trade upheaval, resulting in a price rise for a number of products. A devaluation of silver took place and inflation made itself felt around 1550. Unemployment increased as a result and there was a rise in the number of people without means.

The situation outlined above was one of the causes – though naturally not the sole cause – of why large groups of people were so receptive to the idea of the Reformation, which had begun its spectacular advance in 1517, when Martin Luther published his 95 theses denouncing the sale of indulgences; nevertheless this only took place after an 'incubation period' of many years. An extreme manifestation of the new movement was the foundation of a New Jerusalem in Münster by the Anabaptists; however, the city was captured in 1535 and a massacre followed.

In the Late Middle Ages there had already been various reform movements within the Church, but they had not contested the authority of the Church and its institutions. Examples of such trends were the Modern Devotion in the Netherlands (late 14th century), the observance movement within various monastic orders, and the Councils of Constance (1414–1418) and Basle (1431).

At the beginning of the 16th century the time was ripe for a break with the Catholic Church, which turned out to be irrevocable. In The Netherlands too, the Reformation rapidly gained acceptance, although the greater part of the population remained Catholic.

The Catholic reaction to this was the Counter-Reformation, which found expression, for instance, in the Council of Trent (1545–1563), which represented a breakthrough in the Catholic Church on account of the numerous decisions on reform. A prominent role was also played by the Order of Jesuits, founded by the Spanish nobleman Ignatius Loyola in 1534; the Order saw preaching and education as its principle tasks and could thus be used to combat the 'heretics'.

Such is the historical background therefore against which we must form a picture of the cultural life and attitudes of the people of The Netherlands. Ideas on life and death, religion, the arts, society and human relationships in general were coloured by the situation outlined in the brief survey given above. The man/woman relationship and the picture of woman which emerges from the 15th and 16th century sources were also influenced by the developments previously mentioned, particularly by the social changes and alterations in the previously indisputable role patterns.

II. WOMAN AND MARRIAGE

Marriage and discussion

We do not have a great deal of information on the position of women in marriage and in the family round about 1500. As far as The Netherlands are concerned there has up to now been little research on the subject. There are a number of detailed studies in existence in neighbouring European countries, but because the Netherlands developed along their own lines on account of their lack of feudal tradition and comparatively early[1] and wide-spread urbanisation, it is not always possible to apply these studies to our territories.

What has been the most comprehensively catalogued up to now, consists for the greater part in 'ideological' material: ecclesiastical tracts, legal texts, prints and other visual material. In the pictures which have come down to us from the period in question we see certain themes and representations of women frequently reappearing – the articles in this book endeavour to give a portrayal of them. The themes concern themselves with the position of women within, but especially *outside* marriage: with her role as temptress and threat to individual virtue and social order. But we also show her counterpart: the virgin: the modest wife and chaste widow. Does the fact that these themes were so popular around 1500 point to actual developments concerning marriage and conjugal ethics, developments in which the position of *women* is also or indeed specifically under discussion? So long as we lack substantial information on women's position in society and the history of the family during this period in The Netherlands, such conclusions must remain cautious and tentative. What we can say with certainty, however, is that marriage and women's position within it were topical themes. And that applies not only to the visual arts and to printing – which began to develop in the second half of the 15th century – but also to other types of material, which can give us an idea of the conceptual world of that time: theological writings, tracts by humanists, medical doctors and so on.

Several of the authors in this book have related the impassioned discussions and disputes, which were taking place during this period over the position (and sometimes literally over the *body*) of woman to the development of a bourgeois way of life.

Attention is sometimes drawn to the remarkable family pattern – marrying late and living in a comparatively small group, the so-called 'nuclear family' – which a number of family historians regard as typical of north-western Europe in this modern time.[2] Exactly when this typical Western family pattern may have started is a subject of controversy,[3] and it was associated for a long time with certain social groups. A late marriage was supposed to be connected with the fact that people first wanted to work and save up for their own household, necessary if people did not want to continue living in the parental home. However, such a reason for marrying late carried less conviction amongst the well-to-do and the very poor, for whom there was little opportunity to save. Moreover, for the latter group the principle reason for concluding an official marriage, namely for the law of inheritance, was of little significance. Thus for a long time they continued to marry 'clandestinely' which is to say they exchanged vows and then cohabited without having had any official witnesses, as required by ecclesiastical or civil authorities.

If one assumes that around 1500 a typical Western family pattern was already spreading to some extent and certainly amongst the bourgeoisie, this means that there was a comparatively high number of marriageable, but still unmarried women and men. When under the influence of the Reformation, celibacy in a religious community – in a monastery or béguinage (house of a lay sisterhood) – became less highly regarded, the need to effect a good marriage increased. We can still glimpse these eager-to-marry groups in the numerous prints of this period which depict a young woman or a young man seducing an old, but well-endowed partner.

Be that as it may, the discussions over the significance of marriage and of woman's place within it, blossomed forth about 1500 at various levels. If in the course of the discussion fresh emphasis came to be laid on a number of points, this may be connected with the transition from a more agrarian to a predominantly 'bourgeois' pattern of society, as is contended here by various authors. Another reason for this shift of emphasis would appear to be the fact, that during the period in question, more people – and at this time that meant almost exclusively men – were able to express their views. In the second half of the 15th century an increasing number of laymen had the opportunity of becoming 'lettered' through the establishment and expansion of universities and schools and in particular through the invention of printing. These laymen began increasingly to join in the discussions on morals, which were after all ultimately concerned with their lives and their interests. And what subject lent itself better to lay comment than that of marriage, which had for a long time been one of the most extensively treated themes in ecclesiastical morality, in sermons and in confessional manuals, and had therefore always been approached from the viewpoint of a celibate clergy? The laymen who now joined in the discussion were still predominantly men. And perhaps this was the reason for the relatively large amount of attention paid in these debates to the nature and place of *women*. Now that there were laymen participating in the talks who possibly themselves shared their life officially with a woman, women became all the more compelling an object of care and concern.

As for the rest, these new authors – clerk, humanist or reformer – continued to move within the same *Christian* tradition which had become accepted in Europe in the course of the centuries as the pre-eminent guardian of marriage and of its solemnisation. Most of the authors deliberately harked back to a number of elements from this tradition, precisely to be able to formulate their own criticism and new approach. By falling back on tradition and above all on the Bible, they tried to present their own views as being more in line with an original Christian way of life. In order to give a true idea of these reformulated ideas and to show them in their proper context it is therefore necessary to make a small detour. In the following paragraphs we shall begin with the most important passages from the Bible, which are repeatedly quoted in support of Christian conjugal morality. We shall then given an outline of the most important develop-

Quinten Metsys (1465–1530), *Unequal love*, panel.

ments which preceded our period (the 15th and 16th centuries) and are reflected therein. And finally we shall return to the issues on which these discussions focussed.

Biblical passages which are often quoted in connection with conjugal morality

The first scriptural passage in which the community of man and woman and procreation are mentioned is to be found at the beginning of the Bible, in the story of the creation. And here we are immediately confronted by problems, since there are two different versions of the creation (originating from two different traditions). According to one version, man and woman were created equal in God's image and likeness; in the other versions woman was created from the rib of man. In our own time we prefer the first version whereas ecclesiastical writers clearly preferred the second, until long after the Middle Ages. The majority of them believed that it was possible to conclude from the latter theory that the inferiority of woman was already inherent in the order of creation (and Eve's part in the Fall only strengthened this conviction. It was only in the order of salvation, 'in Christ', they believed, that man and woman could be said to be equal).

Apart from that, the references to the Old Testament were very selective. A number of the practices described, such as polygamy, were after all not exactly in line with Christian conjugal morality. However, later on various figures were happily cited in the context of conjugal morality, as for example faithful Abraham and Sarah, who had a child late in life, or the dedicated, courageous widow Judith.

In the Gospels in the New Testament, which recount the stories of Jesus' life, marriage is not really mentioned very much. Jesus' most important pronouncements on the subject contain criticism of putting away your own wife all too easily (Matthew 9,9). In general Jesus' comments on marriage stipulations are restricted to drawing the attention of men and women to their hardness of heart and the persistency of sin. He does not really institute his own new law. And yet there were

Heinrich Aldegrever (1502–1555), *The creation of Eve*, engraving.

14

numerous theologians who used the fact that Christ performed his first miracle at a wedding (changing the water into wine at the marriage in Cana, John 2) to infer that marriage had received a new significance instituted by Christ. The authors, who later argued that marriage should be recognised as one of the seven sacraments, used this as one of their grounds. That marriage was a good estate for Christians, provided it was experienced as chastely as possible, was also inferred by the Church from the fact that Christ was born from the union of a woman and a man, Mary and Joseph, even though it was a *virgin* mother.

The epistles of St. Paul form a more important New Testament source for marriage morality than the pronouncements of Jesus. In Paul's frequently cited views on marriage, the pronouncement that it is better to remain 'even as he' occupies a central position. This would seem to imply 'do not marry'. 'But if they cannot contain, let them marry: for it is better to marry than to burn.'[4] (1 Cor. 7, 8–9). These pronouncements of Paul must be seen in the light of the early Christians' eschatological expectations. However the interpretation given by the Fathers of the Church amounted to an absolute preference and greater esteem for the virgin state. Marriage was only considered healthy as a remedy against all too great desire. Moreover, even within the married state the satisfaction of lust was not permissable without restriction. According to ecclesiastical morality which took shape under the influence of Augustine (354–430), the sexual act may only take place for the purpose of procreation for God, to save the other from fornication, or to pay the conjugal 'debt' (the claim on your body by the other, 1 Cor. 7, 3–4).

As well as 1 Cor. 7, Paul's epistle to the Ephesians has been the subject of a great deal of commentary. In the fifth chapter of this epistle Paul compares the relationship between man and wife with the relationship of Christ to His Church. He calls this relationship a great mystery. This was another passage which was frequently used later to decide on the sacramental nature of marriage, and in

Hieronymus Bosch (c.1450–1516), *The marriage in Cana*, panel. Museum Boymans-van Beuningen, Rotterdam.

particular to prove the *indissolubility* of the marriage ties. The contention was that Christ could after all have only one Church. The passage did not always have very pleasing consequences for women. It is true that the man is asked to love his wife as Christ loves the Church, but the woman must show obedience to and respect for the man since he is the head, just as Christ is the Head of the Church.

An influential view of marriage and virginity: Augustine

The Church Father Augustine previously mentioned exercised a great and long-lasting influence on conjugal ethics. For Augustine, marriage quite clearly came second in perfection to the virgin state. Yet he did not deny that marriage could also have its merits. In this he turned against manicheism, to which he had himself adhered for some eleven years. This dualistic heretical movement rejected marriage and procreation because procreation was believed to continue the incarceration of the spiritual in the physical. According to Augustine marriage could be called good on account of three *bona*, three good things: *proles* (progeny), *fides* (mutual fidelity, mindful of the teachings of the Church) and *sacramentum*. 'Sacrament' refers here to Paul's pronouncements on marriage as a symbol (Eph. 5,32) and was not yet meant in the sense in which the sacrament is now interpreted. Indeed it was only in the course of the Middle Ages that marriage became part of the seven sacraments and was then accorded the last place. Whether marriage was a sacrament in this later sense – that is to say whether it was instituted anew by Christ and grace was received through the conclusion of the rites – remained a subject of dispute for a long time. A number of Catholic theologians and certainly the reformers refused to count marriage as one of the sacraments instituted by Christ and maintained that the Church had nothing to add to the mutual exchange of marriage vows.

The interpretation of Augustine's views received a renewed impetus and significance, also in the Counter-Reformation, on account of the fact that the reformers turned again to his doctrines – as well as to the Bible – in their theological struggle against the scholastic disputations.

Christian theory and Germanic practice

In the centuries after Augustine, his work and the pastoral directives of Pope Gregory the Great (pope from 590-604) were a particularly important source of conjugal ethics. The admonitions of this pope stem from the time when missionaries were converting little by little Western Europe to Christianity, meanwhile adhering to a principle which Christianity has made good use of ever since the first Roman period, namely whenever possible to adopt the customs and symbols of the prevailing culture and endow them with a Christian significance.

Germanic societies in the Low Countries had their own legal systems. Kinship and marriage relationships formed the basis of these societies. The central role of the kinship, which was organised on patriarchal lines, found expression amongst other things in the important part played by the *bestowal* of the bride in the whole marriage ceremony.

In this ritual bestowal, the father or brother of the girl entrusted her to the protective relationship of the man and his family. However, for a number of the Germanic peoples it was not the ritual bestowal which was the deciding factor in the actual conclusion of the marriage, but the fact that a couple had had intercourse with mutual agreement. This form of marriage was sometimes preceded by abduction, either with or without the foreknowledge of the woman. If the woman consented to the abduction and intercourse had taken place, it was then difficult to annul the marriage. The due marriage portions or gifts were subsequently exchanged with the woman's family, always providing that she had not yet been contractually given away to someone else.

Thus although the ritual bestowal occupied the central place in the Germanic marriage ceremony, the actual marriage was completed in the coitus or 'copula'. This principle was now adjusted to the circumstances and, invested with a Christian significance (the act of becoming one flesh, in which the indissoluble tie between Christ and Church was confirmed), was adopted in the official conjugal ethics of the Church. Up to then the marriage celebration had been based on the Roman rules of law regarding the mutual 'consensus ad idem'.

Towards an ecclesiastical matrimonial law

The linking of the Roman consensus view of marriage with the Germanic emphasis on the 'copula' finally took form in the ecclesiastical matrimonial law, the *canon law*, which came into being from the 10th century onwards. Before that time the Church held certain theological and pastoral views on marriage, which found expression in tracts and confessional manuals, but it did not have its own matrimonial law or its own official marriage ceremony. For the latter, use was made of the civil practices and legislation. From the 10th century onwards marriage ceremonies and the accompanying legal arrangements came increasingly within the power of the church (with the exception of financial and hereditary questions, where people mainly continued to appeal to civil law).

The realisation of canon law owed a great deal to the system and provisions of Roman law, in which the contract occupied a central position. The reversion to Roman law has been linked with the flowering of the towns and the merchant bourgeoisie in Italy (where canon law took form, in particular at the University of Bologna). For the rising merchant bourgeoisie, contracts of course played an important role. Partly as the result of the development of a separate canon law, it was possible from the 11th century onwards to draw clearer dividing lines between the civil-political and the ecclesiastical areas of jurisdiction. Here too the influence of the rising bourgeoisie can be assumed to be a factor. After all it was advantageous for these people to be able to operate autonomously in certain areas, in particular where their political and trade interests were concerned (the Church for instance forbade asking interest on loans). In the marital sphere they attached importance to sound, sanctioned conjugal ethics. Wherever money was in

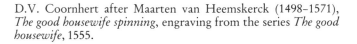

D.V. Coornhert after Maarten van Heemskerck (1498–1571), *The good housewife spinning*, engraving from the series *The good housewife*, 1555.

circulation sexual intercourse should preferably be stable, so as to obviate all sorts of problems connected with care, upbringing and inheritance.

The canonists, who were faced with the task of drawing up a readily usable legal system, reverted to the Roman regulations for matrimonial law concerning a contract between two parties involved. And yet most of them continued to place the actual beginning of the marriage in the 'copula'. This had after all the most practical consequences. The ultimate theological synthesis between the more practical 'copula' view and the 'consensus' view of marriage was formulated in the 12th century by the great Parisian theologian, Peter Lombard, in his famous *libri Senteniarum*. This book served as a manual for theological study until well into the 16th century. All the theological tracts on marriage written in the centuries after Lombard refer directly or indirectly to his Sententiae. Lombard arrived at a synthesis in which marriage *attains legal validity* in the consensus, but only achieves completion in the coitus, the 'consummation'. It is only through the latter that marriage becomes the *indissoluble* symbol of the unity of Christ with His Church (a motive for the undesirability of second marriages, even after the death of the partner; this symbol remained objectively effective and could not be broken, and could not in principle be entered into for a second time in the Church). However, as far as Lombard was concerned the marriage which had not (yet) been 'consummated' was also a valid marriage: marriage as a holy sign already comes into being in the consensus. After all Mary and Joseph also had a full, holy union.

Although from the 10th/11th century onwards the Church was urging an official church solemnisation, for a long time many marriages were still concluded clandestinely. These marriages were considered valid, even though they were forbidden, on pain of exclusion from the sacraments – a measure which is becoming topical again in the Roman Catholic church of our own day.

The great emphasis which the Church has always placed on the free consensus of the partners (whereby the minimum age at which such a decision could be freely taken was also laid down) represented for the woman potential liberation from the paternal authority, to which she was as strictly subject in Germanic as in ancient Roman society. In political tracts, and by the reformers of the 16th century, protests were frequently lodged against the Catholic viewpoint that a marriage could validly take place without the consent of the parents (even though this was indeed desirable).

A new 'rational' foundation for the inferiority of woman: Thomas Aquinas

The great and influential system of thought of Thomas Aquinas (1225-1274), in which he expounded the Christian religious truths with the aid of the Aristotelian philosophy of natural reason, produced a new, 'rational' foundation for the time-honoured views on the inferiority of woman. Thomas argued that man and woman are indeed equal as the work and image of God, but that in the natural order woman is an imperfect being compared to man. Following the line of Aristotle's *De generatione animalum* Thomas maintains that nature is inherently inclined to perfection. When the man's seed enters the woman, the intention is inherent by nature to bring forth a boy. But this intention, this natural objective, can be disturbed; by weather conditions, food, age, and other factors. Then an imperfect being will be conceived, a girl. Because she is inadequate, she will develop an insatiable desire to be fulfilled by the man. For the man is the only one who possesses the generative principle; the female principle only represents the matter to which the male principle lends the form. Although the woman is thus imperfect, her nature does have its function, namely procreation. Apart from this, Thomas considers that in marriage the woman also has a task as the man's companion. However, the man does not really need her.

Thomas, just as most of the Christian writers, emphasised that even though woman is inferior to man in the natural order, as far as salvation is concerned, they are equals. He considered that women could express this relation to salvation better by entering a nunnery than by motherhood. The entry into convents and especially the increase in nunneries and béguinages which can be observed from the 13th up to and including the 15th century certainly cannot be entirely explained by such theological arguments. As we shall see, the convents and béguinages offered women a reasonably free and protected existence.

Scholastics, clerks and moralists, on: towards a lay assessment of marriage

The work of Thomas Aquinas set the seal as it were on the development of scholastic or school theology. This theology was so called after the places where it came into being, in the schools and universities which grew up in Western Europe from the 12th century onwards. These universities were increasingly trying to wrest themselves from the tutelage of the local ecclesiastical authorities, at least in so far as certain faculties were concerned. In the 13th century, the century in which Thomas was writing, this process had not by any means been completed. Nevertheless there were certain subjects which were already being taught by laymen, known as 'clerks'. As a result of the Gregorian Reformation in the 11th century these clerks were obliged to remain celibate, if they wished to continue to enjoy certain advantages which were attached to their state. It can well be imagined that these compulsorily unmarried clerks, who did not live in 'protected' environments, but in towns and at court, not infrequently made a caricature of the Church's views on marriage and woman, and the supposed perfection of the virgin state in particular.

With the increasing number of laymen who had the opportunity of becoming 'learned' or even of teaching and writing, other more profane sounds began slowly to permeate conjugal ethics as they have come down to us in writing. If we look, for example, at the Low Countries in the 14th and 15th centuries, we see a boom in moralistic literature in the vernacular (mirrors of sin, moralising drama etc.) in which the theme of marriage and the relationship between man and woman plays an

D.V. Coornhert after Maarten van Heemskerck (1498–1571), *The good housewife doing business*, engraving from the series *The good housewife*, 1555.

important part. This literature was to an increasing extent being written by laymen. It is true that these laymen made full use of known religious texts which they adapted from Latin into Middle Dutch, but in the course of the adaptation they introduced their own nuances. In the context of our subject this is a very obvious fact. Whereas in religious literature the virgin state is by tradition always more highly esteemed than the marital state, in the secular literature in the vernacular there was already, long before the Reformation, criticism of all those clerics who certainly did not fully live up to their so-called perfect state of life. For those who evidently had great difficulty in leading a life of perfect chastity, marriage presented itself as a good alternative for a Christian life. In marriage lust is tempered in a permissable manner and children are begotten to the glory of God; and who would there be to people the monasteries and nunneries if no more children were to be piously begotten, was the lay moralists' retort to the clergy.

The criticism of an all too externalised, hierarchic Christendom – criticism which is so characteristic of a movement such the Modern Devotion, and which occupies a central position in humanism and the Reformation – was already to be detected here at an early stage. 'Neither status nor habit confer sanctity, only a pure heart leads to holiness', wrote, for example, the author of the *Dietsche Doctrinale* (1345)[7]. This writer and an author such as Jan van Boendale *(Der Leken Spiegel,* (1325) only consider the virgin state superior to the marital if it is perfectly observed. The authors conclude, however, that this is seldom the case. Lay writers such as Jan de Weert[8] or Willem van Hildegaersberch[9] also explicitly defend marriage as a good institution and express severe criticism of the clergy's lack of chastity and hypocritical claim to perfection. All moralists, both clergy and laymen, warned that what made marriage a precarious affair was the vanity, coquetry, voluptousness and unreliability of women. This theme, which is characteristic of a tradition in which it is principally men who express their point of view[10] will be heard again in a variety of forms in the 15th and 16th centuries. Yet gradually some voices begin to be raised in opposition, as we shall see later on.

Criticism of the religious institution

The comparatively high esteem in which marriage was held by the Middle Dutch lay moralists of the 14th and 15th centuries turned into an explicit *preference* for marriage with 16th century humanist authors such as Erasmus. In their defence of marriage (and of woman as wife and mother) the humanists fell back on the ancient original texts, on the Bible and on the classical authors who allotted more room in their work to *reason*, for 'rational' contemplation of human nature. This return to the original texts is characteristic of the humanism of the early modern time.

This humanism developed in 14th century Italy as part of the Renaissance. The renewed interest in the original texts of the classics was inherent in the idea of 'renaissance', literally rebirth. The humanism which spread across Germany, France, England and The Netherlands in the 15th century owes its name to its concentration on man and true humanity. However, this orientation to man did not mean the abandonment of the Christian faith. In northwest Europe in particular, humanism was accompanied by enrichment of the Christian tradition. There was a protest here against sophisticated, scholastic tours de force and a plea for a return to the original text of the Bible (thus Eramus published the New Testament in the Greek text with a translation into classical Latin) and to the simplicity of the early Church Fathers. Thus a distinction must be made between this Christian-oriented humanism and the more classically-oriented humanism which was most widely disseminated in Italy. (However, it is not correct – as sometimes happens – to associate the different trends in humanism all too closely with geographical boundaries.)

In the context of this broad and multiform reorientation of humanism, there were at the beginning of the 16th century a number of authors in the Low Countries who were explicit champions of marriage. As, for instance,

Erasmus, who was mentioned before, the Spaniard Juan Luis Vives, and the doctor and scholar Agrippa of Nettesheim. We shall call this defence of marriage 'philogamy', referring to Erasmus' *Virgo misogamos* (the girl who was opposed to marriage), the title of one of the dialogues in his *Colloquia familiaria*. In the dialogue in question, the young girl Catherine appears on the scene. She made up her mind to become a nun. As a child, she had once visited a convent and it seemed to her like paradise. The person with whom she is conversing tries to dissuade her. He gives a copious description of the negative aspects of convent life. Chastity is certainly not guaranteed amidst the lustful priests and nuns, who have Sappho's manners, but lack her talents. Moreover, do not her parents have other plans for her? And Paul said that children should obey their parents. Catherine nevertheless enters the nunnery, but soon regrets it, as is to be seen from the next dialogue: *Virgo poenitens* (the girl with regrets). In spite of the family drama which was caused by her entry, and the large sums of money which her father had to pay for her marriage to Christ, now her dearest wish is for her parents to rescue her from the nunnery. She will thankfully accept the marriage plans they have made for her.[11] From this short summary of the two dialogues it can already be seen that considerable criticism of the corrupt ecclesiastical institutions was to be found in Erasmus' philogamy. If we are to believe Erasmus then, the glorification of chastity was not by any means always a matter of piety, but a means of ensnaring unwitting children, preferably from well-to-do families.

Erasmus did not only criticise the implicit misogamy of the Church, but also its official conditions for concluding a marriage. As we have already seen before, in these conditions the consensus was considered sufficient for a valid marriage; the 'consummation' made the marriage indissoluble. Even the parental permission, although urgently desirable, was not absolutely necessary. Erasmus, who in many fields defended individual freedom to an extent which seems very modern, considered these conditions extremely liberal. He maintained that,

C.V. Coornhert after Maarten van Heemskerck (1498–1571), *The good housewife feeding and clothing her family*, engraving from the series *The good housewife*, 1555.

though they represented liberation from the tyranny of parents, they appeared to introduce a greater evil: that of the unverifiable marriages.[12]

The civil authorities repeatedly protested against these unofficially concluded marriages. However, the sanctions which they had at their disposal (the disallowance of the material advantages in particular which were attached to a marriage) in general only affected the wealthy. Those who refused to recognise the validity of the clandestine marriages could support their point of view with the many instances in which a marriage, agreed and 'consummated' on an impulse, under the influence of drink or with deliberate seduction, had disastrous consequences. Not least for the community itself, since the illegitimate children often became a public charge either directly or indirectly (via begging or crime).

This politico-legal criticism of the monopoly which the Church had acquired in the course of the preceding centuries with regard to the conclusion of marriages (criticism directed above all at the concrete theological interpretation and elaboration) was not an isolated instance. It fits into the framework of the more comprehensive emancipatory movement of the urban bourgeoisie. The ideological needs of this class and the values of the Church began to diverge on increasingly concrete points. At this period such a conflict of interests took place to a great extent on the ideological plane. And although the Church was mainly in control of the 'media' of that time through its writings, sermons, visual art and last but not least the censure, the foundation of that monopoly was becoming increasingly unstable. Not least because of the lack of conviction, with which the ecclesiastical authorities personified the Church's ethics on poverty and chastity. As we have seen, criticism of the not exactly moral behaviour of the clergy had already been expressed by the 14th century lay moralists. This criticism was to be heard everywhere and since the 12th century had found expression in the poverty movements and, for example, in the founding of the mendicant orders in the 13th century. In the 15th century the various reformatory councils urged reformation 'of head and members', that is to say of the ecclesiastical authorities and of the faithful. Thus at the Council of Constance (1414–1418) the celibacy of the secular clergy was openly discussed. When so many were living in a state of shame, would it not be better for the Church to allow its representatives to marry?

Indeed looking back it is remarkable that Luther remained a protagonist of the celibacy of priests up until 1520, whilst Erasmus was a protagonist of the freedom of choice between celibacy and marriage. For Erasmus chastity was not tied to the estate in life. It is also possible to lead a chaste and virtuous life within marriage, indeed the chance is even greater where the weakness of the flesh does not make the observance of absolute chastity very plausible. And yet even for Erasmus the relationship between Mary and Joseph remained ideal. Man and woman should preferably only unite if they knew that the urge was motivated by procreation.[13]

Towards a reasonable Christianity
One of the objects of the 16th century reforms was the formulation of a new Christian order, in which there would be more room for man's natural condition and his worldly aspirations; a condition and aspiration which the Protestant was to accept in the light of the Fall as indeed a 'fallen', but nevertheless 'given' nature, and which was accepted by humanists such as Erasmus even with a certain amount of confidence in human possibilities. These basic assumptions seemed more down-to-earth than the unrealistic asceticism which was preached by the Church. Thus Erasmus wrote, for example, that people who were dying and who were troubled by a bad conscience sometimes even took the habit at the eleventh hour to assure themselves of a place in paradise; as if God were not capable of recognising a rogue beneath his disguise.[14] No, rational Christianity meant that people lived a decent life in the state in which, to the glory of God and for the benefit of their neighbours, they could give of their best.

Reading between the lines here we discover the burgher

asking for recognition of his way of life. He was the man who worked hard and was irritated by the parasitism of the mendicant friars and the riches of the Church and its financial practices; the man who had enjoyed a certain amount of education and viewed the world with curiosity; the man who was frustrated by the fact that the theologians had appropriated a monopoly in the interpretation of God's word, and discussed it amongst themselves in unintelligible language. After all, had not Christ talked in simple words and to everyone? The Church made the faithful take part in all sorts of ritual as a sign of subjection, whilst Christ had freed his brothers from all too rigid ritual and interpretation of the law. This burgher was happy to read that Christ's own choice for his first miracle had been a wedding. It was understandable that the leaders of early Christianity had chosen celibacy; that was a rational choice for militants who were risking their lives. But times had changed. The continued existence of Christianity called for new insight.

New insight into an old story: appreciation of woman as wife, mother and tutor

In the context of the increased appreciation of marriage and – dependent on the background of the different authors – more or less resulting from the new rationality, we see in the 15th century another striking and comparatively new phenomenon: the explicit defence by men of the female sex. Throughout the 15th century these defenders of the female sex fought a fierce battle against those who ridiculed and accused women – often the previously mentioned, compulsorily celibate clerks.

At the beginning of the 16th century the defenders of woman had some success. The influence of the ladies at the European courts seemed as it were to inject new life into the tradition of chivalry: Italian-oriented neoplatonists gave explicit expression to their appreciation of the stimulating qualities of love. All this came after a long period in which the emphasis had been exclusively on the destructive, addictive nature of love.

Philogamists such as Erasmus, particularly in the

D.V. Coornhert after Maarten van Heemskerck (1498–1571), *The good housewife buys a vineyard*, engraving from the series *The good housewife*, 1555.

23

context of their critical appreciation of marriage, drew attention to the possible positive qualities of woman; an undertaking without which the praise of marriage could not be very convincing. To achieve this, the traditional arguments against woman, which had been collected from the classical writers and the Bible and as such were even published in separate tracts, had to be refuted; a debate in which Agrippa of Nettesheim excelled with his *De nobilitate et praecellentia foeminei sexus.*[15] This contest was carried on with all the more appetite and expertise, since the humanists were able to attack the ecclesiastical ideologists on popular ground. The ups and downs in the balance of power between man and woman formed at that time – just as in our own time and probably throughout history – a subject which occupies many people. This would also appear to find expression in the persecution of witches, which is discussed elsewhere in this book.

The philogamists' books became bestsellers. From the moment that Luther's ideas began to have success, the Church started to react officially to philogamic works which were all too critical. In particular the works of Erasmus, his dialogues and his *Encomium matrimonii* (the Praise of Marriage, 1518) were scrutinised by the censure, and the Council of Trent later placed his entire oeuvre on the Index.

In the Late Middle Ages and the Renaissance the writings of classical authors on *medicine* formed an important source of argumentation in the battle 'for' or 'against' woman. For in these medical tracts the 'nature' of woman was set forth and explained. As we have seen, in the 13th century Thomas Aquinas went back to Aristotle's *De generatione animalium.* His explanation of the nature of woman was seized upon to provide the traditional religious views on woman with fresh arguments, and thus at this period it began to become topical again.

The humanists widened the horizon by publishing the classical texts: Aristotle (*Historia animalium*) Plato, Hippocrates and Galen. The last two were physicians and their work was very popular with medical men, who were critical not only of theological dogmatism (because this impeded medical experiments) but also of the illiteracy of the traditional healers, barbers, midwives and so on. Although the polemics concerning the nature of woman were very complex, the situation can be summarised as follows: in a society which held the lay estate in high esteem and had revalued material pleasures, but which feared the asocial effects of sexuality, woman was looked on with favour as long as she had a *function* to fulfil. The doctors had to demonstrate that woman was a valid member of society as a procreator, but that she nevertheless remained inferior to man physiologically and psychologically. Hippocrates and Galen were quoted for the purpose of revaluing woman's role in procreation: she had an active seed just as man. This meant that her pleasure was functional and that she bore great responsibility for the hereditary aspects. People such as Andreas Vesalius (1514–1564) of Brussels paid special attention to her specific anatomy. Medical historians have pointed out that from 1550 onwards there was a striking increase in the publication of books on gynaecology.

One of the ways in which the inferiority of woman was illustrated was with the help of the theory of the humours (Hippocrates, Galen). Those who saw woman as an active and dangerous being thought – referring in particular to Plato's *Timaeus* – that the specific female organ was a sort of animal, thirsting for liquid when it was parched and for penetration when it was too full. Galen refuted the old theory of the 'animal' by describing the female organ as a male organ turned inwards; he considered the humoral theory as sufficient explanation of the differences in character, the peculiarities and the specific illnesses. As a cold, damp being it was much more difficult for woman to deal with her defects than for man. Man was indispensable for her equilibrium, but man could act freely, ardent in his activity and independent of external influences. One had to be patient and tolerant, he argued, towards a sex which was weak rather than dangerous.

To those who used the innate badness of woman as an argument to prove the impossibility of conjugal friendship, a humanist such as Erasmus retorted in his

Encomium that the bad man makes the woman bad, that good parents have children who follow their example, and that *the upbringing* rather than the nature determines a person's propensities, be it man or woman.

Who can find a virtuous woman, or: the importance of the upbringing

Tracts on the upbringing of woman appeared in abundance in the 16th century, and however different the milieu might be, which the authors had in mind – from the homely German housewife of Luther to the Italian 'cortegiana' of Castiglione – it was always the same virtue which was acclaimed: obedience. In the trading towns of the Low Countries a new type of school developed which offered the daughters of the bourgeoisie a complete education in commercial subjects and in virtuousness, so as to make them perfect marriage partners. These schools were given the name 'French', because the French language was taught there and also to distinguish them from the 'Dutch' schools, where girls and boys received primary education (reading, writing and arithmetic), and from the Latin schools, which – with a few exceptions – were open to boys only. At the French schools girls and boys were kept strictly separate.

From the second half of the 16th century the French schools for girls were particularly flourishing, partly due to the influence of the successful masters and writers of school books from Antwerp.[17] It is evident in a variety of ways, that the philogamic texts from the first quarter of the century were known to these schoolmasters. Thus, for instance, in 1579 two Antwerp masters asked Plantijn to have a new French translation made of the tract *Institutio foeminae christianae (1524)* by the humanist Vives. And in 1592 a son of one of these masters published a translation in Dutch and French of Erasmus' most famous dialogue on marriage *Uxor mempsigamos:* 'Dialogue between a good housewife and a bad housewife'. Here Eulalia ('she who is well-spoken') teaches the still inexperienced and recalcitrant Xantippe how to make an awful husband into a treasure. There is one golden rule:

D.V. Coornhert after Maarten van Heemskerck (1498–1571), *The good housewife feeding the needy*, engraving from the series *The good housewife*, 1555.

25

always do everything to please him so that he realises that he is nowhere as well off as in his own home![18]

Woman and marriage in the Reformation and Counter-Reformation

The regard for marriage and woman's role therein, the initial impetus of which we have outlined in the preceding paragraphs, came to fruition in the Reformation. These themes are to be seen there in the broader context of the theological restatements of the Reformers, in which, in spite of all the differences amongst them, certain central points are to be recognised. Following the line of the first great Reformer Luther, most of them defended the general priesthood of the faithful. The faithful lived through the grace of God and were only justified through their faith. The Reformers therefore rejected the rules of perfection, according to which a distinction was made between clergy and laity. Every Christian was called upon to observe God's word in his daily life, in his or her own place. The Bible should also be present in daily life, accessible to everyone and should preferably be consulted and read or read aloud every day in a Christian family (Luther did a German translation of the Old and New Testament).

The Reformers' ideas on marriage must be seen in this general theological context. As was the case with the Reformation as a whole, their views were characterised by a renewed appeal to the Bible. It would go beyond the scope of this article to go into all the facets, we shall therefore restrict ourselves to the most far-reaching points.

Luther's defence of marriage is linked with his fundamental view that man is branded by sin. Since the Fall, man has been living in a fallen state. On account of this state of sin most people are unable to observe perfect chastity, and to try to do so shows evidence of unnecessary pride. Marriage, which was instituted by God before the Fall – whereby it acquired a sanctified character – provides a good Christian solution to the sexual problem. Luther emphasised that a possible victory over the flesh must be seen as a gift from God, not as personal merit. One cannot count ones good deeds, in this case chastity, like coins with which to buy God's forgiveness. For Luther and the other Reformers, marriage belonged in the first place to the natural order, and it was not a sacrament.[19]

Contrary to the traditional Catholic marriage objectives, special emphasis was laid on mutual companionship and help within marriage, making reference to the story of the creation. Thus procreation was no longer the first or most central objective of marriage. On the other hand the obedience of the wife received renewed emphasis, theologically legitimised by reference to Paul. The master of the house could, if necessary, refer to this all the more, since the family in particular was supposed to have knowledge of the Bible.

Since marriage, apart from being a union instituted by God, was also a social contract which concerned the political community (Luther's doctrine of the two kingdoms is significant here [20]), most Reformers set store on an official, public marriage ceremony. The relevant legislation and administration of the law they left to the secular authorities, who were expected to act in the spirit of the Reformation. The States of Holland, for instance, laid down the matrimonial law in the Political Ordinance of 1580. According to the provisions of the decree, a marriage could be concluded before a clergyman or before a magistrate, and had to be preceded by parental consent (for women under 20 and for men under 25) and by three public announcements, so that possible impediments to the marriage could be submitted.

The Reformers attached great importance to the parental consent, also making reference to St Paul. Without this consent, many of them considered the marriage invalid. This provision was so abused by those who regretted their choice that in 1548 the Emperor Charles V issued an order against it: a marriage, which had been concluded, could not be declared invalid by pleading parental disapproval. However, a possible *divorce* was formally allowable as far as the Reformers were concerned, since marriage was no longer considered a sacrament. Nevertheless in practice divorce appears to have remained a difficult procedure in many cases. Certainly for the woman, who often had no income of her own and also had to stifle her possible dissatisfaction for a long time, on account of the subservience required of her.[21]

The Catholic authorities found themselves compelled to take a stand against the Reformers' re-evaluation in many fields and they did this at the Council of Trent (1545–1563). For them marriage remained a matter for the Church (the obligatory civil wedding required in some countries assumed the nature of a formality). In its provisions and implementation the official marriage legislation did show a similarity to the Political Ordinance on a number of points. Both Catholics and Protestants were confronted with the problem of the clandestine marriages, which on account of the increasing urbanisation – and the accompanying decrease in informal social control by family and milieu – was becoming more and more difficult to keep under supervision. The Catholics had for long been calling for public notification and a marriage ceremony with three witnesses (including an authorised priest), and this was made obligatory at the Fourth Lateran Council (1215). Up to then the Church's views on free mutual consensus as the basis for valid and sacramental marriage had, however, made it impossible to declare unofficially concluded marriages invalid. The authorities in Trent were under considerable political pressure – from amongst others the Kings of France and Portugal – and fully realised the dangers of the clandestine marriages. These risks varied from bigamy, breach of the marriage vows and desertion, uncertainty for the descendants and child neglect, to abortion and infanticide. As time was pressing they arrived at a compromise: though clandestine marriages were declared valid, under certain circumstances the Church could pronounce them null and void.

Various historians and in particular female historians have – from differing points of view – posed the question

Anonymous master after Maarten van Heemskerck (1498–1571), *Jael* and *Ruth*, engraving from the series *Famous women of the Bible*, c. 1563.

27

as to whether the Protestant conjugal ethics represented an improvement of woman's individual and social position. In so far as she was no longer depicted as the dreaded 'gate of hell' for timorous celibates, but became a wife pleasing in God's sight, at first glance this certainly appears to be the case. On the other hand, for women who could not or would not marry, the other esteemed estate, entry into a convent, was no longer open to them. In so far as the nunneries had offered a number of women comparative freedom and opportunities to develop their abilities, this would seem to be a loss. However, as we shall see later on, the Council of Trent also placed fresh restrictions on this freedom for Catholic women, by the reintroduction of stricter enclosure for female members of an order.

III.   UNMARRIED WOMEN

Single women 'in the world'

In the preceding section we have discussed the image of woman as wife and mother. But just as in our own day, there were also women who remained unmarried. Indeed, in the Catholic tradition it was, as we have seen, more highly esteemed to remain unmarried and dedicate oneself to God as a virgin, than to enter into marriage. In the period around 1500, but also in the preceding centuries, there was a striking number of unmarried women – probably not always of their own free will: the numerous wars, epidemics (men often appeared to be more susceptible to illness) and other causes resulted in a considerable surplus of women.[22] Of course not all these women devoted themselves to a religious life, and those who did will not all have been inspired by purely spiritual motives. However, we must be careful in this context not to judge too much according to our own criteria. In the Late Middle Ages social and religious reality were not to be distinguished, 'material' facts were experienced in a religious form or translated into religious terms.

Children were sometimes promised to a monastery or nunnery at birth or in infancy, to fulfil a promise already made to God, or to avoid the problem of caring for them. Having learnt from experience, the convents adhered to an age limit, at which these *oblates* (bestowed on God) had to decide for themselves whether they wished to remain in the convent. Before they had reached the set age, which varied from 12 to 15, they were not allowed to take vows. This was a choice which for many people was probably only a sham, since they were not really prepared for life outside the convent.

Not a great deal is known about the situation of unmarried women who did not live in religious communities, but nevertheless enough is known to suggest that generally speaking, life was not very rosy. Unmarried women, and in particular widows, did, however, have more rights than married women. In most areas and towns they had a certain degree of legal competence – although the regional differences were considerable – and they could often carry on their own business or practise certain occupations. However, the range of possible occupations decreased rather than increased from the 15th and 16th centuries onwards, on account of the restrictive measures of the guilds, which were very powerful at that time. Occupations in which many, or even exclusively women were to be found were, for example, the lighter sections of the textile industry, such as woolcombing, spinning and sewing.[24] In the nunneries and béguinages this sort of activity was often necessary to provide an additional source of income.

In middle class circles and in the country, married and unmarried women usually worked in the business or household of their husband or relatives. After the death of her husband it was usually possible for the widow to carry on the business – depending on the freedom of action to which the woman was entitled by local legislation and the guilds and on the law of inheritance. There again there were considerable regional differences, but comparatively speaking, northwest Europe was not unfavourable for widows and there were usually provisions for restitution of part of the dowry and/or maintenance or usufruct of personal property and real estate. On account of this more well-to-do widows were popular marriage partners, who were sometimes literally taken by storm.

In the population groups where there was little to be inherited, widows and women on their own had the greatest difficulty in obtaining the barest necessities, usually by means of temporary or seasonal work. Not that men or married women who worked with their husbands were much better off; but women had fewer occupations to choose from and the wages were usually lower. In addition there were often children, whether or not 'legitimate', who had to be cared for, which made the unmarried, widowed or deserted women a particularly vulnerable group.

Many of them lived from hand to mouth, went out begging or even travelled with the armies as camp followers (in English this is still another term for a prostitute). If there was something going on in a town, they congregated in large numbers: at the Diet of 1394 in Frankfurt on Main some 800 camp followers were counted, at the Councils of Basle and Constance there were even 1500![25] Other women sought shelter in public houses for women, the brothels in the town. The urban authorities tried to restrict prostitution to certain streets or houses, but recognised and protected it to some extent. Judging by the descriptions and the complaints on the subject, it was considered by some that in German towns in the 15th century there was a striking amount of extramarital sexual intercourse, possibly resulting from the presence of comparatively large groups of unmarried people, both women and men (priests,mates who during their apprenticeship were obliged to remain single, journeymen etc.)[26] The increasing criticism of these practices may also be partly connected with the new social context of the towns, where fresh regulations had to be drawn up for the supervision of sexual practices. The rapid spread of the new veneral diseases in the second half of the 15th century also increased the need for action. In many places

Anonymous master after Maarten van Heemskerck (1498–1571), *Abigail* and *Judith*, engravings from the series *Famous women of the Bible*, c. 1563.

brothels became subject to stricter measures.

The economic expansion at the end of the 15th century exacerbated the contrast between rich and poor, and as far as we have been able to discover, the poor included a comparatively large number of women.[27] The uncertain life of unmarried or itinerant women and the attendant risks may perhaps have attracted some people, but many will have tried to find a steadier basis for the security of their existence. By binding sexual intercourse to a promise of marriage a young woman (or man) could try to catch a wealthy partner, although if these marriages remained clandestine, they could not easily be checked and were somewhat unreliable. However, large groups of women resorted to the comparative security and protection offered by another sort of house for women of that time: the nunneries, béguinages, houses of the Sisters of the Common Life, or other houses for women who lived together on a religious basis and tried to provide for their own livelihood.

The religious women's movement of the 13th century

The phenomenon of large groups of women going to live together in houses, courts or nunneries in order to lead a chaste and sober life was not a novelty in the 15th century. This 'religious women's movement', as it has been called, had already sprung up towards the end of the 12th century. In the 13th century this resulted in the foundation of numerous béguinages and houses, and of a large number of new 'secondary orders' (women's sections of existing orders for men): in the somewhat older orders which followed the rule of Benedict or Augustine; in the Cistercian and Premonstratensian orders which flourished in the 12th century; or in the mendicant orders of Dominicans and Franciscans established in the 13th century.

There has been a great deal of speculation over the background of this 'religious women's movement'. For one thing it took place in the broader context of the reformation movements within the Church: in the criticism made by the poverty movements of the superficiality and 'unchristian' character of the official Church. More or less directly under the influence of these movements, many women went to live together in new forms of communities, which were scarcely tolerated by the Church and were only kept in check with great difficulty. Some historians put forward principally socio-economic grounds for the attraction exercised by this women's movement in the 13th century[28]: the nunneries and béguinages could assure needy women of a reasonable existence. The evangelical poverty which they professed was not only an ideal but often dire necessity, and the life they could lead in the béguinages and nunneries was relatively sheltered compared to the insecurity of existence in the outside world. The older orders, particularly those of the Benedictine nuns, were moreover comparatively prosperous or even rich, but then they only admitted women who could pay a considerable entrance fee or *dos*.

Other historians have come to the conclusion from studying the biographies of these women and from other information about the beginning of this religious women's movement, that it was certainly not only poor women who joined in this communal life. They believe on the contrary that a comparatively large number of women from the nobility and the rising prosperous urban bourgeoisie were to be found at the origin of the movement. Women who wanted to turn their back on the extravagance of their earlier life or who managed with the greatest difficulty to escape from carefully arranged marriages or even occasionally with the husband's consent whilst he was still alive, withdrew into these communities. The observation, that so many rich women in particular became members of these communities, is partly based on the collections of *vitae*, the biographies of these women.[30] However, we must not lose sight of the fact that these vitae were intended for edification: they were written by fellow nuns to be read aloud in the refectory. In consequence the accounts will naturally have been carefully selected and recorded; and rich women who repented of their ways seemed to provide a more spectacular story than women who had difficulty in providing for their existence before they entered a community. As has been mentioned, the poorer women could not in any case enter the older nunneries on account of the large *dos* which was asked. They were, however, sometimes admitted as lay sisters for the housekeeping or the infirmary.

In the 13th century the Church attempted to make more provision for these poorer women, partly in order to counteract what the Church considered as women's 'disorderly' life and communal living. Thus, for example, in Germany the Mary Magdalene orders for penitents (prostitutes) were established from 1227 onwards. However, after a time these orders also began to show traits of the older convents. As a result of benefactions they had achieved comparative affluence and status even before the end of the century. They proceeded to concentrate on the education of girls from the highest circles and thereafter called themselves 'white women' (from their apparel).

The attitude of the male members of the orders will also have had something to do with these developments. Whilst the Curia tried via innumerable bulls and encyclicals to incorporate the various religious women's communities into the recognised orders by forbidding the communities to choose 'monastic-type' living patterns on their own initiative, and whilst the women themselves were often actively seeking to associate with existing orders (in order to escape the paternalism of the local clergy or downright persecution as heretics [31]), the male members of the orders put up stubborn resistance to the incorporation. In the framework of the Church's attempts to restore discipline in the monasteries such an association meant that the tasks of the male members of the orders became much more onerous. The function of the abbess, which from the 6th to the 12th centuries could be very autonomous and powerful, became more marginal in the new orders. Male members of the orders were entrusted with strict responsibility for the supervision and spiritual guidance of their female order members. In view of the fact that religious women far outnumbered the male members and the clergy, the men were afraid that they

Anonymous master after Maarten van Heemskerck (1498–1571), *Esther* and *Susanna*, engravings from the series *Famous women of the Bible*, c. 1563.

31

would be overburdened by the responsibility for these women and thus be kept from their real tasks.[32]

At first the resistance from the orders met with some success, but from the second half of the 13th century onwards the Curia managed to make it obligatory for the orders to admit and look after the new women's communities. The means of livelihood of these communities were often extremely slender, for the very reason that they did not ask such a large entrance fee. In order to provide the community with a means of livelihood, it was naturally necessary for the women to go outside their house fairly frequently, to sell their sewing and embroidery, their spun and woven goods, to care for the sick and to keep vigil over the dead, or if the worst came to the worst, to beg.

However, if these communities wanted to enter an order, then they had to undertake in the first place to maintain complete enclosure or *clausura*, which in the course of the 13th century was laid down again with increasing strictness for the female religious. The male members of the order did not wish to be held responsible for the comings and goings, which it was impossible to supervise.[33] This development came to conclusion in the papal bull *Periculosa* of 1298: the observance of the solemn vows (chastity, austerity and obedience) and of the enclosure were laid down as conditions for gaining recognition as a religious. These stipulations naturally also had consequences for the infrastructure of the community; during the period in which the orders resisted the incorporation of new female members of the order they often made an exception for rich women and communities. The latter would be able to maintain themselves without all that, difficult to supervise, coming and going, but at the same time without imposing too heavy an economic burden on the order.

Apart from the increase in the number of nunneries in the 13th century the béguinages also remained in existence and increased, albeit anxiously watched by the local clergy, the inquisitors and the bourgeoisie (who came to view the béguinages and the nunneries with their cheap labour and often exemption from certain taxes as formidable competitors, especially as regards the spinning and weaving trade). The fact that strict enclosure and supervision were not observed to the same extent in all monastic houses is evident from the numerous attempts of the ecclesiastical reformers to get the monasteries and nunneries to stricter observation, i.e. the upholding of the Rule.[34]

Religious women and church reforms in the 14th and 15th centuries: chastity 'in the world' or behind bars?

One of those in the Low Countries who expressed criticism of the degenerate practices of the monks and nuns and the clergy in the 14th century was Geert Grote (Gerardus Grotius). This Geert Grote, the spiritual father of the Modern Devotion and fervent advocate of simplification and spiritualisation of the Christian life, immediately after his conversion in 1374 placed his parental home in Deventer at the disposal of poor women who wanted to lead a religious life. In the statutes of the house, which were drawn up several years later, the inmates were given protection on two sides; they should not run the risk of being suspected of the same heresies for which many béguines were condemned at the Council of Vienna in 1311, nor should they bear too much resemblance to nuns, since it was forbidden to found a new order without the Pope's consent.

The inmates had, however, to adhere strictly to the rules of the house. They owed strict obedience to the chosen 'mistress', had to support themselves by their own labours, attend mass and prayers and above all promise 'to lead a chaste life all their days. And not to have unedifying contact with male persons'. A sister was free to leave the house, but once she had left she was not readmitted.

Numerous houses of Brothers and Sisters of the Common Life, modelled on the 'Master Geert's house, were founded in the Low Countries and in Germany. The number of sister-houses and the number of sisters per house far exceeded that of the brothers.[35] According to the statutes of the Master Geert's House no *dos* could be asked, preferably poor women were to be admitted and exclusively virgins. On account of restrictive conditions of this kind, but also because the houses could soon no longer cope with the number of postulants [36] and because a life without a recognised monastic rule aroused the suspicion of the church authorities, towards the end of the 14th century a number of convents from the circle of the Modern Devotion were founded which adhered to the Rule of Augustine and which together formed the Congregation of Windesheim. Since the Chapter also opposed the incorporation of too many nunneries – the spiritual care for the sisters would deflect the brothers from their contemplative life – the number of affiliated nunneries lagged far behind that of the monasteries.[37]

Particularly in the 15th century the women who could not enter these nunneries and who continued to live together in houses, increasingly often joined the so-called 'Third Order' of the Franciscans or Dominicans. This Third Order enjoyed a certain degree of recognition by the Church (although on the part of the Curia it was certainly not encouraged!) which made it possible to take official vows, in particular that of chastity. However, the vows were of a provisional nature and solemn vows were not made.

With the consent of her husband a married woman could also become a member of a Third Order, a *tertiaris*. A great advantage of this Third Order for women was that they were not obliged to observe enclosure as were the nuns. The enclosure applied less rigidly to the men of the mendicant orders on account of their tasks in preaching, giving special spiritual care and combatting heresy. It is noticeable that the Third Order numbered many more women than men.

Many béguines also joined the Third Order of the new mendicant orders, especially after the condemnation of béguines and beghards in 1311. This condemnation referred mainly to the heresies which were supposedly to be found amongst them; an exception was made however for really pious women who irreproachably submitted

Anonymous master after Maarten van Heemskerck (1498–1571), *Mary* and *Mary Magdalene*, engraving from the series *Famous women of the Bible*, c. 1563.

themselves to the local priests. The Brethren of the Common Life were also liable to be suspected of heresy; one of the vitae even tells of a sister who had to appear before the inquisition and expose her breasts in order to prove by their virgin state that she was not a heretic . . .[38] Though the Bishop of Utrecht in 1401 recognised the right of existence and the way of life of the Brethren, the ecclesiastical bodies (and the population) remained suspicious. In the course of the 15th century an increasing number of Sisters of the Common Life entered the Third Order, not infrequently under the 'guidance' of male religious and priests, their father confessors.

The growth in the number of religious women's communities and nunneries is especially striking in the first half of the 15th century; in the second half of the century the number stabilised. After the revival in the 12th and particularly the 13th centuries the number of women's communities remained fairly stable in the 14th century before increasing again in the 15th and finally declining in the 16th century, especially after the Reformation. About 1500 the bishopric of Utrecht numbered 10,000 nuns in enclosed orders and 5000 tertiaries as against 3000 monks and 5000 secular priests (not attached to an order). Apart from this there were a number of béguines and Sisters of the Common Life who did not belong to an order.[39]

This revival in the religious life of The Netherlands in the 15th century has sometimes been ascribed to the influence of the Modern Devotion. In spite of the reformation movements within the Church certainly not all the monastic houses in the 15th century were equally sound in the faith. For example, in 1485 Beatrix, daughter of the Lord of Assendelft, entered the Zijl nunnery in Haarlem. For reasons of health the father stipulated that she could do what she liked, eat and drink what she fancied, and could attend services if she felt so inclined. The nunnery agreed to these conditions, probably for financial reasons and to keep on good terms with the powerful lord – which could be of vital importance to a nunnery in the event of vicissitudes of a material or (ecclesiastical) political nature. In many nunneries and béguinages it was possible for well-to-do ladies to buy themselves in, in a similar manner; they took no vows, although they were obliged to observe a certain minimum number of rules, and the nunnery or béguinage acted in fact as a respectable boarding house. Probably the difference between these ladies and the other sisters was not always all that great, or was mainly a question of class distinction. According to the vitae the women of the Modern Devotion certainly needed an eye kept on them to see that they did not take advantage of such class distinctions.[40]

That not everyone appreciated the strict religious practice of the devotees is evident from the downright hostile reception accorded to female devotees when they were sent out or asked as members of the mother convent to reform an over-indulgent abbey or nunnery. 'The devils have come', exclaimed the nuns of such a (Benedictine) nunnery, the Hilweerts House, on the arrival of the devotee sisters.[41] The moralistic literature of that time, particularly in German, gives another very graphic impression – no doubt exaggerated for the purpose, but certainly not totally unfounded, in view of the reponse – of the not always devout practices in the convents and béguinages. And of course the writings of the great Reformer Luther give a similar impression. A certain male prejudice against these women who evaded matrimonial intercourse, may also perhaps have played a part in these tirades.

Reformation and Counter Reformation – some trends
As has been explained above in the section on marriage, the Reformers had little use for organised chastity and the distinction between virginity and the married state, as recognised in the Catholic tradition. Luther himself married a former nun and in one of his after-dinner speeches he let slip the remark that you only had to look at a woman's body to see what she was naturally intended for: 'were not her broad hips and behind created for sitting at home, bearing and bringing up children'?

The decline in the number of religious women – noticeable in the Low Countries from about 1530 onwards – cannot, however, be attributed entirely to the influence of the Reformation. This decrease had already started in the first quarter of the 16th century, after a certain degree of stabilisation in the second half of the 15th century. However, as the Reformation penetrated ever further, the decline rapidly accelerated: true comparatively few women left the orders, but the number of new members was clearly on the decrease. Monasteries, nunneries and other types of religious institutions found it increasingly difficult to meet the rising urban taxes. These points reinforced one another: on the one hand less income, on the other hand higher expenditure. Most of the institutions for women were closed down between 1560 and 1580, because the financial means had been exhausted, the number of inmates had dropped too far or the urban authorities had imposed restrictive measures.

The Council of Trent was confronted with the Reformers' criticism of the monastic houses. This criticism was levelled not only at the distinction in perfection between the two states of life, but also denounced the not very 'Christian' behaviour of many monks and nuns.

In an attempt to restore discipline in the monasteries and nunneries the Council fell back – as far as the nuns were concerned – on the stipulations of the Bull *Periculosa* of 1298 and once more ordained strict enclosure for the nuns. The tertiaries also had to comply with this as far as possible. If the monastic houses did not adhere to the rules, then they were not allowed to admit any more novices and would thus in the long run cause their own demise. The provisions, which are perhaps understandable as a reaction to the criticism of the Reformers, had somewhat the reverse effect at a time in which a practical sense of public spirit and Christian life-in-the-world were increasingly setting the tone. The renewed and strict enclosure behind convent walls ran counter to the views of those who were beginning to allocate an esteemed, albeit subordinate place to woman as chaste wife, tutor, and attendant of the sick, the weak and children. The

D.V. Coornhert after Maarten van Heemskerck (1498–1571), *The good housewife is as a crown on the head of her husband*, engraving from the series *The good housewife*, 1555.

enclosure also countered the initiatives and needs of the women themselves. The Order of Ursulines, for example, founded in Italy even before the Council of Trent, explicitly considered its principal objective to be the Christian upbringing of girls, rather than cherishing their own perfection in isolation from the world. Indeed, in the beginning these Ursulines continued to live at home, but they did have to observe a set rule. Although their objectives quickly found approval, here too it was soon necessary to take restrictive measures. The women had to retreat to nunneries in order to facilitate the observance of the Rule and the supervision; the work of upbringing and education was brought within the nunnery.

IV. IN CONCLUSION

We may conclude then that in the second half of the 16th century in particular, the ideal role and position of woman was being stated with increasing precision. In the Catholic tradition the married woman continued to be esteemed above all as a mother, a task in which she received intensive guidance by means of a great deal of pious and pedagogic advice. The religious state was still more highly esteemed by the Church, but the monastic houses had actually decreased in size and social significance and could offer women only limited freedom of movement.

Within the Reformation the only position which was really granted to women was that of mother and wife. In the radical Protestant movements, women did sometimes play an active part in preaching the Word, but this phenomenon remained mainly restricted to a few women from the upper classes, and disappeared as soon as the movement was established. The Reformers showed more appreciation of the married woman as the husband's (obedient) assistant, and she was assigned an important role in the religious upbringing, which had first of all to take place within the family. But it is questionable whether the advantages of this appreciation outweighed the disadvantages. After all, this 'natural' vocation, intended by God in his Creation, was not in store for all women. From various sources we hear reports of women who could not see that natural vocation as their only task or fulfilment, or simply could not make that the objective of their existence.

We should like to finish with the conclusions of an English researcher, who has made a comparative study of the *pre- and post*-Reformation views on marriage. The aim of her study was to reveal the similarities and differences in the views of Catholics, Protestants and Puritans. She finds that ultimately these ideas according to their tenor and content *as presented to the faithful*, were not so dissimilar. As she remarks incidentally, the ideal family was usually described by all of them in terms of the ideal housewife.[42]

1. Especially from the 12th century onwards. Zutphen was the first town to receive city rights (1190) in the Northern Netherlands.
2. See in particular: J. Hajnal, 'European marriage patterns in perspective' in: D.V. Glass, D.E.C. Eversley, *Population in history*, London, 1965, 101-143. For the period round about 1500, however, Hajnal gives no data.
3. See for a short survey of these discussions, amongst others: D. Haks, *Huwelijk en gezin in Holland in de 17de en 18de eeuw*, Assen 1982, 2-9, 23-30, 226; E. Kloek, *Gezinshistorici over vrouwen*, Amsterdam, 1981. An author such as Peter Laslett argued in his controversial study *The world we have lost*, London 1965, which he and others have since gone into in more depth, that the nuclear family has always been the dominant family type in Western history.
4. The meaning is burning with desire.
5. Cf. Th. Van Eupen, Een eigen kerkelijke sexuele moraal?; in: *Liefde, Lust, Leven* (=Tenminste 4, 1982), 27.
6. See: A.G. Weiler, 'Enige aspekten van de man/vrouw verhouding in de middeleeuwen', in: *Vrouw man kind. Lijnen van vroeger naar nu*, Baarn 1978, 25-43; J. Huisman; De man/vrouw-verhouding in de vroege westerse kultuur, met name in de Germaanse oudheid', in the same volume, 9-24. See the relevant authors for a bibliography.
7. *Die Dietsche Doctrinale*, ed. W.J.A. Jonckbloet, The Hague 1842, 298 ff.: 'That neither habit nor status makes man holy'. Lines quoted 1603 ff.
8. Jan de Weert, *Nieuwe Doctrinael of Spiegel van Sonden*, ed. J.H. Jacobs, The Hague 1915. Jan de Weert was a surgeon, and wrote at the beginning of the 14th century.
9. Willem van Hildegaersberch, *Gedichten*, ed. W. Bisschop and E. Verwijs, The Hague 1870. Van Hildegaersberch probably wrote for a living, on commission. He worked round about 1400.
10. Little by little women begin to make themselves heard and discuss subjects such as love and marriage from their point of view. One of the first and most important of them, the Frenchwoman Christine de Pisan (1364-1430?), for instance, asked the men, who were already privileged enough on account of the social norms, to stop circulating nauseating jokes, mean accusations and patent lies about women. She asked husbands in particular to take their marriage vows more seriously. De Pisan considered that clerks amongst others were responsible for the dissemination of hatred of women. The discussion over the nature and position of woman which was initiated by Christine de Pisan and continued by many women after her is known as the *Querelle de Femmes*.
11. *Opera Omnia Desideri Erasmii Roterodami. Ordonis Primi III*, Amsterdam 1972. 'Virgo misogamos', 289-297; 'Virgo Poenitens', 298-300. The two dialogues were first published in 1523 (in *Familiarum Colloquiorum Formulae*, published in Basle by Frobenius).
12. See for a summarising study of Erasmus' point of view on marriage: E.V. Telle, *Erasme de Rotterdam et le Septième Sacrement. Etude d'évangélisme matrimonial au XVIe siècle et contribution à la biographie intellectuelle d'Erasme*, Geneva 1954. The author defends the idea that Erasmus' 'philogamy' was primarily anti-monachism; a standpoint which is not shared by all scholars.
13. Erasmus refers to the exemplary marriage of Mary and Joseph several times in his *Institutio Christiani Matrimonii*. The humanist Vives also refers to it in his *Institutio Foeminae Christianae*.
14. Amongst other places in the dialogue 'Exequiae seraphicae', *Opera Omnia*, op. cit., I.III, 686-699.
15. *De Nobilitate* was written in 1509 and printed and presented to Margaret of Austria in 1529. In this work the traditional arguments against woman were turned in favour of women. The argument that woman is inferior and subservient to man by nature, because God is said to have created her from Adam's rib, is explained by Nettesheim as follows: God created woman from matter which had already been enriched by the divine intelligence, and she therefore possesses physical perfection.
16. See for ideas on woman in medical science: Ian Maclean, *The Renaissance Notion of Woman. A study in the fortunes of scholasticism and medical science in European intellectual life*, Cambridge 1980; and Yvonne Knibiehler, Catherine Fouquet, *La femme et les médecins*, Paris 1983 (in particular I, ch. 1, 2, 3 and II, ch. 5).
17. Two standard works on the French schools are: K.J. Riemens, *Esquisse historique de l'enseignement du Francais en Hollande du XVIe siècle au XIXe siècle*, Leiden 1919; en M. Sabbe, *Peeter Heyns en de Nimfen uit den Lauwerboom. Bijdrage tot de geschiedenis van het schoolwezen in de 16e eeuw*, Vereeniging der Antwerpsche Bibliophilen, no. 41.
18. 'Uxor mempsigamos', in: *Opera Omnia*, op. cit., I.III, 301-313. A relation between philogamy and the flowering of the French schools for women is posited and elaborated in J.M.J.L. Noël, 'L'école des filles et la philosophie du marriage dans les Pays Bas du XVIe et du XVIIe siècles' in: *Onderwijs en opvoeding in de achttiende eeuw*, Amsterdam/Maarssen 1983, 137-153. This is discussed in more depth in the same author's forthcoming thesis, particularly in ch. 2 (as regards the influence of Erasmus and Vives on the school literature).
19. Most of the Reformers only recognise baptism and holy communion as sacraments instituted by Christ. For them the sacrament is not a means of grace, but a sign of God's promises, to strengthen faith.
20. Following on the ideas of Augustine amongst others Luther distinguished two kingdoms. In the one (represented by the state) the political leader rules – and, if necessary, by force. The aim of this kingdom is the maintenance of peace and justice. In the other kingdom (embodied in the Church) Christ rules, not by laws, but by the Word and sacrament. Both kingdoms must serve the rule of God, but they are distinguished according to power and authority.
21. See amongst others E. Kloek, 'De Reformatie als thema van vrouwengeschiedenis. Een historisch debat over goed en kwaad', in: *Jaarboek voor vrouwengeschiedenis 4*, (1983), 120-121, and the literature cited therein (with reference to some detailed studies).
22. Weiler, op.cit., 36, referring to Karl Bücher, *Die Frauenfrage im Mittelalter*, Tübingen 1910², 6-7.
23. See for a survey of the legal position of women in The Netherlands

in about 1500: Mr B.H.D. Hermesdorf, *Rechtsspiegel. Een rechtshistorische terugblik in de Lage Landen van het herfsttij*, Nijmegen 1980, ch. XIII: 'De vrouw in recht en rechtsleven'.

24. See for an impression of the scope of professions and activities for women in about 1500 in four Dutch towns ('s-Hertogenbosch, Utrecht, Leiden, Dordrecht): Jenneke Quast, 'Vrouwenarbeid omstreeks 1500 in enkele Nederlandse steden', in: *Jaarboek voor vrouwengeschiedenis 1*, (1980), 46–64. In contrast to some of the foreign studies (as for example in Regine Pernoud, *La femme au temps des cathédrales*). Quast finds a relatively large labour market for women in the towns studied, although she also finds signs of women being kept out of the guilds.

25. Bücher, op.cit., 49.

26. Idem, 60

27. See amongst others idem, 51–52.

28. See in particular Godfried Koch, *Frauenfrage und Ketzertum im Mittelalter. Die Frauenbewegung im Rahmen des Katharismus und des Waldensertums und ihre sozialen Wurzeln (12.-14. Jahrhundert)*, Berlin 1962.

29. The Church did not officially permit divorce, but in certain cases – and entry into a nunnery could be a reason – a judicial separation could be granted with mutual consent.

30. As, for example, in Herbert Grundmann, *Religiöse Bewegungen im Mittelalter*, Hildesheim 1961[2], 188–198. Also studies which are based more on the material history of various institutions for women, and use sources such as lists of inmates, testamentary dispositions, statutes and property enactments, show that some of the inmates were far from needy or humble. However, institutions such as the béguinages also took in poorer women, in separate houses or in the service of richer béguines. Cf. Florence Koorn, *Begijnhoven in Holland en Zeeland gedurende de middeleeuwen*, Assen 1981.

31. Sometimes the desire to lead a chaste life, and particularly resistance to possible attempts at seduction by a priest, was sufficient to be accused of heresy. Cf. Grundmann, op.cit., 180.

32. For instance preaching and combatting heresy in the case of the Dominicans.

33. Grundmann, op.cit., 271 ff, passim.

34. Cf. for example M. Hüffer, *Die Reformen in der Abtei Rijnsburg im 15. Jahrhundert*, Münster 1937. The abbey of Rijnsburg was near Leiden.

35. See amongst others: E. Persoons, 'De verspreiding der Moderne Devotie', in: *Geert Grote en de Moderne Devotie*, Zutphen 1984, 57–100.

36. Almost all institutions had a probationary period for postulants to see if they were suited to this life. The duration of the novitiate depended on the institution and the progress of the candidate. The novices received guidance from older nuns and sometimes lived in a separate house in the town.

37. Persoons, op.cit., 81.

38. *Hier beginnen sommige stichtige punten van onsen oelden zusteren*, ed. D. de Man, The Hague 1919. The story concerns Fye Van Reeden (d. 1429), sister in the Master Geerts House, who had to appear before the inquisitor in Cologne (99–101). That she had to expose her breasts – 'in order to see whether she was a pure virgin, for they said of her that she had a child' – is not told in this account, but in the collection of vitae of the sisters from Diepenveen (Fye was related to one of them) *Van den doechden der vuriger ende stichtiger susteren van Diepen veen* (Ms. D), ed. D.A. Brinkerink, Leiden 1904,297. Grietje Dresen is working on a thesis over the development of moral and religious awareness in the women's communities by means of exercises, devotional pictures etc. The vitae of the devote sisters are one of the sources.

39. R.Post, *Kerkelijke verhoudingen in Nederland vóór de Reformatie van ca. 1500 tot 1581*, Utrecht/Antwerp 1954, 165.

40. It is said that rector Johan van den Gronde impressed on a sister, who was using her noble birth as an excuse, that 'If you are born from the shield and from arms then you are from a line of thieves and murderers'; De Man, op.cit 46.

41. Brinkerink, op.cit., 353.

42. Kathleen M. Davies, 'The sacred condition of equality – how original were Puritan doctrines of marriage?, in: *Social History 5* (1977), 564. The Catholic sources used by Davies (sermons, edifying tracts) date from about 1500. In these lay-oriented instructions Davies also finds the emphasis on mutual companionship and help, mindful of course of the authority of the husband.

RENÉE PIGEAUD

Woman as temptress

Urban morality in the 15th century

Apart from the image of woman as witch and saint presented elsewhere, we want to focus attention here on woman as temptress. It is not difficult to find illustrations of this aspect – there are both prints and texts which depict the danger of the voluptuous woman. Why was it that the theme of the concubine, the mistress who beguiles man into adultery, was so popular in the 15th century? Did people find it risqué, or was there some other intention behind it?

For us the aesthetic function of art, artistic enjoyment, is taken for granted, but it was only in the 19th century that this view developed. Certainly in the Middle Ages art was intended to have a didactic function, even though it might at the same time provide entertainment. By means of telling examples people were taught how to live a good and proper life. These examples were mostly taken from the Bible, but sometimes also from sagas and legends. There are two kinds of example which you can use to propagate virtue: one is to show how things should be done, the other is to illustrate what happens to those who are irresponsible and lead a wicked life. Examples of sinners were very popular, because it was assumed that a moralizing message was most effective when the instructive and the piquant were combined.

The sexual morality of the 15th century burgher was fairly strict; adultery for instance was condemned and punished, as can be seen from civic regulations and guild statutes. Literature, drama and the visual arts all reinforced and propagated this morality by portraying woman as a dangerous temptress and demonstrating how famous men had met their downfall through their mistress. In this way two goals were achieved: art served morality and at the same time people were able to enjoy risqué stories and lewd scenes. The danger of lust or lechery is always one of the central themes. In the majority of cases woman is regarded as the source of all evil: through her charms and wiles she tempts man to commit adultery and thus to stray from the straight and narrow path.

I. URBAN VALUES AND NORMS IN THE 15TH CENTURY

The town and sexual morality

Whilst the Church had of old regarded itself as responsible for the moral conduct of Christians, in the 15th century town councils and other urban organisations, such as the craft guilds, began to take a hand in the morals of the townspeople. As far as morality was concerned efforts were made to control prostitution and to punish adultery. From 1428 onwards the guild statutes of 's-Hertogenbosch (Bois-le-duc) contained a more or less standard article, in which it was punishable to associate with prostitutes (idle women), commit adultery and do dishonest business (profiteering and acting as an illicit middleman).[1] For as long as a person was guilty of committing one of these offences, he was forbidden to practise his craft. If he paid no heed to this, he was obliged to pay a fine

'If a person commits adultery, publicly engages in dishonest business or consorts with prostitutes, the guild masters shall forbid him on oath to practise his

Anonymous master, *The cloth market at 's-Hertogenbosch*, c. 1500, panel, Noord-Brabants Museum, 's-Hertogenbosch. In the foreground the patron saint of the clothiers' guild, St Francis.

craft for as long as he engages in any of the matters mentioned above.'[2]

The town council of 's-Hertogenbosch insisted on legitimate birth as a necessary condition for holding public office. The guild statutes also emphasised that to be eligible for an official function a person must both have been born in the town and also be the issue of a legal marriage.[3]

Although the towns had come into existence much earlier,[4] and there had for some time been an urban patriciate (certain magisterial families and well-to-do merchants) and a large number of crafts[5], it would seem that in the 15th century a specific urban morality developed.[6] In the towns of northwest Europe the town councils gained an ever increasing influence over the life of the burghers, and the burgher for his part felt himself responsible for his town, to which he was bound by rights and obligations (the burgher oath)[7]. The burghers saw the town not only as a practical institution, but also as the place which God had allotted to them. The civic laws were God-given, the town received God's punisment if it behaved in a sinful manner. Every year the townspeople held a procession with the relics of the patron saint of their own town. People saw a close connection between the material prosperity and the godliness of the town, in short there was a desire to integrate the secular and religious functions of the town. The town considered itself 'Christian' and used this as grounds for taking over from the ecclesiastical authorities ever increasing responsibility for the behaviour and spiritual well-being of the burghers.[8]

The town council of Basle, for example, declared in about the mid-15th century that the most important function of every civic authority was to combat sin and crime in the name of God.[9] Sin and crime included blasphemy, violation of the Christian festivals, adultery, gambling and all possible excesses. Concubinage and adultery certainly found no favour with the Council of Basle. In 1441 adulterers were threatened with exile and in 1457 adultery was brought under the civic criminal law.[10] The adulterer was fined or received corporal punishment, the adultress was expelled from the town. In the Seventies illicit love affairs and lechery of all kinds were also threatened with punishment.[11]

Such measures were not restricted to Basle; in Leiden in 1444 the city court also pronounced against adultery. Just as in Basle this was done in order to maintain God's order on earth.

> 'Thus the court of the town has truly learnt and proved that many people within the town of Leiden have publicly engaged in adultery and are still doing so every day, which is a sin against God and the Holy Church . . .'

The court pointed out that the guilty had already been 'talked to' in vain by the church. Leiden could not tolerate this transgression and it was decided that all those who at that moment committed adultery publicly were to separate between then and the coming Palm Sunday and were not to come together again in any way whatsoever.

A firm line was also taken with prostitution. Prostitutes were indeed recognised as a social group, but they were only allowed to settle in certain quarters of the town, mostly in the vicinity of the city gates.[13] The town council supervised them and rented the brothels out to the brothelkeepers.[14] Whores had to wear special clothes, so that they could be taken into custody if they were in prohibited areas.[15]

A middle class value pattern?

As has been said, the urban middle class – both the patriciate, the town councils (sometimes composed of members of the patriciate with representatives of the guilds) and the craft guilds – had its own set of values and norms. Particularly in the course of the 15th century these norms became more clearly formulated. Various modern authors have tried to define this middle class value pattern; characteristic aspects mentioned included the attention paid to work and individual achievement, the need for knowledge and insight into temporal affairs,

the concern for good morals and urban patriotism. Behind all this lay the conviction that what is good for the individual automatically benefits the community as a whole.[16] Linking rational thought with practical examples for good behaviour is characteristic of the late Middle Ages; this has been termed 'ethical practicism'.[17] The contrast with the values of the 'upper class', the court circles, is most striking; in the 15th century the latter occupied themselves principally with aesthetic pleasures such as hunting, tournaments, feasts and banquets.[18]

The ethical practicism of the late medieval burgher was on the one hand modern in the emphasis on rational knowledge and practical use, whilst on the other hand there was no question of a purely pragmatic attitude in a secularized society. Religious and secular affairs were not strictly separated; a virtuous life on earth could be a guarantee for a good place in heaven. Natural disasters and economic recession were experienced as divine punishment and many people looked forward to the year 1500 with apprehension, because that would be the end of the world.

Within Christian thought itself there was a development from strong emphasis on metaphysical knowledge and systematics (scholasticism) to a philosophy which was more oriented to direct experience and to ethics. In some of the European universities – especially those founded in the 15th century – a struggle was in progress between two scientific views: the 'via moderna' and the 'via antiqua'. It was a question of a conflict between an orthodox and a modern view of knowledge, albeit that both remained within the Christian philosophical context. The via antiqua was based on the classical scholasticism of Thomas Aquinas, which came into existence in the 13th century and placed science at the service of religious truths. The via moderna believed that the objective of knowledge was to serve the happiness of material man and to study the world on that basis.[19] The universities were being attended by an ever increasing number of burghers, as well as the clergy.[20] The students from middle class milieus saw their university studies as higher vocational education in subjects including law, theology and medicine. What mattered to them was the practical use, theory was there for the sake of practice, and practical ethics were preferred to metaphysical reflections. This could explain the fact that at the end of the Middle Ages the universities were propagating a new view of philosophy: a real philosopher is someone who lives 'wisely' and not a philosophically trained scholar. Erasmus expressed this in his letters as follows:

> 'The great philosopher is not he who knows the premises of the Stoics or the Peripatetics by heart, but he who expresses the meaning of philosophy through his life and his morals, for that is the purpose of philosophy.'[21]

In one of his *Adagia* (proverbs) Erasmus mentions a number of heathens and Christians who measure up to his criterion of wisdom, including Socrates, Diogenes the Cynic, Epictetes, and as far as Christians are concerned, John the Baptist, the apostles, St Martin, St Francis and Christ himself.[22] They represent the ideal of exceptional behaviour (atopia). As can be seen from these examples, Erasmus wanted to reconcile classical and religious ideals.

Both the Modern Devotion movement and also neo-stoicism emphasised the 'honest life', practical ethics. The followers of the Modern Devotion put more stress on the ethical aspect, whilst considering philosophical knowledge of less importance. According to them the individual tries to attain his own salvation in imitation of Christ or certain saints. The neo-stoic way of thinking of Seneca, for example, was more popular in circles interested in philosophy. In stoic ethics the greatest importance was attached to obeying reason, without allowing oneself to be influenced by the misfortunes of fate. Above all one must not allow oneself to be carried away by feeling, must not grieve, but must keep a cool head and an unsullied soul. One must learn self-control, both in behaviour and in emotions.

The late medieval entrepreneurs evidently felt the need of a practical moral philosophy which would reinforce and justify their work ethic. The merchant must not be put off by misfortunes, but boldly proceed to take risks, especially in business. The book *Der foertuynen troost* of about 1512 from the list of the Brussels' printer Thomas van der Noot contains a dialogue between Reason and Emotion: Emotion is complaining; Reason offers comfort for all her complaints. Reason is the weapon against fate (chance, catastrophe), intellect makes a man insensible to misfortune. The book, which van der Noot appears to have translated from the French, was originally a commentary on Seneca - one of the most important Stoics from the first century of our era. [23]

In many different fields, both within the Church, the universities and also in the towns, the 15th century saw the development of a practical moral theology and moral philosophy. People felt the need of guidelines for the practice of daily life and were clearly seeking examples of 'wise' behaviour. The burgher's behavioural ideal consisted amongst other things of hard work, the use of rational knowledge and irreproachable conduct.

Middle class concern about good morals
As we have seen, people in the towns were keen to regulate prostitution and to counter promiscuity. It was not so much a case of an expression of puritan meddling on the part of the town councils and the craft guilds, as a striking preoccupation of the middle class as a whole with the distinction between moral and immoral behaviour. This moralism appears to have increased in the course of the 15th century and around 1500 there is a veritable peak in moralising texts and illustrations, as we shall see in the second half of this article.

The development in the Middle Ages of a classification of occupations into 'honourable' and 'dishonourable' (shameful) is a good example of the need for an ever more refined distinction between respectable and reprehensible occupations. Both in the German and in the French-speaking areas there had already been an occupational hierarchy in the towns since the 12th century.[24] The classification of occupations was based on the criteria of the two highest estates, the nobility and the clergy.

Merchants were despised by these classes because they dealt with money. With the rise of the towns the middle class merchants acquired more influence, and thus in the 12th and 13th centuries the occupational hierarchy also altered because the non-middle class taboo on earning money was dropped.[25] Within the towns a clear division of labour gradually emerged, which in turn resulted in the need of a more differentiated status hierarchy, in which new groups of merchants, craftsmen and other occupational groups could be classified.[26]

The classification into honourable and dishonourable occupations reflected to a high degree the new socio-economic structure of the towns. People established their identity not only towards one another, but also in a religious form, in that each craft chose and venerated its own patron saint. The criteria for this classification was based partly on socio-economic grounds, but also partly went back to deep rooted pre-Christian taboos, such as that on blood (this applied for instance to the occupation of butcher, executioner and surgeon) and that on uncleanliness (for example the occupation of fuller, dyer and cook – work that made you dirty).[27]

Groups which were already despised from of old were the prostitutes and the jongleurs: people who in any way traded their bodies. According to a scholastic classification they were not only bad 'ex occasione' (in certain cases), but 'ex natura' (by nature).[28] The voluptuous behaviour occurring in prostitution probably played the greatest part in the contempt shown for this occupation; earning money was not in itself considered so wicked. There is even a 13th century theological tract which draws a distinction between 'good' and 'bad' whores.[29] A good whore does indeed hire her body out, but she performs 'work'. In so far as she receives money for her 'work', she is lawfully engaged. However, if she prostitutes herself for lust, then she is doubly evil: the deed is shameful and so too is the reward; in that case there is no question of 'work', but of the 'satisfaction of lust'. At the end of the argument the author suddenly remembers that prostitution is bad by nature, thus that really no distinc-

Siegburg funnel-necked cup with picture of a fool, 16th century, Nijmeegs Museum 'Commanderie van Sint-Jan', Nijmegen.

tion may be made with regard to the motives for the behaviour. Further there is a passage in the 13th century *Sachsenspiegel*, a Saxon statute book, which includes the following: 'the jongleurs and whores resign their honour for money or goods and exhibit themselves publicly.'[30] Thus apart from the money aspect, dishonourable behaviour is evidently that which is especially connected with the exhibition of the body. This applied to a greater extent to prostitutes than to jongleurs, since they not only exhibited their body, but also received bodily secretions from different people, things which in this context counted as filth and waste.[31]

Adulterers and illegitimate children formed another dishonourable category. Sexual intercourse which had not been sanctioned by the Church through the consecration of marriage placed those involved in the 'dishonourable' category. From the beginning of the 13th century onwards a proof of 'honourable' birth, i.e. birth in wedlock, was required for admission to the guilds. Children who were born 'too early', that is to say within nine months of the marriage ceremony, were also debarred from membership of the guilds when they grew up.[32]

All categories of dishonourableness have in common the connection with the bodily, the organic and the animal element in man. An increasing number of things which were associated with the human body and which were reminders of the animal element in man, were designated unclean, contagious and dishonourable.[33] You could see in the development of the notion of dishonour a symptom of the advancing process of civilisation, a hypothetical process of a socio-psychological nature. In the beginning people draw up rules for social intercourse which gradually become spiritualised, so that they assume the function of a 'conscience'. This applies in particular to the rules concerned with the control of instinctive impulses, such as primary passions and spontaneous outbursts of temper. In the course of time people become ashamed of things to which they previously took no exception.[34]

The development of a new middle class morality can be explained by a fusion of various factors: psychological, cultural and socio-economic. From the psychological point of view the burgher exhibited an inclination to emphasise self-control, amongst other things in the sexual field; culturally he wished to distinguish himself from the nobility and the clergy and also from the uncivilised countryfolk. The desire to maintain the distinction in status between honourable and dishonourable occupations certainly played a part; through his morals and his behaviour the burgher wanted to distance himself not only from certain despised occupational groups, but also from the poor countryfolk who flocked to the towns. The fact that the guild statutes placed so much emphasis on good morals is probably connected with the social fear of being identified with dishonourable, unrefined people.[35] The smaller the social distance between honourable craftsmen and dishonourable, the greater the fear of the former to be contaminated by the latter, that is to say put on a par with them. The more elevated circles and the authorities naturally attached less importance to the middle class notions of virtue.

At the end of the 15th century economic recession was in evidence. The drift of impoverished farmers and countryfolk to the towns was on the increase. This placed heavy economic pressure on the towns; the population expanded whilst wages dropped and grain prices rose. During the years 1481–1483 there was a general economic crisis throughout northwest Europe, due in part to the failure of the grain harvest.[36] If there is indeed a connection between diminishing social differences on account of economic decline and increasing fear of losing social status, that is to say of being identified with socially despised groups, then this could well be one of the important explanatory factors for the striking concern by the middle class, and especially the guilds, for their 'own' good morals at the end of the 15th century. In other words, tolerance towards 'asocial people' thrives more in an economically prosperous society than in one threatened by poverty. A means of elevating yourself above others is to pass judgment on dangerous newcomers.[37]

The crisis of the Eighties also made itself felt in The Netherlands there were often strikes in the towns and the guilds tried to make the best of the difficult economic situation. To add to the problems there were continual wars with France and between the various territories.[38] In these crisis years the cloth industry also went through a bad period with greatly increasing competition and a mounting burden of debts.[39] It was not until 1494 when Philip the Fair came to power that the situation began to improve and numerous towns took vigorous measures to restore the economy.[40] A first report on the penurious state of the people of Leiden dates from 1486. In 1491 a plan to levy a new tax was dropped because it was feared that with the prevailing poverty there might be danger of 'great inconvenience, which could proceed from riots, commotions and rebellions'.[41] 1480–1500 was also a bad period in France, during which there was growing hatred and suspicion of the poor and vagabonds and increasing prostitution due to the impoverishment in the towns. Even needy middle class women were forced by lack of money to become prostitutes.[42]

The drift of the countryfolk to the towns resulted in a decrease in the informal control exercised by family and neighbours, people became alienated from the close social ties which existed in the country. The urban middle class reacted to the newcomers by formalising and tightening up the social control within the towns. The burgher symbolised the distinction between him and the new-comers in an idiom of virtue and refinement. Prostitution, for example, had for centuries been a 'dishonourable' occupation, but people now felt the urge to portray the whore's lust as particularly pernicious. A legal marriage and legitimate birth had for long been conditions for membership of a guild, but at the end of the 15th century they became extemely important as proof of irreproach-able behaviour. The middle class concern with good morals was motivated not so much by the idea of educating the lower social classes, but was much more a proof of their own virtue and unsullied morals. One

Master of Leiden, *Worldly pleasure*, c. 1510–1515, painting on glass, Stedelijk Museum de Lakenhal, Leiden.

could still make ones mark by good morals, whilst in the economic field the distinction with the dishonourable section of the urban population was growing increasingly small.

Lucas van Leyden (1489/94–1533), *A man with a torch, arm in arm with a woman, followed by a fool*, c. 1507, engraving.

II. ART AND MIDDLE CLASS MORALITY AT THE END OF THE 15th AND BEGINNING OF THE 16th CENTURIES

In this section an attempt will be made to show a relation between the sexual morality of the burgher and various literary and visual themes of the late Middle Ages. As has been said, the moralising function of art was fully accepted as a matter of course by 15th century man. The more the didactic message was translated into concrete - often exemplary - pictures, the more impression it made on people.

Through the printed book, illustrated with woodcuts, certain themes gained great popularity, the more so as the texts were translated into the vernacular of the different countries.

A remarkable amount of interest was shown in the figure of the 'fool'. At about the end of the 15th century books even appeared in which the fool, or the personification of 'folly' was the principal character. A famous example is the *Narrenschiff (Ship of Fools)* by Sebastian Brant dating from 1494. It has been translated into numerous languages; around the turn of the century a Latin, a French and a Flemish version were in circulation in the Low Countries.

Another popular theme was that of 'women's wiles', in which woman's role as temptress was emphasised and men were warned against falling into her trap, victim to her cunning. Lucas Van Leyden used the subject of women's wiles for many of his prints. The paintings of Hieronymus Bosch contain a more general warning against all forms of sexual temptation.

In humanistic circles the theme of 'Hercules at the cross-roads' was very popular, especially for Latin school texts. This subject gives a learned view of the choice between virtue and lust.

The 'fool' around 1500

In German literature of the late Middle Ages the fool often plays the principal role, both in farces (shrovetide plays) as well as didactic poems. The fool is the antipode of the wise man. A wise man is one who knows the divine laws and has the ability to live his life in accordance with them, whereas the fool possesses neither the knowledge nor the ability to live wisely.[43] In the Bible 'foolishness' is a religious-ethical, not a psychological notion; the foolish man is a sinner, but not mad or deranged. The fool is, as it were, foolishness in the flesh, not an abstract conception, but a figure which makes a direct appeal to the imagination. He is immediately recognisable by certain attributes, such as the fool's cap with ass's ears and bells and the marotte, the fool's sceptre. Both the ass's ears and the marotte probably point to the sensuality of the fool.[44] The ass is not only a symbol of stupidity, like the monkey and the cuckoo, but also of sensuality. The fool exhibits himself with animal attributes; he is a human being, but at the same time his head is entirely enveloped in a fool's cap with ass's ears. He personifies the sinfulness, but also the animal nature of man. In the shrovetide plays the fool's significance is usually ambivalent; he behaves both comically and irresponsibly. Finally there is also a positive view of the fool: with Erasmus 'Stultitia' (folly) steps outside society and unmasks so-called wisdom, whereby she has a precisely clarifying effect.[45] However, the fool is usually intended as a negative example, especially in the moralising didactic poetry of the end of the 15th century. He behaves stupidly, dissolutely and sinfully, in short he personifies the very characteristics which the respectable Christian burgher should not exhibit. He is the prototype of the late medieval 'anti-burgher', who has no Christian sense of responsibility and allows himself to be carried away by his passions. Particularly as regards sex the fool allows himself far more liberty than the burgher. He frequently succumbs to the temptation of Venus' hand-maids, but he also receives his due punishment in that he comes away worse than he went.[46]

The negative aspects of the fool - his sinfulness and irrationality - are most clearly expressed in Sebastian Brant's moralising satire *Das Narrenschiff (The Ship of Fools)*. In Brant's work the fool loses his grotesque and humorous aspect as seen in the shrovetide plays and becomes a figure of negative identification; you must above all not behave like a fool, because then you make yourself ridiculous and you come to a bad end.[47] What exactly are the fool's sins? They amount in fact to the seven deadly sins: pride, envy, covetousness, lust, gluttony, anger and sloth. It is striking that in Brant's examples from everyday life he stresses the very aspects of these sins which are 'anti-middle class'. The virtues which are highly valued by the burghers, such as simplicity, thrift, punctuality, perseverance and sexual discipline are exactly the opposite of the sins of the fool. These virtues are characteristic of the urban middle class and were the very virtues which were propagated in various forms as practical ethics.[48] Thus in Brant's work we see on the one hand that he reverts to the biblical significance of foolishness - living a life of sin - and on the other hand that he expresses a contemporary view of the fool as the reverse of the late medieval burgher's moral ideals.[49]

Das Narrenschiff (The Ship of Fools) by Sebastian Brant

This book dating from 1494 occupies a key position in the literature on fools at the end of the 15th century. Its enormous popularity was due not only to the text but also and more especially to the woodcuts accompanying each of the 112 chapters. Each woodcut depicts a male or female fool behaving 'foolishly'.

Sebastian Brant was very closely involved in the urban society of his day. He was born in 1457 in Strasbourg, where his father was the owner of the well-known inn 'Le Lion d'Or'.[50] He studied civil and canon law in Basle, where he was later appointed professor of law, and finally returned to Strasbourg, where he became town clerk in 1503. Brant wrote in both German and Latin; in 1494

The woodcut contains the following text labels:

Das Narren **schyff**

Ad Narragonia

har noch

Title page of Sebastian Brant's *Das Narrenschyff* (*The Ship of Fools*), Basle 1494, woodcut.

apart from *The Ship of Fools* he also wrote the Latin *Carmina*. In 1497 *The Ship of Fools* was translated into Latin by his pupil Locher Philomusus (1471–1528) and was subsequently translated from Latin into other European languages. [51] The form of the book is based on an old carnival theme: the 111 fools who sail to Narragonia.

Brant associated with craftsmen as well as with the urban patriciate and intellectuals. Like most of his contemporaries he dreamed of the time when the Church would return to its original evangelical mission. He may be counted as one of the first generation of German humanists, whose cult of Antiquity did not yet lead to the renunciation of the Church, but who tried to purge the existing mentality from within. Geiler von Kaysersberg, the writer of numerous penitential sermons, was their mentor. [52] In Brant's work the world is both a 'dwelling place of the devil' and a 'fool's abode', thus not only the realm of sin, but also a place where folly and not wisdom has the last word. [53]

With regard to woman Brant exhibits the same 'middle class' attitude as in the rest of his thinking. True he does not revile women, but he does not admire them either. There is certainly no question with Brant of an exalted song of praise to the 'lady' as was customary in chivalrous culture. He considers that 'courting by night' (a nocturnal serenade to the beloved) is ridiculous and foolish. Dancing is also a source of trouble, since physical contact inflames the passions. [54] Furthermore he warns men against marrying women whose only quality is their beauty. Such a woman only encourages adultery.

'And then it seems to me 'twere right
If many a guest you'd not invite,
This is preeminently true
In case your wife is fair to view;
On no one can one quite depend,
Of falsity there is no end.' [55]

Brant is by no means the most anti-female writer, but he too issues continual warnings about the voluptuous woman, the wife who commits adultery. The voluptuous woman makes herself up too much, plays cards with men and addresses men in the street.[56] In the chapter on 'Of Bad Women' he mentions a number of women, whose charms enticed men to their downfall. He gives not only well-known examples from the Bible, such as the concubines of Solomon and Herodias with her daughter Salome,[57] but also women from classical Antiquity such as Medea, Clytemnestra and the Danaides. Brant's knowledge of the Bible and the classics is also displayed in other chapters, such as 'Of Amours' and 'Of Sensual Pleasure'. In 'Of Amours' he gives a whole list of famous men whom Venus had made a fool of, such as David, Samson, Solomon, Amon, Joseph (the son of Jacob), Aristotle, Virgil and Ovid. A number of heroes constantly occur in a set combination as the victim of love in the 'women's wiles'.[58]

In the preface to *The Ship of Fools* Brant apologises to the good and honourable women - it was not his intention to offend them in his poem. He values the role of woman as wife, housewife and mother. (He was married himself and had a son). The basis of the successful marriage is not love, but the friendship and trust between partners. Such a union is a source of joy and a good example for the children. The moral conduct of the mother determines that of her children. It is especially important not to give any occasion for adultery.

> 'A wife who would be modest found
> Should cast her eyes upon the ground
> And not coquet when'er she can
> And not make eyes at every man,
> Nor heed what'er one says and does.
> Panders will often wear sheep's clothes.'[59]

As we see, Brant is not possessed by hatred and fear of woman, nor does he exalt her cultural and social contribution to society, as did some of his contemporaries amongst the Italian humanists. He shared the middle class family ideals of his milieu, in which the man was the person of authority and a subservient role was allotted to the woman.[60]

The danger of lust portrayed in the visual arts

It goes almost without saying that certain middle class

'If through his fingers one can see And lets his wife promiscuous be, As cat she views the mice with glee.'
Title print to chapter 33 *Of adultery* from: Sebastian Brant, *Das Narrenschyff*, Basle 1494, woodcut.

49

Master E.S. (end 15th century), *Large garden of love*, engraving.

norms concerning marriage and sexuality were also propagated by means of visual representations. It has been pointed out by a number of art historians that in the 15th century a form of middle class art developed, that is to say, art by burghers for a burgher public.[61] Apart from copper engravings, woodcuts were especially favoured as a medium to give visual expression to certain themes. Woodcuts were also much in use for book illustration, as in *The Ship of Fools*.

What were these middle class themes – so often chivalrous and biblical subjects, newly interpreted in the visual arts? The most important motif is certainly the representation of the danger of lust. There are various ways in which that can be portrayed. In the first place the presence of a fool in the company often indicates the 'sensual' character of a gathering of men and women, whether it takes place in a love garden[62], an inn or on a fool's ship. The fool represents, as it were, the key to the type of message being illustrated: he seems to indicate that there is something sinful and irrational going on here.[63] In order to give the content of the message more conviction, the fool also behaves in a shameless manner and, for example, exhibits his genitals. The burgher knew only too well that whatever he did, he should not imitate the fool's behaviour; conjugal fidelity and control of the passions were the very qualities by which he could distinguish himself from the uneducated.

The theme of women's wiles presumably also had a moralising intention: it illustrates the danger of lust by showing the humiliation of the hero at the hands of his beloved. The theme had already been in use for centuries, though its significance shifted over the years. When it became popular in middle class circles in the 15th century, it finally assumed the meaning of a warning against adultery. The theme was first used in the visual arts in the 13th century, though it was already known in literature. It shows famous men, such as Samson (example of strength), Solomon (example of wisdom) and David (example of sanctity) who met their undoing through their beloved.[64] Adam is often added to these examples as being the first man who was tempted by a woman. The Malterer tapestry from the beginning of the 14th century depicts noble heroes at the height of their fame and then at the moment at which they were ruined by a woman.[65] The subject was eminently suited to the chivalrous culture, in which the contrast between honour and humiliation was so important.

The knight fought for honour's sake, but ended up in utmost misery through low, perfidious Love. The tapestry also shows how love for Christ (medallion with woman and unicorn) is ultimately higher than the love between man and woman.[66] Women's wiles were often cited in sermons as a warning against worldly love. However, when the subject occurs in secular poetry it sometimes has an apologetic significance: if famous men have fallen a prey to love, how can I, as an ordinary mortal, hope to escape this fate?[67]

In the 15th century this subject, which had been used in the chivalrous and religious applied visual arts, found its way into prints. The meaning was now adjusted to the needs of a middle class public, which was not so much concerned with the contrast between spiritual and worldly love, as with the distinction between conjugal fidelity and infidelity. Since the emphasis was laid on the ignominious consequences of illicit intercourse (adultery), the prints implicitly propagated conjugal fidelity and legal marriage. Supporting evidence for this interpretation of the late medieval women's wiles is to be found in the fact that numerous town halls of the period contain representations of women's wiles.[68] In most cases it is decorative art, such as ornamentation on chairs or ceilings. As has been noted earlier on, the town council felt itself responsible for the moral behaviour of the citizens; adultery had no place in the social-religious order. Lucas van Leyden's two series of woodcuts (dating from 1514 and 1517), each comprising six illustrations of women's wiles, were most likely intended to be moralising: if even heroes can be tempted to commit adultery, then as an ordinary burgher you must certainly be very careful that it does not happen to you.

Georg Pencz (c. 1500–1550), *Aristotle and Phyllis*, engraving.

Lucas van Leyden (1489/94–1533), *Aristotle and Phyllis*, c. 1515, woodcut.

The subject was also frequently to be found in late medieval literature. An early 16th century work, in which the stories of the wiles are recounted, is the book *Dat bedroch der vrouwen* (The deceyte of women). Apart from all sorts of other love stories with a bad ending, the book also describes the women's wiles depicted in Lucas van Leyden's little series of woodcuts.[69] A description has also survived of a festival of snowmen in Brussels in 1511, in which the writer Jan Smeken gives a list in verse of what there was to be seen in the city in the way of snowmen and snowhouses. There are for instance a variety of contemporary figures such as the bossy wife and the henpecked husband, but also traditional figures such as Aristotle and Phyllis, one of the classic couples from the women's wiles.[70]

The subjects depicted by Hieronymus Bosch can also be linked with middle class morality. Bosch was to portray visually what was usually expressed in words in his time. Attempts have been made to interpret Bosch's pictures as a visual translation of metaphors and verbal puns.[71] For someone in the 20th century these expressions are no longer comprehensible, but for the inhabitants of 's-Hertogenbosch at the end of the 15th century they were presumably readily understandable. An example of this is the painting 'The Temptation of St Anthony'.[72] Anthony is tormented by the presence of a house, the roof of which is formed by the head of an old woman. On her head the woman bears a dovecot. In the door opening there is a naked woman who has sunk into the earth up to her knees. Another woman is seated at a small table and a third is looking out of a window. There is a flag with a swan protruding from the house. All this becomes comprehensible when we know that 'dovehouse' was another word for a brothel and 'dove' for whore, and that 'cock pigeon' referred to lover or adulterer. The swan on the flag indicates a harlot or whore. The woman who is up to her knees in the earth has sunk into the pool of destruction. There are many more things to be found in the painting which are connected with fornication and unchastity, but the most striking is certainly the fusion of

Copy after Hieronymus Bosch (c. 1450–1516), *The temptation of St Anthony*, panel, Rijksmuseum, Amsterdam.

the brothel with its owner, both of which afford opportunity for committing fornication.

Apart from unchastity Bosch also criticises sins such as gluttony and drunkenness - in short the sins of the foolish jester.[73] In reality these sins were mainly ascribed to the lower classes, who had been reduced to beggary as a result of their dissolute life. The label 'dishonourable' is certainly applicable to this group of people. Bosch himself is said to have come from the middle class and as a 'pictor doctus' (learned painter) to have portrayed the humanistic, intellectual and cultural aspirations of his class.[74] The penurious people who commit all sorts of sins represent the negative ideal of the burgher; their unrestrained and brutish behaviour was contradictory to the middle class values of virtue, rationality and refinement.

The choice between Virtue and Lust

In the chapter 'Of reward for wisdom' in the *Ship of Fools* Brant describes true wisdom: only he who is humble and conscious of his own fool's cap shall belong to the small group who will find favour in God's sight; but the self-conceited will be punished. Many think that they are on the right path, but still choose the wrong road. Up to this point Brant's argument fits completely into the medieval tradition of divine punishment and reward, but he adds an example of a totally different order, namely the original classical Greek parable of Hercules at the cross-roads.[75] On the path of life Hercules meets two women, each of whom tries to win him over. One is Virtue, the other Lust. Hercules finally chooses of his own free will the severe figure of Virtue and not the attractive figure of Lust.

'The other one seemed pale, hard, sour,
Her mien was joyless every hour,
She said: "No joy I promise you,
No rest, and labors not a few,
On virtue you will virtue heap
And recompense eternal keep."
Then Hercules went where she led,
Joy, idleness, delight he fled.'[76]

The motif of Hercules at the cross-roads is totally alien to medieval thought. It was only through the first generation of humanists, including Brant, that after several centuries the theme became popular again in both literary and visual form. Brant himself is really standing at a sort of cross-roads, namely between two different ethical views. On the one hand he believes that man is essentially a sinner and can only be saved by belief in Christ, but on the other hand he recognises the idea of free will, the conscious choice between good and evil.[77] With a philosopher such as Erasmus we find the view that man is good by nature, and can achieve virtue by his own efforts much more emphatically expressed than with Brant. As the source of the parable of Hercules at the cross-roads Brant took the Latin version of the Church Father Basil (329–379 AD).[78] Basil does not describe Virtue as beautiful, but ugly, serious and severe, as was customary in some early Christian ascetic writings. This view fitted very well into the way of thought of the late medieval burgher, who also attached great value to self control, rationality and ethical gravity.

In the Latin translation of *The Ship of Fools* by Locher Philomusus, *Stultifera Navis*, use is made of yet another version of the Hercules fable. Locher almost literally follows the text of the Roman poet Silius Italicus (1st century AD).[79] The latter paints a completely different picture of Virtue from that of the pale severe woman who advises you to toil in sweat in order to attain to the joys of heaven. His 'Virtus' promises those who follow her political power, literary fame and military victories, in short worldly fame and not heavenly peace. Locher's Latin translation of the fable is based on his Roman model both in form and content. We may assume that he was not unsympathetic towards the Roman way of thought and that the combination of virtue and worldly fame was not alien to him. He was the exponent of a new ideal for men of letters; with him we reach the second generation Humanists, whose emphasis is more on Renaissance than on medieval ideals.

If we look at the woodcut which accompanies Locher's

'Concertatio virtutis cum voluptate', we are back as it were in the late Middle Ages, in the world of Sebastian Brant.[80] The woodcut shows a dormant knight (Hercules), behind him rise two hills, on the left hand hill there is a naked woman (Lust), on the right hand the chaste figure of Virtue. Beside Lust a rosehedge is visible, behind her stands Death, smiling sardonically, and above her head lap the flames of hell. Virtue is portrayed as a woman with a distaff in one hand and a Bible and a rosary in the other. Beside her are thistles and thorns and above her head a starry sky. Brant himself probably gave directions for the composition. Contrary to the text of *The Ship of Fools* the two women do not approach Hercules, but are standing at the end of two paths.

This interpretation of the Hercules fable is to be traced back to the Greek poet Hesiodus (8th century BC).[81] A theme related to the two ways or 'The straight and narrow path' is however also to be found in the Bible, both in the Old and New Testament.[82] In late medieval drama this theme of the 'via mortis' and the 'via vitae' was very popular.[83] To make things even more complicated the parting of the ways in the woodcut is in the form of a Greek y; this points to Brant's knowledge of the pythagorean letter symbolism.[84]

If we return to the two women, it appears that they also have a rich iconographic tradition behind them. Lust is depicted as the naked 'Unchastity' (one of the seven deadly sins) - unchastity is often symbolised by nakedness in Christian iconography. Death standing behind her refers to the 'danse macabre' motif of 'Death and the girl'. The rosehedge is a biblical motif, roses grow along the broad path of sin, whilst the narrow path of virtue leads over thorns.[85] The flames of hell behind Lust speak for themselves. If we look at her opponent, Virtue, then we are immediately struck by the distaff, from olden times the symbol of female activity, the rosary and the Bible point to her godliness. However, she must not be seen as a picture of a housewife selected at random; she too is a traditional symbol, that of Dame Poverty.[86]

On another woodcut, also made for *The Ship of Fools*, it

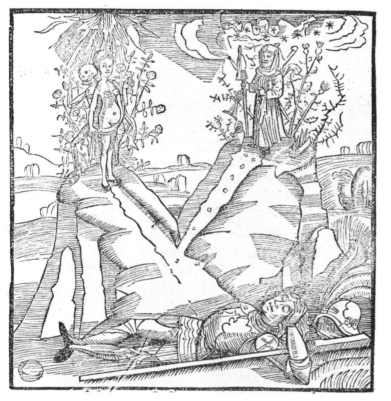

Hercules at the crossroads, woodcut from: Sebastian Brant, *Stultifera Navis*, Basle 1497.

can be seen even more clearly that Virtue wears ragged garments and worn-out sandals. Dame Poverty is not a beggar, but a symbol of ascetism and renunciation of the world; she cares nothing for sensual pleasure and worldly riches, but she is virtuous, poor and meek. In her appearance she reflects the ideal of poverty of the Franciscans for instance; modesty and humility are more important than beauty and self-assurance. In particular in the large woodcut of Hercules and the two women, we find a unique synthesis of classical and medieval motifs. One single print contains a depiction of the ethical-religious views and the classical-humanist erudition of Brant and his fellow burghers.[87]

III. CONCLUSION

The preceding sections have given a broad sketch of the morals of the urban middle class in the 15th century; an attempt has been made to show a connection between sexual morality, as propagated in the town by the town council and craft guilds, and the moralising content of certain works of art of the period. The view that the 15th century saw the development of a specific middle class morality, supported by codes of behaviour, is gaining increasing ground.[88] Ethical practicism in its various forms is characteristic of this morality; the emphasis on rational knowledge; and the condemnation of all forms of behaviour which have anything to do with man's animal instincts. As far as marriage is concerned the moral norms were directed at combatting any form of unchastity and dishonour. The honourable woman does not make herself up, remains in the background and is above all a faithful wife. Marriage is the best guarantee for man and woman against unchastity, it helps maintain the social stability of the town and the distinction from the dishonourable is emphasised by a lawful marriage.

In this context we must remember that the distinction between religious and secular values as we know them was not applicable. For the late medieval burgher there was still a close connection between sinfulness, irrationality and social dishonour. Religion, ethical and social values were not to be separated from one another.

Virtus and *Voluptas*, woodcut from: Sebastian Brant, *Stultifera Navis*, Basle 1497.

1. Cf. N.W. Posthumus, *De geschiedenis van de Leidse lakenindustrie*, The Hague 1908.
2. This article occurs for the first time in the statutes of the bakers' guild of 9 September 1428 (art. 13). See N.H.L. van den Heuvel, *De ambachtsgilden van 's-Hertogenbosch voor 1629*, I (sources), Utrecht 1946, 105; and: van den Heuvel, *De ambachtsgilden van 's-Hertogenbosch voor 1629*, (thesis) Utrecht 1946, 152 ff.
3. Van den Heuvel (sources), op.cit., 104; Van den Heuvel (thesis) op.cit., 109.
4. The towns had already come into being in the early Middle Ages; cf. E. Ennen, *Die europäische Stadt des Mittelalters*, Göttingen 1975. 's-Hertogenbosch acquired city rights in 1185.
5. The oldest guild of 's-Hertogenbosch is that of the smiths, whose statutes date from 1302. In 1494 there were 18 craft guilds in the city. Cf. Van den Heuvel (thesis), op.cit., 11.
6. The development of a burgher morality in the 15th century has been postulated amongst others by H. Pleij in *Het gilde van de Blauwe Schuit. Literatuur, volks-feest en burgermoraal in de late middeleeuwen*, Amsterdam 1979, and in *De wereld volgens Thomas van der Noot*, Muiderberg 1982. Some criticism may be made of this socio-economic interpretation of medieval texts; cf. the review of *Het gilde van de Blauwe Schuit* by J.B. Drewes in: *De nieuwe taalgids 74* (1981), 253-275.
7. B. Moeller, *Imperial cities and the reformation*, Philadelphia 1972, 45.
8. Idem, 48 ff.; F. Rapp, *Réformes et Réformation à Strassbourg*, Paris 1974, 453 ff.
9. R. Wackernagel, *Geschichte der Stadt Basel*, Basle 1916, II, chapter 2, 871.
10. Idem, 923.
11. Idem, 924.
12. P.J. Blok, *Leidsche rechtsbronnen uit de Middeleeuwen*, The Hague 1884, 73.
13. Wackernagel, op.cit., 922 (Basle); Blok, op.cit., 267 (Leiden).
14. J. Rossiaud, 'La prostitution dans les villes francaises au XVe siècle, in: *Communications 35 (Sexualités occidentales)*, Paris 1982, 68 ff.
15. P. Blok, op.cit., has included a case against a certain Geertrui, who was suspected of keeping a brothel in a 'forbidden' area.
16. Cf. Rapp, op.cit., 442 ff. (for Strasbourg); Pleij, *Thomas van der Noot*, op.cit., 66 (for Brussels).
17. This term is derived from J. Domanski, 'Ethischer Praktizismus als eine Kategorie zum Beschreiben des Bewusstseins der Philosophen im ausgehenden Mittelalter', in: A. Zimmerman (Hrsg.), *Soziale Ordnungen im Selbstverständnis des Mittelalters I*, Berlin 1979, 298-313.
18. Cf. J. Huizinga, *Herfsttij der Middeleeuwen*, Haarlem 1921. English translation F. Hopman, *The Waning of the Middle Ages*, 1924.
19. M. Markowski, 'Soziaie Grundlagen des Praktizismus und Naturalismus an der Krakauer Universität im 15. Jahrhundert', in: A. Zimmerman (Hrsg.), op.cit., 314-322.
20. Ennen, op.cit., 218-219, points out that a great many medieval universities were founded by the towns.

21. Quoted by J. Huizinga, *Erasmus*, Haarlem 1924, 153.
22. See Domanski, op.cit., 312, note 47.
23. Pleij, *Thomas van der Noot*, 34 ff.
24. A. Blok, 'Infame beroepen', in: *Symposium III* (1981), 104-128. J. Le Goff, *Pour un autre Moyen Age*, Paris 1977, the essay 'Métiers licites et métiers illicites dans l'Occident médiéval', 91-107.
25. Le Goff, op.cit., 97 ff.
26. Le Goff names the 'technicians', such as doctors, surgeons, and writers, as a separate occupational group (op.cit., 104).
27. Le Goff, op.cit., 93 ff.
28. Idem, 97 ff.
29. This refers to the *Poenitentiale* of Thomas of Cabham, subdeacon of Canterbury. He also divided the jongleurs into useful and shameful entertainers. Cf. E. Faral, *Les Jongleurs in France au Moyen-Age*, Paris 1910, 67.
30. A. Blok, op.cit., 112 ff.
31. Idem, 111 note 10.
32. Idem, 115.
33. Idem, 116
34. I am making use here of the theory of Norbert Elias, as expressed in *Ueber den Prozess der Zivilisation*, Bern 1969[2].
35. Fear of social contamination by foreigners is also used by A. Blok as an explanation of the strict distinction between the honourable and the dishonourable. A. de Swaan in his column 'Sociale sortering' (Social grading) *NRC/Handelsblad*, 15.12.1984) arrived at a similar interpretation of the racism of certain population groups. 'Xenophobia and related forms of fear of social contamination are connected with class consciousness . . . Envy of another person's status is heightened by the present social and economic stagnation.'
36. L. Dresen-Coenders in *Het verbond tussen heks en duivel*, thesis Baarn 1983, 122 ff. connects economic recession with the increased fear of witches.
37. See my quotation from A. de Swaan in note 35.
38. The death of Charles the Bold in 1477 also contributed to the social unrest. In 's-Hertogenbosch the guilds revolted against the patriciate and temporarily seized power in the city. Cf. A.M. van Lith-Drooglever Fortuyn, 'De stad 's-Hertogenbosch en haar houding tot het landsheerlijk gezag ca. 1470 -ca. 1500' in: *Varia Historica Brabantica, V*, 's-Hertogenbosch 1976, 55-119.
39. Cf. Posthumous, op.cit., 337 ff. In 1478 there was a great strike amongst the fullers of Leiden, which lasted two months.
40. Cf. Van den Heuvel (thesis), op.cit., 302, and Van Lith-Drooglever Fortuyn, op.cit., 93 ff (administrative reform in 's-Hertogenbosch).
41. Posthumus, op.cit., 388.
42. Rossiaud, op.cit., 80 ff.
43. See amongst others B. Könneker, *Wesen und Wandlung der Narrenidee im Zeitalter des Humanismus*, Wiesbaden 1966, 10. She points to the biblical antithesis sapientia/stultitia in the Books of Wisdom (Proverbs, Ecclesiastes etc.) in the Old Testament.
44. J. Lefebvre, *Les fols et la folie*, Paris 1968. In particular the paragraph on 'Le concept et l'image, 16-22, has

influenced my interpretation.

45. Huizinga, *Erasmus*, op.cit., 99 ff.
46. Könneker, op.cit., 7 ff. Especially in Shrovetide plays, such as the 'Gouchmat' by Pamphilius Gengenbach, the 'fool' often represents the lecherous lover.
47. Könneker, op.cit., 14.
48. Lefebvre, op.cit., 116–119, speaks in connection with Brant's ethics of 'ascesis within the world' and 'the moral of the golden mean'.
49. In chapter 112, 'The wise man', of *Das Narrenschiff* Brant pictures the positive ideal of the burgher. This chapter is actually a translation of the poem 'Vir bonus' by Pseudo-Virgil.
50. Rapp, op.cit., 160. In view of his father's occupation Brant appears to have come from the middle class. See further for Brant's biography: K. Manger, *Das 'Narrenschiff'*, Darmstadt 1983, and D. Wutke, 'Sebastian Brant', in: *Lexikon des Mittelalters, II*, 1982, 574–576.
51. For this motif see also Pleij, *Het gilde van de Blauwe Schuit*, op.cit.
52. See Manger, op.cit., for the influence of Geiler von Kaysersberg on Brant.
53. See the lucid epilogue by H-J Mähl, in: Sebastian Brant, *Das Narrenschiff*, Stuttgart 1980.
54. See Brant, op.cit., ch. 61, 'Of dancing' and ch. 62 'Of serenading at night'.
55. Ch. 33 'Of adultery', verses 59–64. I use the modern English translation by E.H. Zeydel, *The Ship of Fools*, New York 1944, the only straight verse translation which has appeared in English. The first English adaptation by the priest Alexander Barclay, *The Shyp of Folys*, appeared in 1509.
56. See ch. 77 'Of gamblers' and ch. 92 'Presumptuousness of pride'.
57. Cf. I Kings 11,4: 'For it came to pass, when Solomon was old, that his wives turned away his heart after other gods...' This motif is to be found as 'Solomon's idolatry' in various series of 'women's wiles'. See also Th. Vignau Wilberg Schuurman, *Hoofse minne en burgerlijke liefde in de prentenkunst rond 1500*, Leiden 1983. Herodias incites her daughter Salome to ask king Herod for the head of John the Baptist (Matthew 14, 1–13). This subject does not belong to the set theme of 'women's wiles'.
58. I go into the 'women's wiles' in more depth below.
59. Ch. 32 'Of guarding wives', verses 25–30.
60. See also: E. Shorter, *The making of the modern family*, New York 1975; and L. Stone, *The family, sex and marriage in England, 1500–1800*, London 1977.
61. See Vignau Wilberg-Schuurman, op.cit.; further K.P.F. Moxey, 'Master E.S. and the folly of love', in: *Simiolus, II* (1980), 125–148, and P. Vandenbroeck, 'Over Jheronimus Bosch', in *Archivum Artis Lovaniense*, Louvain 1981, 151–188.
62. 'Love garden' refers to the chivalrous theme of the 'garden of love' or 'hortus conclusus', in which chivalrous love was elegantly practised.
63. Cf. Vignau Wilberg-Schuurman, op.cit., 9 ff.
64. For the history of Solomon see note 57. Delilah deprived Samson of his strength by cutting off his hair (Judges 16, 4–22). David committed adultery with Bathsheba, the wife of Uriah, after she had tempted him during her ablutions (II Samuel 11).
65. See F. Maurer, 'Der Topos von den Minnesklaven', in: *Dichtung und Sprache des Mittelalters*, I, Munich 1967.
66. For the antithesis spiritual/carnal love see: Vignau Wilberg-Schuurman, op.cit., 46. See also: Susan Louise Smith, *To women's wiles I fell. The power of women topos and the development of medieval secular art*, thesis, University of Pennsylvania (type-script) 1978.
67. See idem, 43. This refers to the so-called 'more and less' topos of the minne-poets: how could I (the poet) who is after all less strong and wise than they, withstand love.
68. Vignau Wilberg-Schuurman, op. cit., 50. She mentions amongst others the town halls of Courtrai, Damme, Döbeln, Regensburg, Cologne, Reval and Lübeck.
69. See H. Pleij, 'Een fragment van de oudste nederlandse novellenbundel in Cambridge', in: *Opstellen door vrienden & vakgenoten aangeboden aan Dr. C.M.A. Kruyskamp*, The Hague 1977, 142 ff.
70. See Vignau Wilberg-Schuurman, op.cit., 44. The wise Aristotles was so captivated by the beautiful Phyllis that he complied with her request that she should ride him as a horse.
71. See W.S. Gibson, *Hieronymus Bosch*, London 1973. D. Bax was the first to engage in deciphering Hieronymus Bosch. See also Vandenbroeck, op.cit.
72. In the Rijksmuseum, Amsterdam. See D. Bax, 'Jeroen Bosch en de nederlandse taal', in the catalogue *Jheronimus Bosch*, 's-Hertogenbosch 1967, Contributions, 61 ff.
73. These sins are also denounced in Brant's *Narrenschiff* in ch. 16 'Of gluttony and feasting'.
74. Vandenbroek, op.cit., 174.
75. See E. Panofsky, *Hercules am Scheidewege* (Studien der Bibliothek Warburg XVIII), Leipzig 1930.
76. Ch. 107, 'Of reward for wisdom', verses 29–37.
77. Panofsky, op.cit., 45.
78. Idem, 53.
79. Idem, 70.
80. See also Manger, op.cit., 204–205. He gives here a synopsis of Brant's *Narrenschiff* and Locher's *Stultifera Navis*. The 'Concertatio' does not occur in the *Narrenschiff*, nor do the three accompanying woodcuts. They were probably added to the *Navis* at Brant's own instigation.
81. Panofsky, op.cit., 64.
82. See R.P. Zijp, 'The narrow and the broad path; an alternative throughout the centuries', in the catalogue *Vroomheid per dozijn*, Rijksmuseum het Catharijne Convent, Utrecht 1982, 35–42.
83. See W. Helmich, *Die Allegorie im französischen Theater des 15. und 16. Jahrhunderts*, Tübingen 1976, 166 ff.
84. See W. Harms, *Homo viator in bivio. Studien zur Bildlichkeit des Weges*, Munich 1970.
85. See Panofsky, op.cit., 56. This is to be found in the vulgate text of Matthew 7, 13.

86. Panofsky, op.cit., 57.

87. Brant probably wrote a play in 1512 which was also inspired by the Hercules fable; see S. Brant, *Tugent Spyl*, ed. by G.L. Roloff, Berlin 1968. D. Wuttke went into the dating and attribution in his article 'Zu den Tugend-spielen des S. Brant', in: *Zeitschrift für deutsches Altertum*, 1968, 235–246.

88. See Pleij, A. Blok, Vignau Wilberg-Schuurman, Moxey and Vandenbroeck.

LÈNE DRESEN-COENDERS

Witches as devils' concubines

On the origin of fear of witches and protection against witchcraft

I. DEVILS' CONCUBINES

The witches who began being persecuted in the 15th century must be distinguished from the sorceresses who had been operating within and without Christian culture down the ages and who used their magic powers for good or evil purposes. The authors of the famous handbook for exterminating witches, the *Malleus Maleficarum* or *The Hammer of Witches* (1487) were deeply convinced of the difference and accordingly referred to them as the 'modern witches'. The inquisitors Jacobus Sprenger and Henricus Institoris said that the most pernicious heretical sect of witches only came into existence in their time.[1] The eminent authority to whom they appealed was their fellow Dominican, the famous Johannes Nider (died ca. 1439). He completed his influential *Formicarius*[2], in which a chapter was dedicated to the sect, at the time of the Council of Basle (1431–1437). A printed edition of this appeared in Cologne no later than 1473 and was followed by many more.[3] The emphasis on women in the *Formicarius* is nevertheless not as strong as in the *Malleus Maleficarum*. The rapid spread of the ideas from the *Formicarius* probably benefitted from Nider's prominent position among the councillors, who came from far and wide. Possibly the disaster of the first major European grain crisis of the 15th century which occurred just at this time (1437–1439), enhanced the credibility of Nider's argument. In fact in the *Formicarius* it is the male sorcerers, who are able to conjure up hailstorms among other things, who play an important part.

The *Malleus* argues that in contrast to the witches of earlier times the modern witches freely consecrate themselves to the devil with body and soul.[4] They enter into a pact with him, a pact which must be viewed in the light of the rapidly approaching end of time. Bearing this in mind, the devil's kingdom assiduously endeavours to extend its bounds. The most useful weapons in the battle against the Kingdom of God are those lecherous women whose unchaste desires make them prepared to give themselves wholly to the devil and to fornicate with him. There are also some men who enter into the unholy pact but their number is smaller, mainly because their lust is not so insatiable. In contrast to the female parties to the pact, the men have to be forced to copulate with devils in human form.

Thus it is only the very lowest sort of devils in the hierarchy of hell who have to carry out the dirty business, as incubi, by copulating with these lewd women. The succubi, demons in female form who copulate with men, belong to a rather higher order of devils.

On account of the preponderance of women in the new sect, the authors of the *Malleus* characterized the parties to the pact as female in the very title of their book: maleficarum and not maleficorum. The concentration on women was at variance with the Papal Bull on witches which the two inquisitors had obtained in Rome in support of their work in 1484. The fact that Rome had its hands more than full with male dissidents probably played a part in this. Thus the Bull needed to be supplemented.

In addition to copulation with a devil in human form the main characteristics of the 'modern witches' are the killing of unborn and newly born children, preferably unbaptized, along with the dedication to the devil of those children who do live. Naturally it is mainly mothers who have the opportunity of committing these shameful deeds. Moreover, midwives also have special power with regard to the unborn and recently born. According to the authors, the special power of women in the field of reproduction even explains the devils' preference for female accomplices.[5] The position of women within the new sect also explains why men are frequently the victims of witchcraft, particularly in the sexual area. Witchcraft can cause impotence and irresistable feelings of repugnance for men's own wives together with great passion with regard to other women.

But also by means of other 'maleficia', that is to say pernicious acts of magic, the witches are obliged to contribute as much as they can to the extension of the devil's kingdom. The victim of the maleficia would undoubtedly be even more susceptible to demonic enchantment in their desperation. Black magic of old, in which the devil only took part at most as an assistant, was thus incorporated into the new doctrine on witches. Even the term 'maleficium' became interpreted anew. This came to mean: 'male de fide sentire', which is to say 'treat faith with malice'. As the authors of the *Malleus* themselves point out in their introduction, their doctrines on witches consist of old elements which each had a long history. However, their systematic integration in the doctrine of the pact with the devil was new. The great question is why this integration which evidently met with such a response, occurred just then in the 15th century. Were there perhaps social problems involved which lent the pact between devils and witches a degree of plausibility? Do these problems come through in the *Malleus*?

Contemporaries on the danger of witches

The prolix argumentation of the *Malleus* concerning the

A woman being wooed by the devil.
A man being bewitched.
Two witches creating storms and thunder.
Woodcut from Ulricus Molitorus, *De lamiis et phitonicus mulieribus*, Reutlingen, 1489.

existence of the new sect sometimes contains interesting references to the social problems of those days. This is thanks to the disbelief that the doctrine of witches encountered among the clerical and secular authorities. It was the authors' top priority to convince above all clergymen and judges that the evidence they had gathered as inquisitors during the investigation into witchcraft was not just a figment of their imagination.

An objection which was frequently heard was that God can punish mankind with (natural) plagues even without witches.[7] At the time of the appearance of the Malleus plagues were not a feature of the distant past. Thus the second major European grain crisis of the 15th century (1481–1483) was still clearly remembered. It was just at this time that the inquisitors were summoned to Ravensburg because two women had been accused of having caused the total destruction of the grain and grape crops. At the trial the inquisitors were not only able to gain confirmation of this accusation but also the confession of the pact with the devil, which no one had suspected until then and which had been expressed in fornication with the devil down the years. And it was precisely as a result of this pact which was entered into freely that God allowed disasters to be brought about in unnatural ways.[8]

A kindred objection to the doctrine of witches was that witches were really not necessary if God permitted the devil to afflict mankind with misfortune. The Old Testament figure of Job was the most obvious example of this. The authors replied that at that time there were not yet any 'modern witches' as there were now in the crucial endtime. By means of them the devil was able to affront God to an even greater degree.

Another sort of objection concerned the sanctity of the sacrament of marriage. How could God permit that as a result of witchcraft on the community of marriage and by interference with reproduction the human race should be led to destruction? The *Malleus* replied that this was permitted because of the repugnance of the sexual act. This act had of course always been connected with lust

Witches and their maleficia, woodcut from U. Tengler *Der neü Layenspiegel*, Augsburg, 1511.

since the sin of Adam and Eve and had at the same time transmitted original sin to their descendants. At frequent points in the *Malleus* it is evident that the authors experienced great difficulties with the question of the protection of the institution of marriage and the social control of sexual relationships outside marriage. For example, where they explain how the devil misuses the social situation to seduce witches they mention three groups of problems. In addition to the poor married women who are afraid of losing their possessions they refer to young girls who are easily seduced from fear that they will not find a husband and, in connection with this, the category of vengeful young women who despite promises of marriage have been left in the lurch.[9] This group was so suspect that the authors announced elsewhere: 'truly the current increase of witches essentially goes back to the sorrowful struggle between married and unmarried men and women. As a result of the vengeance of women it is not surprising that there are so many witches.[10] In so saying they indirectly referred to 'clandestine' marriages, that is to say those contracted only by mutual promises of fidelity. As poverty increased and social control of the family and village diminished as a result of the drift to the city there was a high chance that these alliances would end in the desertion of the wife and/or child.

Another objection concerned the verification of witchcraft; illness, for instance, can also have an unknown natural cause. The authors' reply includes a set of three indications of witchcraft. There is reason to be afraid of witchcraft, first, if a qualified doctor cannot form a diagnosis on the basis of external symptoms; the next, if an illness seems to be incurable or even becomes worse despite medication; and finally, if an illness occurs suddenly or unexpectedly. Considering the state of medical science, these indications offered every opportunity to accuse people of witchcraft. We only have to think of the explosion of venereal disease at the end of the 15th century. The epidemic of syphilis which broke out at that time was also called 'the incurable disease'.

Witches' scene, woodcut from Joh. Geiler von Kayserberg *Die Emeis*, Strasbourg, 1517.

Finally there were opponents who claimed to observe certain elements of contradiction in the doctrine of witches. If the witches were so powerful, why were they themselves not rich? According to the *Malleus*, witches were above all to be found among the poor and illiterate who certainly had nothing to lose. Why did they not ensnare their enemies then, particularly the noblemen, judges and clergymen who were persecuting them? The authors replied simply that the demons affronted God even more if they got the witches as cheaply as possible. As a matter of fact, if they were rich they would take fewer risks. Moreover, concerning their enemies, they are unassailable as a result of carrying out their functions. They are protected by God and the angels.

Behind the dispute between the supporters and opponents of the doctrine of witches loomed a world full of threats: a world where disease, poverty and famine reigned; a world where those who had suffered became set on revenge; above all, a world in which the social and moral controls on the cohabitation of man and woman, and thus also on reproduction, appeared to be unenforceable. It was not the first time in the history of Christianity that many people thought that the Day of Reckoning had dawned and also not the first occasion on which scapegoats were sought in the adversity of the times. The Jews had frequently been the victims of this. However, it was most certainly the first time that the behaviour of women had come to be at the centre of fear and aggression to such an extent.

Fear of the power of women

It is all too easy to lay the blame for the doctrine of witches and the concomitant persecution of witches on the sexual frustation of celibates in the manner of popular psychoanalysis. If this interpretation were valid the doctrine of witches would certainly not have found so much credence among non-celibates in the Catholic world and then later also among Protestants.

What is remarkable with the authors of the *Malleus* and also with other theoreticians of the doctrine of witches is their great apprehension of the power women can exert, both individually and as a group. This was thought to be particularly so, not only in the inalienable power of mothers over unborn and newly born babies but also in their power over children's upbringing, especially when it came to girls. Thus the daughters of witches were always suspect.[11]

Apprehension is also evident on the position of dependence that courtship, love and marriage can bring a man. The influence of paramours is especially feared, particularly if they are the mistresses of secular or clerical authorities. There is the continual danger that a man who has once been seduced will fall victim to a woman's secret greed and lust for power.[12]

There is also fear of the whole 'women's network' which excludes men as it does. This does not only hold with regard to midwives, women who run brothels and marriage-brokers, but also when it comes to the covert information and gossip network of women among themselves. Women's talkativeness, which makes them incapable of keeping secrets, is frequently cited in connection with their predisposition to witchcraft.[13]

Also in the description of the many other unfavourable female qualities which the authors detail, following in the footsteps of previous writers, the question of fear of 'the power of women' crops up again and again. One of the overlapping categories that they use in the description is based on a well-known pattern: reason, will, memory and desire.[14] Concerning reason, women are inferior. The word itself even bears this out: 'femina' means less (minus) belief (fe = fides). Concerning the will, it is interesting to note how love can change to hate in the case of women. The hatred of Potifar's wife as a result of her unrequited love for Joseph is held up as an example. Women's lust for power is so strong that it affects their memory. Women have a selective and therefore unreliable memory. The lust for power exists in rich and poor women alike. Married women will not rest until they have enslaved their husbands. And once they are widowed, their pride and presumption go completely to their heads.

Medea's raging shows what women's desire for power is capable of. However, they do not only lust after power on a personal plane: women such as Helen, Jezebel and Cleopatra show that they can destroy entire kingdoms. It is no wonder then that the contemporary world suffers under the malevolence of women. Finally there is her sexual passion. A woman's desire is unsatiable. As we have already said, this is her most disastrous characteristic: to satisfy her desire she will even consort with demons.

This sensual desire, particularly in combination with lust for power, vengeance and greed, is described in the *Malleus* as the most dangerous female characteristic. And this is not only maintained by the supporters of the doctrine of witches. The art and literature of the 15th and 16th centuries contain innumerable indications of the fear of 'the power of women' which lurks in this combination of characteristics. The popularity of the theme of 'women's wiles' in 15th and 16th century prints and drawings is just one of the many symptoms of this.[15]

In this connection we are not only concerned with works of art by men. The writer and teacher Anna Bijns (1493–1575) of Antwerp apparently shares this opinion. In her didactic verse she frequently warns men against casual intercourse and impetuous marriage. In one poem of 1525 for instance ('I did marry her, but oh how I should like to leave her'), a man allows himself to be seduced by the enchanting appearance of his wife in the first verse. In the second he is led astray by her money and in the third he has overlooked the fact that she wants to have control: the filthy slut wants to wear the breeches. In the fourth he has not realized that she is out to get his money: 'She wants to embezzle my money, the dirty ugly shrew!' In the prince-strophe he exclaims: 'I'll smash the chairs about her ears'.[16]

Similar motifs came to the fore in a poem of 1527, this time as a warning for bachelors and widowers, ('Best to be unbound to woman, Rich the man without a wife'). Here it is successively argued that: women want to wear the trousers; she confronts her husband with abuse when he comes home late; it is quite incredible what it costs to

Anon, *The battle for the trousers*, 1555, woodcut, Rijksprentenkabinet, Rijksmuseum Amsterdam.

keep a wife; and, finally, women want to go everywhere, want to go to the fair and generally make good cheer. However, Anna Bijns also considered it from the other side. In an earlier poem that contains a warning for young girls and widows ('I do not despise marriage but how much better to be unattached') she complains, 'A good husband is like a white raven'.

The motifs used by Anna Bijns continually recur in the graphic art of the 15th and 16th centuries. Seduction by feminine beauty is generally portrayed in extra-marital scenes, such as Aristotle being mounted by Phyllis.

A favourite subject was also that of the 'unequal marriage': the young woman who marries an old man for his money, offset by the rich old woman who catches a young man, implying that adultery was in store for the younger party in both cases.[17] Perhaps even more popular was 'the fight for the hose', in which the man who allows his wife to dominate him and who lets himself be forced to take care of the housekeeping and the children's upbringing is ridiculed. This subject has maintained its attraction right up to our own century, albeit that the popularity has been transferred to another public. Indeed via popular art it became the most popular children's picture from the 17th century up to the beginning of the 20th century and especially as a cartoon strip about 'Jan de Wasser en zijn Griet'.[18] That the 'battle for the trousers' was a favourite subject also among the affluent urban bourgeoisie in the 15th and 16th centuries is evident from the quality of some pictures. It is obvious that the middle class division of roles assigning the husband the function of breadwinner and the wife responsibility for the housekeeping and the children's upbringing was clearly not yet adhered to at that time. In the following centuries the role division became such a fundamental ideal that the exaggerated role-swopping in the 'fight for the hose' was no·longer a joke. The subject was no longer 'bon ton'. In lower middle class circles the wife was frequently forced to work from economic necessity, and had to share the function of being bread-winner. 'The fight for the hose' remained in evidence

Hans Leifrinck (ca. 1518–1578) *The henpecked husband*, woodcut, Prentenkabinet, Museum Plantin-Moretus, Antwerp.

Hans Baldung Grien (1484–1545) *Witches preparing for the Sabbath*, 1510, woodcut.

here. The warning for boys against an over-hasty marriage adorned the Jan de Wasser pictures, usually as a rubric.

Bourgeois morality and the ethics of marriage

It was in the urban bourgeoisie that the division of roles between the husband as breadwinner and the wife as the subordinate housekeeper/childraiser first established itself. In the rural milieu being the breadwinner and doing the housekeeping were not so sharply distinguished. Taking the farm as a whole, husband and wife did indeed have their own duties. The wife's responsibilities included not only looking after young children and seeing to water and fire, but also caring for the vegetable garden and the smaller animals. Thus the wife certainly did have tasks that we would call productive. Both marriage partners derived authority of their own from the responsibility they had for their individual tasks, although the husband bore the responsibility for the whole, particularly with regard to the outside world. But if the husband died or if he was away for a long time the wife had to take on the entire responsibility. This demanded robustness on the part of the woman right from the beginning. The division of male and female tasks was not so much characterized by our typology of work on the one hand and care on the other, but rather by a functional division of different areas to be attended to and the work which this entailed.[19]

This functional division was also maintained in the class structure of artisans and tradesmen within the developing culture of the Middle Ages. In addition, married and unmarried women practised other professions to make a living. As the bourgeoisie developed further and began to occupy a more dominant position both financially and politically, the task division between husband and wife gradually became more disparate. The woman's area became increasingly the field of caring, the man's a specialized field of work that required training. The universities of the Late Middle Ages which were exclusively reserved for men made their contribution to this too. The male world, which was far more focussed on the control of nature, became increasingly alienated from the female world, which was inclined to stick to traditional women's tasks and the authority connected with them. There is a connection between the hostility towards 'the power of women', which had been increasing particularly since the 15th century, and its most extreme application in the doctrine of witches.

The core of the inalienable 'power of women' resided, as we have already said, in the field of seduction, reproduction and upbringing. The control of this area, which from the citizen's point of view was of such vital importance, in particular the protection of marriage and the family, became consequently an area of increasing concern. The emphasis of both clerical and secular writers on the chastity, austerity and obedience of women and girls became heavier and heavier. Moralists increasingly concerned themselves with the education of girls, pointing to the necessary segration of girls not only from the evil world of men but also from association with girls and women, often from another background, who did not meet the ideal standards. Segregation, vigilance, training in housekeeping (the devil finds work for idle hands!) and the mother's good example were at the forefront. The portrayal of the steadfast lives of famous chaste women of the past served as an example with the deterrent of wanton or evil women who came to no good by way of contrast.

The origin of the doctrine of witches and the response it received must be viewed against the increasing need to restrict the omnipresent power of women. In the doctrine of witches the contrast between the world of women who are good and those who are evil is displayed as far as, in the last instance, 'the pact with hell' (see the introduction to the *Malleus Maleficarum*).

The witch as devils' concubine in a topsy-turvey world

During the transition from the Middle Ages to the New Age the image of the devil became increasingly terrifying. We can see the expression of this in paintings of the Last Judgment, for example. The depiction of punishment for

Albrecht Dürer (1471–1528) *The weather witch*, ca. 1500–1501, engraving.

Hans Baldung Grien (1484–1545) *Three witches with new year's greetings,* 1514, drawing, Albertina, Vienna.

sins and various sorts of sinners became more and more fantastic.[20] As spirits, devils are able to assume all sorts of appearances or to summon these up by changing people into such forms. According to the doctrine of witches the witches make continual use of this. The doctrine concerning diabolic illusion gave the artist the opportunity of creating all sorts of physically impossible combinations of images for the depiction of sin or punishment for sins committed and of the devil's kingdom as a counter image to the kingdom of God. This counter world is the false, that is the inverted world par excellence. The topos of the 'topsy-turvy world' was not new. It had already been used in antiquity to express moral undesirability along with and by means of physical absurdities. In the 15th and 16th centuries it was lavishly used by artists to depict more or less profane moral injunctions. In popular art it has been used in this way right up to our own century. It frequently concerns 'false' relations with authority, for example between parent and child, man and wife, ruler and subject, doctor and patient, master and apprentice and so on. The representations of this were alternated with those of physical absurdities such as a fish in the air or a ship on dry land. In the depiction of the kingdom of the devil in contrast with the kingdom of God, the 'topsy-turvy world' took on cosmic, metaphysical dimensions.

With the increasing fear of the devil and his extreme 'false world' it is not surprising that the thought occurred to a number of authorities that 'hell' had formed a pact with women and their 'false world'. In many respects clerical and secular authorities felt powerless to attain the hold on social matters that they desired. One could, of course, try to control midwives by imposing conditions on their practising their profession. One could also make prostitution more difficult and attempt to connect adultery with negative social consequences, though to what extent all this was to be at all successful remains questionable. However, it was not possible to bring marriage under strict social control until the 16th century. The free choice between celibacy and marriage, despite social pressure, was such an important point for the Catholic Church that she had a great deal of trouble with declaring clandestine marriage, which was so undesirable, as invalid. The Protestant code of marriage, which in principle drew marriage away from the Church, fell upon fertile ground.

When, after long arguments and great external pressure, the Council of Trent declared clandestine marriage invalid in 1563, people's attitudes, particularly among the unpropertied groups, were naturally not changed on the spot. For a long time the Churches remained in combat with the 'subversive' means of power which girls and women fell back on especially in emergencies. Moreover, social control over officially contracted marriage was comparatively weak, particularly in a society in which people married late as a rule.[21] Official marriage could also appear as a trap for the man who only noticed after his marriage what his wife was really like. Then he was stuck.

As long as 'the power of women' could not be brought under the control of an established social system, it remained dangerous even if it was combatted with the weapon of juridical regulations, the teachings of the moralists, and ridicule in literature and art. It is indeed remarkable that the end of the persecution of witches in various regions of 17th century Europe occurred at the same time as the establishment of a stable authority and genuine peace and welfare.

II. ST ANTHONY AS PROTECTOR AGAINST WITCHCRAFT

It was obvious that in the Catholic world the Saints should also become involved in the fight against the dangerous power of women. The fear of witches required a saint who could serve not only against witchcraft but also as an example in the fight with the devil. The life history of St Anthony, the abbot of the desert, lent itself to this end particularly well. The fear of witches gave his veneration a new impulse as is shown by many illustrations.

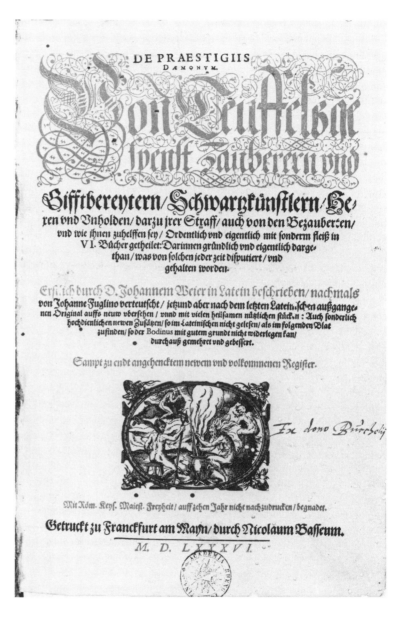

Title page of Johannes Wier *Von Teuffelsgespenst, Zauberern und Gifftbereytern...*, Frankfurt, 1586.

He is also held up as an example in the *Malleus Maleficarum* in this context.

Two forms of devotion to the devil are distinguished in the *Malleus*. The first is individual and not ritualistic and the authors do not waste many words on it. The second is official devotion in the company of other witches. The novice who has been 'converted' to the pact must promise the devil, who appears in human form, to forsake Christian worship and carry out all the acts of witchcraft that the pact demands. She also has to vow expressly to renounce the veneration of the Virgin Mary. Witches, however, do not refer to her by the name 'Mary'. They talk about her as the 'fat woman'. The Virgin Mary is so sacred that her name cannot even be spoken in the utterly false world of witches.[22] In the Christian world, Mary had traditionally been viewed in contrast with Eve, who caused Adam to sin. Ever since then their descendents had been burdened with original sin, although Mary was an exception to this because of her exalted motherhood. The theologians were not in agreement as to whether grace had fallen on her before or after her own conception in the womb of her mother St Anne. The dispute surrounding the 'immaculate conception' would still last for centuries. However in the practice of venerating the Virgin Mary this did not make a great deal of difference. It was unthinkable that Mary had been open to temptation by the devil. Even though she was pre-eminently regarded as the advocate of Christians in sin and need, and despite the fact that she could offer the most powerful protection against witchcraft in that capacity, she was unable to provide a concrete example of how people could protect themselves against the devices of the devil.

St Anthony (ca. 251–356), the abbot who was so often waylaid by devils and diabolic hallucinations during his long stay in the Egyptian desert, was able to provide an example however. The first biography of St Anthony appeared just after his death and was written by Athanasius, a Father of the Church and Patriarch of Alexandria. His aim was primarily to be able to hold up the ascetic life of the abbot of the desert as an example to the monks in the West. Nevertheless, the veneration of St Anthony only gathered momentum in Western Christendom shortly after the year 1000 when his relics were transported from Constantinople to Didier in France. The order of the brothers of St Anthony spread out from Didier, with the care of the victims of epidemics as its primary aim.[23]

As a protector against the plague St Anthony became a dearly beloved popular saint. His veneration reached its zenith around 1350 at the time of 'the black death' and his popularity continued into the 16th century. During the rise of the persecution of witches in the 15th century he became increasingly the saint who could be set against the terrifying 'plague of witches' (the picture from the *Malleus*). This was as a direct result of the story of his life.

The life of St Anthony by Athanasius was retold and elaborated throughout the Middle Ages. The well-known and widely distributed *Legenda Aurea* (Golden Legend), a collection of the lives of the saints by the 13th century Dominican Jacobus de Voragine, also referred to Athanasius concerning St Anthony. A great deal of stress was laid on the diabolic hallucinations which St Anthony had to endure as a hermit. When he was still a young man the devil tried to tempt him with carnal desire. But Satan, who appeared to him in the form of a black child, had to concede that St Anthony had beaten him. Evil spirits later menaced him by half beating him to death, by appearing in the form of all sorts of repulsive animals and by attacking him in the air, where he had been carried by angels. The devil also appeared to him in the form of a giant whose head appeared to reach up to the sky. The *Legenda Aurea* also reported a number of statements which St Anthony made to monks who came seeking his advice, for example, 'Mankind is moved by three sorts of desires: one from his natural predispositions, one from excessive eating and drinking and one from the devil.'

The warning against 'the power of women' is not expressly present in Athanasius' biography. This is more frequently taken up in the medieval *Vaderboek* (Book of Fathers), a Middle Dutch adaptation of a series of biographies of fathers of the desert which was known as *Vitae patrum*. They are based on various authors, although they are so complex that their origin is not always clear. It was in this way that a number of legendary passages which do not occur in Anastasius' account nor in the *Legenda Aurea* were added to the life of St Anthony as it appeared in the printed edition of the *Vaderboek* in 1490.[24] The book tells in great detail about a devilish queen who tries to attract St Anthony's attention while she is bathing in the river with her companions. On the pretext of placing herself under his spiritual leadership she entices him away to her city where she attempts to impress him with expressions of charity, magic powers of healing and riches. Finally she suggests that they marry. When she wants to defrock him by this means St Anthony sees through her and calls to Jesus for help. She immediately changes into a black pig. The inhabitants of the city are transformed into devils who seize him and torture him protractedly.

The *Vaderboek* and *Legenda Aurea* can be regarded as exemplary literature in the service of popular preaching. It is not therefore surprising that the learned writers of the *Malleus Maleficarum* do not refer to them when they discuss St Anthony. Within the scheme of the extensive theological speculations of the *Malleus Maleficarum* on the power of the devilish host, St Anthony is frequently presented as the great example of incorruptibility. The authors refer to a highly respected source, namely the *Collationes* by Cassianus (ca. 360–432). In this work Cassianus the monk gives an account of a year's journey through the Egyptian desert with the aim of questioning the holy fathers of the desert. He recorded the commentaries which he and his companion were able to extract. We know of a large number of manuscript copies of the *Collationes*. Directed as it was towards the promotion of a virtuous monastic life, the copies were to be found in a large number of monastery libraries. It is remarkable that the earliest printed version in the vernacular was written by Johannes Nider, who was mentioned above. His book, which contains sermons adapting the *Collationes* to

Copy after Hieronymus Bosch (ca. 1450–1516) *The temptation of St Anthony*, panel, private collection, 's-Hertogenbosch.

contemporary needs, had already been printed in Augsburg in about 1470.[25] The earliest Latin version of the *Collationes* was printed by the Brothers of the Common Life in Brussels in 1476. A printed translation in Middle Dutch followed in Antwerp in 1506.[26]

In the case of the *Collationes*, the *Malleus Maleficarum* quotes two conferences with the abbot Serenus in particular. These deal with the influence of diabolic powers and protection against them. St Anthony repeatedly serves as an example here.[27] Serenus explains that not all devils are capable of tempting anybody just like that. Every sort of human passion or sin corresponds with its own sort of devil. Unchastity, blasphemy, vengeance, pride and so on are each aroused by special devils, namely amongst those people who according to their own circumstances of time and place are open to their influence. In the Bible demons are often described with names referring to their specific evils: sirens, satyrs, witches, gargoyles, scorpions, dragons and so on.

The atmosphere between Heaven and earth is filled with a great multitude of evil spirits. Luckily, however, providence prevents people from seeing them. The sight of the forms they can assume at will are said to be even capable of making people mad with fear or seducing them into imitating them shamelessly.

Not all devils are equally malicious. Some are nothing more than teases. Others go much further with actual attacks of violence, lust (incubi/succubi), pride and, worst of all, heresy. The scale of evil among the demons is elucidated by the example of the two pagan philosophers who, out of jealousy of St Anthony's great following, tried to drive him from his cell by means of arguments and magical arts. When this did not succeed they sent three hordes of demons after him one after the other, each more powerful and perfidious than the one before. St Anthony, however, who had crossed himself and was deep in prayer did not even notice their presence. In the version of this passage occurring in the *Vaderboek*, the devils nevertheless attacked the saint brutally.

Hieronymus Bosch (ca. 1450–1516) and the Malleus Maleficarum

Of the many representations of St Anthony[28] in the pictorial arts of the 15th and 16th centuries, the triptych painted by Hieronymus Bosch in about 1500 is certainly one of the most famous. As it can be demonstrated that Jacobus Sprenger, the most influential author of the *Malleus Maleficarum*, was not unknown to Bosch and as his doctrine of witches had certainly been the subject of sermons in 's-Hertogenbosch, and probably the subject of dispute there too, it is quite tempting to view the triptych in the light of the *Malleus*. Sprenger, who stood at the head of the strict, reformed wing of the Dominican province of Brabantia had waged a sensational campaign against the monastery of his order in 's-Hertogenbosch in 1483. In so doing he made use of his good relationship with Maximilian, who had recently become regent for Philip the Fair. On the orders of Maximilian the city fathers felt themselves forced to stand at his side and take a strong stand against the monastery in order to force it into submission. Whoever would not comply had to leave the monastery. Of the original members, many were linked with the city either through their families or as a result of other connections. Sprenger appointed new superiors in order to carry out his policy. He took the prior from the monastery in Brussels which had links with Maximilian and the sub-prior from his own monastery in Cologne.[29] One can thus safely assume that the religious precepts of the *Malleus* were taken seriously in the monastery in 's-Hertogenbosch.

Knowledge of Sprenger's contentious actions probably aggravated arguments about the doctrine of witches in 's-Hertogenbosch. In any case it is remarkable that it is only towards the end of the century, that is to say after the appearance of the *Malleus*, that Hieronymus Bosch's diabolic figures lost their traditional character.[30] The symbolism of the customary figures, which was inspired by people or animals, became far more complex. The extensive discussions in the *Malleus* on hallucinations and demonic apparitions which were used both by devils and

Copy after Hieronymus Bosch (ca. 1450–1516) *The temptation of St Anthony*, triptych, Koninklijke Musea voor Schone Kunsten van België, Brussels.

by witches readily lent themselves to this.

Unfortunately we do not know who commissioned the triptych. Nevertheless, even if we did know that would probably not provide a satisfactory answer to the question of whether Bosch and whoever commissioned the triptych had their doubts about the doctrine of witches. The *Malleus* stresses that whoever rejects the doctrine of witches and defends the 'witches', must themselves be suspect of collusion in the pact with the devil. Public rejection could also be dangerous for political reasons as a result of the close relationship between Sprenger and his supporters on the one hand and Maximilian and Philip the Fair on the other. As Roman king of the German Empire Maximilian issued the authors of the *Malleus* with a written recommendation for their work as inquisitors in 1486. It is also known that Philip the Fair, who was raised by a confidant of Sprenger's, was one of Bosch's patrons.[31]

Nevertheless, the *Malleus* itself admits that there were many who had their doubts as has already been mentioned. We can find confirmation of this in the fact that the persecution of witches in Brabant only became comparatively widespread a century after the appearance of the *Malleus*. This occurred during the rule of Philip II, who supported the Counter Reformation.[32]

The St Anthony triptych of Hieronymus Bosch in the light of the Malleus

The St Anthony triptych does not stick closely to the traditional stories about the life of the desert father. This is most clearly apparent in the left hand panel. Here Athanasius' story about St Anthony's being attacked by demons is taken as grounds to pillory contemporary corruption and the spiritual decline of the Church, prelates and clergy. The symbols of this are easy for us to interpret because we know that not only Bosch but also many others with him expressed their criticism of this corruption in words and pictures. The *Malleus* does this too, albeit only in a short passage.[33] As examples of the symbols used by Bosch the only ones mentioned here are the monster prelate with the Bull under the bridge, the brothel in the shape of a large male body to which another demonic prelate is pointing and the church tower on a fish with wheels. (The fish is a well-known phallic symbol and the wheel represents military equipment.)[34]

To do the triptych justice, however, it should first be considered as a whole. St Anthony appears in all three panels although the main significance lies in the central panel. There we see St Anthony kneeling, surrounded by diabolic figures, pointing to the beatifying Christ behind him, Christ who by His suffering - symbolized by a crucifix - has conquered evil.

When the panels are closed the grisaille paintings that show Christ's sufferings are visible. In the left hand panel Christ falls to the ground, surrounded by the soldiers and servants that the high priests and Pharisees have sent to Him. Judas is slinking away with his bag of silver while Peter attacks the high priest's servant with a sword. Thus there is a clear parallel with the inner side of the panel, where the story of the Church of that time is depicted. In the right hand panel Christ falls to the ground under the cross. Among all the male torturers who correspond with the left hand panel, here we encounter two female figures who suggest an antithesis. The one is the compassionate St Veronica, the other an enormous, apathetic shrew carrying a naked child on her shoulders and holding another child by the hand.[35]

Just as women may be found in the right hand grisaille panel there is also a (debauched) scene with women occupying the central position on the inner side of the panel. This is usually regarded as a free interpretation of attempted seduction by the queen of the devils in the *Vaderboek*. St Anthony was said to turn away from this only to find himself confronted with the other source of sensuality: excessive consumption of food and drink (gluttony). However, is it really so clear that St Anthony

Hieronymus Bosch (ca. 1450-1516), *The temptation of St Anthony*, grisaille, left and right outer wings, Museu Nacional de Arte Antiga, Lisbon.

is aware of the scene behind him? The naked woman in the hollow tree over whom a red cloth is draped does not look at him at all but rather in the direction of a fish with an arrow (two phallic symbols at the same time) which is being shown her by an apelike devil. An old woman like a typical marriage-broker pours a drink for a toadlike devil. He is lifting up the red cloth like a tent over the naked beauty. All sorts of other sexual symbols complete the scene.[36] Could a contemporary possibly miss the reference to those sensual women who are even prepared to copulate with the devil and tempt others to do so too? A fish flying through the air with a fat-bellied little man sitting with a woman in red on its back also indicates the doctrine of witches. The man is carrying a stick with a sort of cauldron on it. In the *Malleus'* detailed plea for the truth of witches' ability to fly it is claimed that the devil can also transport his witches through the air to their gatherings on animal apparitions or simply without any attributes. But it expresses the preference that they use witches' unguent which they have made from the limbs of children, preferably ones who had not been baptized. They rub it on a piece of wood or on something to sit on and in so doing affront God even more.

The image of St Anthony in the middle panel corresponds with the way he is held up as an example in the *Malleus* with reference to Cassianus. St Anthony is said to have declared that the devil only has power over people who had previously rid their souls of all holy thoughts. The way he lived his life confirmed this proposition. This is followed by the Cassianus story about the two philosophers who, jealous of the hermit's following , sent him demons one after the other, after they had attempted to drive him from his cell with the most highly ingenious arguments. However, these malevolent, heathen sorcerers as the *Malleus* calls them, have no hold on him at all because he protects himself with the sign of the cross and uninterrupted prayer.[37]

Bosch certainly does portray the saint as totally oblivious of the devilish figures that are right next to him. The demonic forms surrounding him on the plateau seem to be taking part in a rite which appears from its symbolic attributes to be blasphemous and dissolute.[38] All around the plateau other forms dominate, forms whose symbols primarily indicate lust. Some monstrous freaks in the water could possibly symbolize witches. For example there are two women whose flesh has merged with a withered tree. One of them, fitted out with all the accoutrements of hostility, comes storming in from the left. Her armoured hand rests on the figure of a devil so that she forms a couple with him as it were. The other tree-woman figure is sitting on top of a rat draped in a red cloth. She is clutching a baby in her arms and there is another child standing at her demonic tail. She can be seen as a sort of image of the antithesis of how a good wife and mother ought to be, perhaps even as the antithesis of the Virgin Mary.[39] In the distance, above the group she belongs to, towers a grotesque brothel. A whore is drinking a toast with a monk while a 'madame' looks down from an upper window as if she were surveying the 'false world', that is *her* world.

Sinister monsters move in the air at the top of the central panel. They are once again composed of the sexual symbols of fish, bird and ship. A fish in the air was a traditional motif in the profane representation of the 'topsy-turvy world.' The mounted fish in the air in all three panels add further sexual significance. Confirmation of this intention of the symbolism of the false world can be inferred from a group of four little figures 'on their heads'. They accompany the toadlike devil that the imperturbable St Anthony carries away into the air in the left hand panel. There is a small man and a fish in a barge and they are dragging along a little monster, which is upside down, behind them in a boat. The naked little man looks between his legs and contempuously displays his backside.[40]

Hieronymus Bosch (ca. 1450–1516) *The temptation of St Anthony*, central panel, Museu Nacional de Arte Antiga, Lisbon.

Pieter Huys (ca. 1519–1584) *The temptation of St Anthony*, panel, Koninklijke Musea voor Schone Kunsten van België, Brussels.

St Anthony's success as a patron saint

Hieronymus Bosch's triptych on the temptation of St Anthony struck a chord among his contemporaries. Simply the many copies that were made are sufficient evidence of this. The painting also inspired other artists. It seems to have been as successful among those who tended to accept the doctrine of witches as among those who had their doubts or who thought that the blame for all misery had been laid too one-sidedly upon women. Bosch refers to the sinfulness of men, especially among the clergy, rather more outspokenly than the *Malleus* does. For those who doubted the doctrine of witches the picture could also be interpreted to imply that the doctrine of witches was itself a delusion of the devil.[41] It is obvious that ordinary sinful people could also enjoy the scenes that are so skilfully depicted.

That it was above all the central panel that was highly regarded and probably best understood by Bosch's contemporaries can be deduced from the fact that there are a very large number of contemporary copies of precisely this panel. This is all the more remarkable because later, particularly around the middle of the 16th century, Bosch's many disciples showed a preference for the theme of the naked seductress or queen of the devils.[42] In the copy of Bosch in the Rijksmuseum, where a female brothel keeper forms a human brothel and a devilish figure (a witch?) is flying through the air on a fish, St Anthony at prayer is quite clearly the main figure. The representation of the dissolute contemporary world in the background can be seen as underscoring the example of St Anthony for Bosch's times. Also other pictures of Bosch's, whether authentic or only copies, repeatedly reflect the basic idea of Cassianus: St Anthony's holiness protects him from the influence of the devil. The picture of St Anthony surrounded by monsters ('s-Hertogenbosch) can be seen in this way. The two small figures reading among the monsters might possibly be a reference to the two philosophers/sorcerers who sent the monsters to St Anthony.

St Anthony at prayer is also the principal figure in a painting by Aertgen van Leyden (1516) in the Museum voor Schone Kunsten in Brussels. Here his protection against the demons is less unequivocal as they are approaching him from behind.

An early disciple of Bosch's was the artist Jan Wellens de Cock of Louvain. His woodcut of 1522 shows traces of Bosch mainly in his representation of monsters. The principal subject is the attempted seduction by the queen of the devils, but other episodes from the life of St Anthony are also depicted.

The encounter with the queen of the devils is also prominent in a painting by Pieter Huys (ca. 1519-1584) in the Museum voor Schone Kunsten in Brussels. The queen is portrayed both naked and in her official vestments. St Anthony, who is near the side of the picture, is represented as admonitory and not at prayer. Some devilish figures are reminiscent of Bosch.

The warning against the power of women is even more evident in a panel by a disciple of Pieter Huys', also in the Museum voor Schone Kunsten in Brussels. St Anthony at prayer is portrayed on the left with the naked queen of the devils closer towards the centre. A large, morose man's head dominates the right-hand side. The man helplessly bites his diminutive arm, which is attached to his headgear with a bandage. The 'fight for the hose' is represented on it. A woman embraces a man while two other women beat a male victim on the behind. He admonishingly points to the large head which is condemned to silence.

Jan Mandijn (ca. 1500-1560) painted the temptation of St Anthony (Haarlem) in which various sorts of monsters which recall Bosch's triptych predominate. The saint is sitting reading in a corner. Van Mander describes Mandijn as an artist whose work was just like Hieronymus Bosch's, full of monsters and mockery.[44]

Less important artists also played to the demand for monsters à la Bosch but without achieving the visionary coherence of his diabolic forms. This was only approached by Pieter Bruegel the Elder, for example in his 'Dulle Griet' (Vile Dame) (ca. 1562). Bruegel's vision is inspired

Disciple of Pieter Huys (ca. 1519–1584) *The temptation of*
St Anthony, panel, Koninklijke Musea voor Schone Kunsten
van België, Brussels.

by contemporary events of his own society: a world of war, power struggle and oppression. The world in which Bosch painted was a world of obsession with sin, fear of the devil and thoughts of doom. Within this St Anthony represents a symbol of possible salvation from the hold of the devil and his accomplices.

III. CONCLUSION

In the above we have attempted to place the rise of the doctrine of witches against the background of its own times. The power of women particularly, in the field of sexuality, reproduction and upbringing was experienced as a threat at a time when the need for social and moral control in that field was just beginning to increase. It was mainly poor women, who had no other means of power, who were feared. That the devil should choose principally women as his accomplices in his final assault had a certain plausibility on the basis of this. As concubines, witches were united with the hellish enemy and were made out to be extremely dangerous as a consequence. As a result of fear of and discussion about witches the veneration of St Anthony received a new impulse and quality. The traces of this can be found in the St Anthony triptych by Hieronymus Bosch.

1. Jacobus Sprenger and Henricus Institoris, *Malleus Maleficarum*, 1487 (three volumes). Page numbers refer to the translation by J.W.R. Schmidt (1906) in the 1974 Darmstadt edition under the title *Der Hexenhammer*. The fact that the sect of witches is new is already mentioned in the introduction by Sprenger.
2. *Formicarius* means *Book of Ants*. The industrious ant is repeatedly held up as an example to Christians who became disillusioned with the Church. Nider would like to stress through his book that a virtuous life is possible even in his own sinful age.
3. Lène Dresen-Coenders *Het verbond tussen heks en duivel. Een waandenkbeeld aan het begin van de moderne tijd als symptoom van een veranderende situatie van de vrouw en als middel tot hervorming der zeden*, Baarn 1983 (37 ff.)
4. Sprenger and Institoris op. cit. (I, 2, 37 ff.).
5. Idem (I, II, 157).
6. Idem (I, 6, 99).
7. Idem (I, 18, 206).
8. Idem (II, 15, 159 ff.).
9. Idem (II, 1, 19 ff.).
10. Idem (I, 6, 100).
11. Idem (II, 13, 145).
12. Idem (inter alia I, 6, 107).
13. Idem (inter alia I, 6, 98 ff).
14. Ibid.
15. Thea Vignau Wilberg-Schuurman, *Hoofse minne en burgerlijke liefde in de prentkunst rond 1500*, Leiden 1983
16. J. van Mierlo S.J., *Studiën over Anna Bijns*, Koninklijke Vlaamse Academie voor Taal en Letterkunde, Ghent 1950.
17. Ellen Fleurbaay, *Ongelijke liefde in de zestiende eeuw*, graduate dissertation, Gemeentelijke Universiteit Amsterdam 1979.
18. Maurits de Meyer, *De volks- en kinderprenten in de Nederlanden van de 15e tot de 20e eeuw*, Antwerp/Amsterdam 1962 (404 ff. and 495 ff.). 'Wassen' is the Dutch word for 'wash'. Thus 'de Wasser' really means 'the washerman'. 'Griet' is the short form for the Dutch equivalent of Margaret, namely Margriet.
19. Régine Pernoud, *La femme aux temps des cathédrales*, Paris, 1980. Translated into Dutch as *Vrouwen in de Middeleeuwen*, Baarn 1985.
20. Jean Delumeau, *La peur en Occident, XIVe-XVIIIe siècles*, Paris 1978 (232 ff.) and Jean Delumeau, *La péche et la peur. La culpabilisation en Occident XIIIe-XIIIe siècles*, Paris, 1983 (129 ff.). For the 'false world' in popular art see De Meyer, op. cit. (428).
21. Marrying late, at about the age of 25, among the poor in the northwestern Europe of the 16th century is first mentioned by Hajnal. Laslett and other demographers believe that it occurred in some regions even earlier. The large numbers of unmarried young people first had to save, for instance by going into service or by acquiring a social position in some other way.
22. Sprenger and Institoris, op. cit. (II, 2, 29).
23. At the end of the 11th century an epidemic of the disease which is today known as ergotism broke out. This was known as 'St Anthony's fire' in the Middle Ages, probably because a certain

phase of the illness is characterized by hallucinations. From gratitude for his son's being healed, a knight in Didier founded a lay-brotherhood for care of the sick, which was later to be transformed into the Order of the brothers of St Anthony. The primary aim of this order was the care of the sick and the establishment of hostels increased considerably in the following centuries even beyond the French borders. St Anthony, who came from a prominent family and was a courageous adversary of the devil, was also revered as patron saint of knights from the start.

24. The first printed edition of the *Vaderboek* is that of Gerard Leeu in Delft in 1480. This does not include the life of St Anthony. The second edition (Zwolle, 1490) commences with it. In the interim the *Malleus* appeared in 1487. There is a connection here. For the *Vaderboek* see C.G.N. de Vooys, *Middelnederlandse legenden en exempelen, Bijdrage tot de kennis van de prozaliteratuur en het volksgeloof der Middeleeuwen*, Groningen/The Hague 1926 (6 ff.).

25. The book appeared under the title *Vierundzwanzig guldin Harfen halten den nächsten Weg zum Himmel*. This is the only one of Nider's works that did not appear in Latin. See Dresen-Coenders op.cit. (37 ff.).

26. *Der ouder vaders collaciën* was published by Michiel van Hoochstraten in Antwerp.

27. Sprenger and Institoris op.cit. (II, question 1:12, 32; 3, 45; 7, 82 ff.; 10, 108 ff.; question 2:2, 209; 5, 225 ff.; 6, 253 ff.).

28. St Anthony the abbot, the hermit, should be distinguished from St Anthony of Padua (1195–1231), the Franciscan.

29. G.A. Meyer O.P., *De predikheren te 's-Hertogenbosch (1296–1770)*, Nijmegen, 1897; Dresen-Coenders, op.cit. (69–77). Jacobus Sprenger died in 1495. In 1508 Maximilian presented the then famous abbot and humanist Trithemius a number of questions about the doctrine of witches. Trithemius confirmed the doctrine of witches in his replies, In 1508, at the request of the Elector of Brandenburg, published another book on the subject, *Antipalus Maleficiorum*.

30. Dirc Bax, *Ontcijfering van Jeroen Bosch*, dissertation 1948, (133). Bax places the change around 1490 but fails to mention the connections with the *Malleus* (op.cit. 112). It is clear that he only knew an abridged version of the *Malleus*.

31. Dresen-Coenders, op.cit. (71 & 137). It concerns the Dominican, Michael van Rijssel. Philip the Fair commissioned a Last Judgement in 1504.

32. The persecution of witches began to increase from about 1560 and reached its zenith in northwestern Europe between 1580 and 1630. Philip II pronounced several edicts to support and control the persecution of witches. Cf. Dresen-Coenders, op.cit. (196 ff.).

33. Sprenger and Institoris, op.cit. (I, 6, 95).

34. Bax, op.cit. (29).

35. This negative image of a woman (mother) with children is frequently interpreted as being of a beggar as it is by Bax. He also does this for the comparable extremely negative image of the woman with the tail in the central panel. Bax has a general tendency to see references to the sins of beggars and other vagrants, whether

connected with the observance of Shrove Tuesday or not. It is clear that he has not gone into the demonological doctrine of witches very deeply. His approach mainly concerns the linguistic background of the symbols. There is a comparatively negative type of woman on the exterior (the grisaille painting) of the panel of the Last Judgement (Vienna). For the rest the doctrine of witches refers to the 'evil poor' and the symbols which are predominantly sexual according to Bax in fact reflect the doctrine of witches.

36. Bax, op.cit. (107 ff.). Concerning the 'red cloth of witches' Sigrid Schade refers to A. Stöber *Die Hexenprozesse im Elsass, In Alsatia*, Mühlhausen, 1857 in her *Schadenzauber und die Magie des Körpers*, Worms 1983 (108). This indicates that the 'red cloth' frequently occurs in myths about witches.

37. Sprenger and Institoris, op.cit. (II, 7, 82–83).

38. See Dresen-Coenders, op.cit. (138 ff.) where the description of the sect of the Free Spirit in the *Formicarius* is referred to. People of these times possibly associated the two exotic figures behind the table with the 'heathen sorcerers'. The figure in the top hat in front of St Anthony is probably the devilish magician.

39. Bax, op.cit. (107).

40. In Dürer's *Weather Witch* one of the putti is trying to do the same. There are various symbols of inversion present in this copper engraving of around 1500. A witch also peers through her legs in a drawing by Baldung Grien (1514). Cf. Sigrid Schade, 'Zur Genese des voyeuristischen Blicks', in *Frauen Kunst Geschichte. Zur Korrektur des herrschenden Blicks*, Giessen 1984 (73 ff.), which also takes this position on the symbolism of the false world.

41. Agrippa von Nettesheim (1486–1535) and his disciple Johannes Wier (1515–1588) were later to try to combat the doctrine of witches in this way.

42. Cf. *Hieronymus Bosch*, Noordbrabants Museum, s-Hertogenbosch, 1967 (p.62).

43. Cf. Renée Pigeaud's article in this book.

44. Cf. *Hieronymus Bosch*, (230).

ELLEN MULLER

Saintly virgins

The veneration of virgin saints in religious women's communities

I. INTRODUCTION

At the end of the 14th and in the first half of the 15th century the religious life exerted a tremendous power of attraction in particular on women.[1] They entered the new nunneries, béguinages and houses of the Sisters of the Common Life, which were being founded in the towns by the rising bourgeoisie. A number of factors contributed to this renewed interest in religious women's communities. Certainly the development of the Modern Devotion at the end of the 14th century, which through Geert Grote (Gerardus Grotius) voiced strong criticism of the abuses in the Church, and the establishment of the first sister houses played a role.

The young women's choice to lead a life of chastity, withdrawn from the world, will not always have been an equally well-considered one; the average age of entry was 15. The number of those with a vocation must not be underestimated, but worldly motives were also a factor. Such a life offered a single woman, spinster or widow, shelter and protection. This did not apply solely to women without money or social provisions, but also to girls from the nobility or from the upper classes. The difference was that the latter, provided with a good *dos* (dowry), were placed in a nunnery, so that often they could to a great extent continue to lead their old existence.

All the institutions required the postulant to have a pious, chaste attitude to life. During a novitiate under the guidance of older sisters she would prepare herself for her future life. The length of this period depended on the type of institution and the candidate's progress. It sometimes happened that a postulant failed to complete the novitiate because she could not or would not cope with the isolated life, or because her superiors in the house or nunnery did not consider her suitable. This probationary period was also a sensible system from the political point of view: neither the secular nor the religious authorities were keen to see miscarried sisters ('verlopen susters'). After this period came the entry and the profession or taking of vows.

The new members were received by the community in groups, as 'brides'. Certainly for the béguines this was a festive occasion, which was accompanied by all sorts of celebrations, paid for by the new béguine.[2]

In contrast to many of the nunneries no dowry was required when entering a béguinage or sister house, which also made it possible for poorer women to join a religious community. Sisters of the Common Life and béguines led a religious life without being bound to the Rule of a recognised order. On entry they took vows of chastity, piety and obedience for the duration of their sojourn in the béguinage or sister house; they were not subject to enclosure. For these reasons the ecclesiastical authorities regarded both groups with suspicion and kept a strict eye on them. Thus many béguines and sisters, often under pressure from the Church, entered the 'Third Order' of the Franciscans, which was a recognised order, and became tertiaries. However, this did not call for eternal vows or subjection to enclosure either. For the houses of the Brethren of the Common Life there was, moreover, the possibility of affiliation with the Canons of Windesheim, a congregation of monastic houses which had originated from the Modern Devotion and adhered to the Rule of Augustine.

The period during which all these religious institutions for women grew and flourished lasted until about 1450, after which the number remained stable. However, towards the middle of the 16th century there were clear signs of decline. Monastic houses and other types of religious institutions began to be confronted with increasing financial problems: there was a rise in (civic) taxes, whilst there was a sharp decrease in the number of inmates and consequently in the income from work and property. Although it was in this period that the influence of Luther's ideas began to make themselves felt in The Netherlands, it was nevertheless mainly due to the problems mentioned above that between 1560 and 1580 most of the institutions for women were closed down. Only rich nunneries with good connections survived this stormy period.[3]

The devotion of béguines and Sisters of the Common Life was oriented principally to the life and suffering of Christ. The latter concentrated above all on His Passion. As can be seen from *vitae*, biographies of the sisters, meditation on Christ's Passion, together with the practice of virtues, was a regular daily occupation. Some sisters tried not only to evoke the suffering of Christ in thought, but also to imitate it in reality, for example by self-flagellation. However, such excesses of mystic experience met with disapproval. Geert Grote had had good reason for prescribing work; so that the sisters could provide for their own keep and so that they would not indulge in too much mystic contemplation on account of idleness. The observance of such virtues as humility, piety, chastity and absolute obedience were a sister's objectives. Although the piety of the béguines and Sisters of the Common Life was christocentric, they had, just as the monastics, a lively veneration of Mary, Holy Virgin and Mother of God, the pre-eminent example for all women.

Hortus conclusus

From the time of the Church Fathers onwards the virginity of Mary has been compared with paradise, but has also been connected with the *hortus conclusus* (enclosed garden) and the *fons signatus* (sealed fountain) from the Song of Solomon.[4] This was based on the passage in which the bridegroom characterises his bride as: 'A garden enclosed is my sister, my spouse, a spring shut up, a fountain sealed. . .' (Song of Solomon 4, 12). In medieval Bible exegesis the Song of Solomon is connected with Mary: she is the enclosed garden, the sealed fountain. The flowers, herbs and trees with which the bridegroom compares the beauty of his bride symbolise the virtues of Mary: thus the white lily represents her virginity and the violet her humility.[5]

In the 13th century the court, the garden, was interpreted as an allegory for the human soul. In order to achieve spiritual union with Christ the pious person must plant virtues in his garden – the soul – like flowers and must remove the vices – the weeds. In devotional literature different kinds of allegorical gardens are to be distinguished, entirely corresponding with medieval reality: the orchard, the herb (vegetable) garden, and the medicinal herb garden.[6] When in about 1400 not only the scientific, but also the aesthetic interest in flowers increased, the allegory of the flower garden developed from that of the herb garden. This was often called 'Rose Garden' after the most beautiful flower, the rose. Ever since early Christian times the rose has been the epithet for Mary, the heavenly rose in eternal bloom, because her body was not destroyed by death. In spite of her descent from Adam and Eve she was untainted by original sin, the lily among thorns (Song of Solomon 2, 1-2).[7]

In the middle of the 14th century Mary's virgin body was compared with paradise which, by shutting out the temptations of the world, has retained the radiance of Creation before the Fall. Ludolph of Saxony explains in his *Speculum humanae salvationis (1324)* that the enclosed aspect of the garden is not only a symbol of the virginity of the Mother of God, but also of Mary's liberation from original sin in the womb of her mother Anne. On account of this clearly evident relation between the allegorical garden and the virtue of virginity it is possible to apply the allegory in the same way to virgin saints.

An important aspect of the *hortus conclusus* has not yet been discussed: Mary is not only the Mother of Christ, sitting at His right hand in heaven, she is also His bride. This is how she is addressed in the Song of Solomon. This element too is to be found in the devotional literature of the 14th and 15th centuries: the human soul is seen as the bride of Christ. The Mystic Marriage of Catherine of Alexandria, to which we shall return later, is an appropriate illustration of the soul which is turned towards God in love and chastity.

This aspect was also present in the practice of religious life. As has been mentioned earlier, women entered the institution of their choice as 'brides'. The names of some of the convents point to the symbolism of the enclosed court, such as Mariëngaard (= Mary's orchard). The nunnery, the béguinage and the sister house were the places where virtue must blossom in isolation from the world and where the inmates strove to achieve their ideal of communion with God. When they died, the Sisters of the Common Life, for instance, entered into a mystic marriage with Christ, their belovèd Bridegroom. This signified that at death the soul departs from the body and is united with Christ in the heavenly paradise.

In the Western church tradition the Church Fathers Ambrose and Jerome had already made use of the term bride (*sponsa*) in the symbolical sense for both male and female virgins.[8] Jan van Ruusbroec (1293–1381) has elaborated this metaphor into an allegory in his work *Van de chierheit der gheestelijke brulocht*, in which he describes the three stages in the development of man's spiritual life towards a personal encounter with God. In the preface Ruusbroec says that God sent His only begotten Son down to earth 'in a glorious temple, which was the body of the Virgin Mary. There He married the bride, our nature, and united this with His person of the purest blood of the noble virgin. The priest who performed the

Reliquary, *Hortus conclusus of St Ursula*, triptych, Hôpital Notre Dame, Malines.

85

Atelier of Hans Memling (1435/40–1949), *Mary in the rose bower – St George with founder*, diptych, Alte Pinakothek, Munich.

marriage of the bride was the Holy Ghost. The Angel Gabriel did the annunciation and the glorious Virgin gave her consent'.[9]

From devotional prose, poetry, sermons and vitae it can be seen that these mystic garden allegories had a great influence on the development of the inward piety of nuns and sisters. Sister Bertken (c. 1426–1514) speaks in a poem of her 'little court' where she wants to remove the thistles and thorns in order to plant beautiful flowers to please Christ.

Jesus is his name, the lover mine;
Him will I serve eternally and be his own.[10]

In popular art we find a very special expression of this piety. In Malines a number of small altars have been preserved which are all called *hortus conclusus*. They date from the beginning of the 16th century and were made by nuns and béguines in co-operation with painters and woodcarvers. They are in the form of a triptych, in which the middle section consists of a case with glass windows. This case or shrine, has been completely decorated by the religious women with silk and metal flowers – the garden – amongst which there are carved wooden figures of saints. On the painted wings there are portraits of the donors with their patron saints.[11]

In about 1400 the *hortus conclusus* motif found its way into painters' circles in Cologne.[12] It arrived in the Low Countries a little later and was a popular theme in Bruges in particular in the second half of the fifteenth century. We also find these representations in the art of the miniature. It is striking how meticulously the painters and miniaturists have reproduced the flowers and grasses of the eternally green and blossoming garden of paradise. The theme is expressed as follows in painting: Mary with Child, meekly seated in a flowery meadow in front of a grassy bank, sometimes alone and sometimes in the company of angels or virgin saints.

The depiction of 'Maria im Rosenhag' (Mary in the Rose Bower), which was so popular in the early painting of Cologne and the Rhineland, is also to be found in Netherlandish painting, albeit later in the century.[13] A fine example is a diptych of about 1480 from the atelier of Hans Memling.[14] On the inside of one of the panels we see Mary with Child on a grassy bank in front of a hedge with red and white roses, which fences the garden off from the world and places it outside time. She is accompanied by angels playing musical instruments; one of them holds an apple out to the Christ child, symbol of paradise lost. In the garden there are flowers such as lilies, columbines and anemones, which symbolise the virtues, joys and sorrows of Mary. On the righthand panel we see the founder with his patron saint, St George, whose cuirass reflects the events on the other panel. As has been mentioned above the *hortus conclusus* is the symbol of the virginity of Mary and of her flawlessness. This latter aspect is shown in a picture of three generations, Anna-te-Drieën (St Anne with Virgin and Child), which was once on the outside of one of the panels. In this type of representation Anne, Mary and the Christ child are united in one composition. In this particular case Mary with Child is sitting in front of Anne, who is seated on a great throne. The Child has not only an apple in his hands, but also a butterfly, symbol of the Resurrection.

For an early example of the portrayal of Mary with Child in the company of virgin saints we retrace our steps in time and look at a Cologne triptych from the first decades of the 15th century.[15] On the middle panel Mary with Child is seated in the garden of paradise. She has four female virgin saints with her, with their attributes; in this arrangement they are known as the 'Virgines Capitales' and were especially venerated in the bishopric of Cologne. From left to right they are: Catherine with the wheel and the sword, Dorothea with her basket of flowers, Margaret with the cross and Barbara with the tower. They are gathered in a sisterly way round Mary in paradise, in which they are allowed to participate because of their chaste life on earth. Such a portrayal is sometimes called 'Virgo inter virgines' (Virgin amongst virgins). The presence of these saints, whoever they may be, does not really add anything essential to the significance of the *hortus conclusus*. They share with Mary the joy of abiding

Atelier of Hans Memling (1435/40–1494), *St Anne, Virgin and Child*, panel, outside of side wing *St George with founder*, Alte Pinakothek, Munich.

Anonymous Master of Cologne, triptych, c. 1410–1420: central panel *Mary with Child and Saints Catherine, Dorothea, Margaret and Barbara in a hortus conclusus*, left wing *St Elizabeth of Thuringia*, right wing *St. Agnes*, Staatliche Museen Preussischer Kulturbesitz, Berlin-Dahlem.

in paradise and act as her attendants. It is striking how small most of these panels are: they were probably used as devotional pictures, representations to aid meditation, just as is possible with texts.

Representations of 'Virgo inter virgines' were very popular in Bruges at the end of the 15th and beginning of the 16th centuries. The painting by the Master of 1499 shows Mary with Child seated on an imposing, richly decorated throne in the company of four virgin saints.[16] Dorothea offers the Child a flower, Barbara has a kind of diadem in her hands, whilst Catherine and Agnes are sitting with a book on their lap. The painter gives the viewer a subtle hint to the identification of St Barbara and St Catherine. They are both wearing their attribute, respectively a tower and a wheel, as a pendant round their neck. Catherine playing with the ring on her finger represents a discreet allusion to her mystic marriage with Christ. Dorothea's flower could point to marriage symbolism, but flowers, usually in a basket, are the set attribute of this saint. Behind the throne there is a low wall, whereby Mary and the saints paying her homage are shut off from the world and placed outside things temporal.

If we look at the picture more closely and compare it with the previous one, then we see that the flowery meadow and the grassy bank have been partly replaced by a celestial throne and a tiled floor. The painter has probably been indirectly influenced by older, 14th century Italian representations of the *hortus conclusus*. All that is left of the meadow is the strip of grass with flowers in front of the tiled floor and the flowers growing in front of the stone bank. The irises on the left of the throne symbolise the incarnation of the Son of God. The lilies on the right represent the purity of Mary; they are usually to be found in pictures of the Annunciation. That the lily refers here to the immaculate conception is emphasised by the words on the throne: (Ave) Maria Plena Gratia (Hail, Mary, thou that art highly favoured), with which the angel greeted Mary in the Annunciation. The dove in the halo above the throne is the symbol of the Holy

Master of 1499, *Mary with Child and the Saints Catherine, Dorothea, Barbara and Agnes*, panel, Virginia Museum, The Arthur and Margaret Glasgow Fund, Richmond.

Ghost, which became incarnate in Christ in Mary's womb.

Another 'Virgo inter virgines' picture is a painting by the Master of the Lucia Legend.[17] This panel was placed on the altar of 'De Drie Sanctinnen' in the Church of Our Lady in Bruges by a chamber of rhetoric whose patron saints were Catherine, Barbara and Mary Magdalene. A great throng of virgin saints has collected round Mary, who sits enthroned with Child, backed by a brocade curtain, which refers to heaven and is held aloft by two angels. The three patron saints are close to Mary. The Child is putting a ring onto Catherine's finger, Mary Magdalene is kneeling before Him with her jar of ointment and Barbara, sitting on the right, gives the Child a flower. These three saints symbolise the divine virtues Faith, Hope and Charity. Whilst the other saints have their attributes in their hands, those of Catherine (wheel) and Barbara (tower) are woven into their gown. Moreover Barbara is wearing a chain round her neck with towers as pendants. Whereas there was little vegetation in the previous painting, here it appears in profusion. The bushes and trees on either side, the meadow with flowers in the foreground and the scarcely discernible grassy bank behind the curtain rightly make it into a green and blossoming enclosed garden.

Let us now look at the 'sacra conversazione' (literally: holy conversation) by the Master of the Ursula Legend. Although the term suggests that something is happening in the painting, whereby an extra dimension is added to the content of the picture, this is not the case. One of the characteristics of a 'sacra conversazione' is the very fact that nothing happens. Just as the related 'Virgo inter virgines', it is a designation for a type of representation: a number of saints grouped round Mary. This representation, which originated in Italy, developed from the 13th century polyptych, on which the saints and Mary were shown separately. In both types of picture, 'Virgo inter virgines' and 'sacra conversazione' the saints have above all a representative function and are situated in a timeless environment.[18]

In the painting the figures in the foreground are screened off from the enclosed garden and the landscape beyond by the throne and the gothic architecture. On the panel of the Master of 1499 the Incarnation of Christ forms the central theme. Here the presence of Anne and, in the left background, the meeting of Joachim and Anne at the Golden Gate, indicate the glorification of Mary's virgin motherhood and her immaculate conception. Mary sits meekly with the Child on the edge of Anne's throne. The Child has an apple in his left hand and in His right a ring, which he gives to St Catherine. She offers him a carnation, symbol of betrothal and marriage. Behind her stands John the Baptist, who in the background is baptising Christ in the Jordan. His mother, Elizabeth, is depicted in a scene in the right background, where Mary visits her cousin Elizabeth, who is also pregnant (the Visitation). On the left of the throne Barbara is sitting reading, behind her stands St Louis, who was probably the patron saint of the man who commissioned this panel. In the 16th century this type of representation, just as the 'Virgo inter virgines', lost a good deal of its eloquence, because people became interested in pictures with more action and a more 'earthly' character (less contemplative). The earth became the scene of action for the representation of the saints.

Master of the Lucia Legend (Bruges, end 15th century), *Mary and Child with female saints*, panel, Koninklijke Musea voor Schone Kunsten van België, Brussels.

Master of the Ursula Legend (Bruges, end 15th century), *St Anne, Mary with Child between Saints Catherine, John the Baptist and Barbara and Louis The Pious* panel, Koninklijke Musea voor Schone Kunsten van België, Brussels.

Pipe clay statuettes, left *St Barbara*, right *St Catherine*, Netherlands 15th/16th century.

The women who chose a religious life followed in the footsteps of the virgin saints, who embodied the ideals to which these pious women aspired: chastity and perfect unity with Christ in isolation from the world. It appears that many nunneries, béguinages or sister houses had one of these early Christian virgin saints and martyrs as their patron saint. It is striking how often the names of Barbara and Catherine occur in this connection, whereby it must not be forgotten that the naming was usually determined by the founders of the nunnery and not by the inmates. Unfortunately the reasons for the choice of a particular saint are seldom known to us. But this does not detract from the fact that these saints were evidently very well loved.

The flowering of this veneration of virgin saints in the 15th century ran parallel to the renewed interest by women in a religious life, and in the wake of the worship of the Virgin Mary. The popularity of these saints was not solely due to their veneration in religious institutions, they also received a not inconsiderable impetus from popular worship. Expressions of this are to be seen in the 'enclosed gardens' of Malines mentioned above, in which virgin saints were almost always present and sometimes formed the principal figure. The large numbers of small pipe clay statuettes, which were produced in series in Utrecht and other places in the 15th and 16th centuries are more direct expressions of this veneration. Their low price made them suitable for private devotion in houses, convent cells and chapels. Their production took advantage of the 15th century trend towards a more personal religious experience amongst both laity and monastic inmates. Although statuettes of Margaret, Dorothea, Mary Magdalene and Agnes have survived, the principal representations are those of Mary with Child, the Infant Jesus and Catherine and Barbara.

Catherine, Barbara, Margaret and sometimes Dorothea belong to the group of the fourteen Auxiliary Saints who give help in times of spiritual and physical need. According to the legend these four virgin saints turned to Christ just before their execution with the entreaty that He would help all those who asked for succour in their name. Thus Barbara comes to the aid of the dying in their last hour, so that they shall not die without the administration of the sacraments. Margaret and Dorothea help women in labour and Catherine's help can be called on in almost all cases of need. To most of this group, the rest of whom were male, powers of healing were attributed, which largely explains their popularity during epidemics of the plague.

Apart from helpers in distress, Catherine and Barbara were the patron saints of a diverse company: the former of knights, philosophers, lawyers, pupils and the latter of millers, gunners and miners. We come across these two virgin saints very frequently both in the visual arts and also in edifying and religious literature. Their praises were sung in sacred songs, their example quoted in sermons and their lives recounted in poetry and prose.

Catherine and Barbara

In their construction the legends of Catherine and Barbara exhibit, just as those of all early Christian virgin saints/martyrs, a similarity with the life and passion of Christ. After a prologue there is a description of their life and conversion to the Christian faith. Then follow details of the tortures they had to undergo for their faith and how they finally met their death. All these martyrs suffered in order to confirm their own faith and to stimulate that of others, and thus gained admittance to paradise. The struggle of these saints for a worthy Christian life can be compared with the 'pilgrimage' which every sincere Christian has to make. In the theological tracts which provided people with guidelines on the subject, the lives of these saints were used as examples.[20]

Apart from the question of faith, marriage was the second important subject in the histories of early Christian virgin saints and martyrs. The legends betray an anti-matrimonial attitude, that is to say that marriage is seen as an evil which the virgins must avoid at all costs if they are to attain to the status of saint. In that respect the legends are variations of the theme: it is better to burn than to marry. The opposite of what Paul says in I Corinthians 7, 8-9.[21] The marriage proposal always comes from a heathen. The Christian virgin rejects it in advance, because according to her she already has a celestial Bridegroom. The spiritual form of marriage disavows the values of the 'ordinary' matrimonial union, because this evidently lacks spiritual values by definition. It is more difficult for the female martyrs than for their male counterparts, since apart from suffering excruciating torture, they also had to overcome the weakness of their sex. The struggle to preserve their chastity and the price they were prepared to pay for it indicate the high value which was attached to chastity in the Christian way of thinking.[22]

The elements previously mentioned are always present in the legends of Catherine and Barbara. Both saints chose the Christian faith independently, refuse to renounce it and to marry a heathen because of the 'presence' of a celestial Bridegroom. In order to break down their resistance they are subjected to dreadful torture, but by a miracle the torments do them no harm. Finally both Catherine and Barbara are beheaded.

Catherine

The earliest version of the life and sufferings of Catherine dates from the 10th century and is in Greek. Historically nothing is known about her and her name does not appear in early Christian texts. Various versions of her legend were in circulation in the Middle Ages. The *Speculum Historiale* by Vincentius van Beauvais and the *Legenda Aurea* (Golden Legend) of Jacobus de Voragine are the most commonly used sources. They give the following story.

Catherine is a well educated princess, who lived in Alexandria at the time of Diocletian. She spent her days in study, meditation and the propagation of the Christian faith. When she heard about a sacrificial ceremony, which had been ordered by the emperor Maxentius, she went to see him. She outspokenly confronted him with the mistakenness of this idolatry and invited him to become a Christian. Maxentius gathered fifty heathen philosophers together to refute Catherine's religious beliefs. She defended her faith so brilliantly against them that she convinced them all and converted them to Christianity. The Emperor condemned the philosophers to the stake and Catherine to be tortured on a wheel with knives and spikes. A miracle occurred: an angel destroyed the instrument of torture. Maxentius thereupon had Catherine beheaded. However, milk flowed from her neck instead of blood as a miraculous symbol of Catherine's virginal way of life. Angels bore her body off to Mount Sinai and buried her there.

The element which was to play such an important part in her veneration, the Mystic Marriage, is not to be found in the earliest versions of the official collections of legends. We find it in French poems of the 13th and 14th centuries and in Latin prose versions, the earliest of which dates from 1337.[23] In the *Legenda Aurea* we come across it for the first time in an English translation of 1438 by Jean de Bungay.[24] The gist is as follows. Catherine only wanted to marry a man who exceeded her in wisdom, beauty and power. Her mother took her to a hermit to ask advice on this problem. The hermit showed Catherine a picture of Christ, whereupon she said that He was the only person who could be her husband. She received instruction in the faith from the hermit and was baptised by him. During an ardent prayer Jesus appeared to her as King in the company of saints and angels. As a sign of her marriage to Him, He placed a ring on her finger. When, on account of her faith and her refusal to marry, Catherine is tortured and finally beheaded, after the prayer before her execution she hears a heavenly voice saying: Veni, dilecta mea, sponsa mea, ecce tibi coeli janua est aperta (Come, my beloved, my bride, see the gate of heaven is open for you).

In the legend of Catherine the symbolic title *sponsa Christi* (bride of Christ) becomes reality through the marriage. This distinguishes her from all other female saints. Through her betrothal and marriage to Christ Catherine becomes the daughter-in-law of Mary, and the most important intercessor after the Virgin. It is quite common in medieval texts that the author tries to include Catherine in the family of Christ. If we examine the innumerable representations of Catherine, she always appears to occupy the place of honour, on Mary's right hand.

There are no convincing arguments as to why it was Catherine in particular who was accorded this honour, through the addition of this episode to her legend. There are other saints whose legends also include this element, such as the early Christian Agnes and Catherine of Siena (1347-1380), of whom Catherine of Alexandria was the patron saint. In North Netherlandish painting in particular, there are a number of pictures known of the betrothal of Agnes, since this saint was highly venerated in the bishopric of Utrecht on account of the presence of relics.

In the visual arts of the 15th century the Catherine legend has on several occasions been depicted in the form of a 'comic strip', for example in the miniatures of the ms. *Vie de Madame Sainte Katherine*, which was produced in 1457 for Philip the Good.[25] Individual scenes such as the debate with the philosophers are to be found on the orphrey of a cope dating from 1520.[26] But both in the 15th and 16th centuries the Mystic Marriage was the theme most frequently portrayed.

From the preceding paragraphs it has been possible to gain an impression of the 15th century manner of portrayal. In the 16th century the theme was treated in a different way; thus an artist such as the Master of Frankfurt (1460-1533), who depicted the subject several times, still chose nature as the decor and showed Barbara reading, but often added the donor and his patron saint. In a painting by Marcellus Coffermans, an artist from the second half of the 16th century, we see not only Barbara reading, but also Joseph as an onlooker in the interior where the event takes place.[27]

Catherine is depicted in a royal robe with a crown on her head to denote her birth and with her set attributes, the wheel and the sword. Sometimes she has a book in her hands to indicate the contemplative life which she personifies. In the 16th century representations she is more fashionably dressed.

However, the life of a saint is not complete without miracles, wonders which are brought about by the saint after his or her death. Sometimes they were even used as examples in sermons. Miracles serve to edify and to promote devotion, for from almost all miracles it appears that faithful worshippers can count on the help of the saint.

One of the oldest miracles, which is already to be found in the *Legenda Aurea*, is a good example of this. The story tells what happens to a pious man who, after faithfully worshipping Catherine for years on end, finally neglects her. In a dream he sees a host of maidens, the most beautiful of whom covers her face. When he asks one of the others who that is, he is horrified to hear that it is St Catherine. She will no longer show herself to him, now that he has forgotten her. The man regrets his negligence and ardently serves Catherine for the rest of his life.

A somewhat more elaborate version is the 'beautiful miracle of a rich youth'. This young man has the same vision in his sleep: the most beautiful of the ladies hides her face from him. One of the other damsels, Barbara 'handmaid of the saintly maiden, friend, companion', notices this and asks why she is so angry with the young man. Catherine says that she is upset by his infidelity, for he is intending to get married. Barbara tells the young man this and he promises 'to stop doing anything which displeases the glorious virgin St Catherine'. With Barbara he goes to Catherine, who restores him to grace and predicts that he will soon die. The next morning the young man tells his confessor what has happened and dies to be united with Catherine for ever.

A marriage to the saint can also take place in another manner, as is told in 'How St Catherine received a ring on her finger, offered her by a clerk'. A priest is praying before the statue of Catherine and asks if he may marry her and give her a ring in token of this. The statue stretches out its hand so that he can place the ring on the finger, after which it resumes its normal position.[28]

These miracles must be seen in connection with Marian examples, since the latter have exercised considerable influence on the legends of female saints. Indeed, all three of the miracles mentioned above go back to Marian examples. Barbara too has a bridegroom in the miracle 'How a young man had a pleasing vision and did not get married'. The relationship of the lovers towards Mary, Catherine and Barbara respectively can be compared to the spiritual love which the virgins and religious women cherished for Christ as their celestial Bridegroom.[29]

On account of her origin and the philosophical debate Catherine was venerated in the first place as the patroness of knights and of divine philosophy. In the course of time she not only became the patron saint of students, but also of young spinsters. Her cult spread over Europe through the transfer of her relics to Rouen in 1027. The veneration of Catherine reached The Netherlands via Westphalia.[30]

At the end of the 15th and beginning of the 16th century two important changes took place in the devotion of Catherine. As has been said, Catherine was originally the patron saint of divine philosophy (scientia divina), just as St Jerome. In the 16th century she became the patron saint of (human) philosophy (scientia humana), whilst the Church Father Jerome, who was more and more often portrayed as an ascetic, retained his patronage of theology.[31] The second change was concerned with the position of Catherine as the most important intercessor after Mary. As has been explained elsewhere in this book, at the end of the 15th century the devotion of Anne, the mother of Mary, was strongly promoted. This took place at a time when the veneration of Catherine – as a helper in time of need – was on the decrease. This is reflected in the fact that the number of independent editions of her legend, which also included a number of miracles, was very small.[32] About 1500 text editions of the history and miracles of Anne were quite clearly of greater topical value. As a result of this propaganda Anne gradually superceded Catherine as the principal intercessor.

Barbara

The earliest surviving mss. which give an account of the life of Barbara date from the 9th century and were written in Greek. In the *Legenda Aurea* her biography is contained in the appendix.[33] Just as with the legend of Catherine, there were various versions of her legend in circulation in the Middle Ages. One of the most elaborate versions is by the Flemish Augustinian Jan van Wackerzeele who died sometime after 1390. He embroidered the legend with an extensive account of the conversion of Barbara and the part supposedly played by Origen. Jan van Wackerzeele connects Barbara with the family of Christ by representing her mother as a descendant of the house of Jesse.[34]

Wackerzeele recounts the legend as follows. Barbara, the beautiful daughter of the rich heathen Dioscurus, lived in the third century in Nicodemia. Her father shut her up in a tower to protect her against evil worldly influences. Whilst contemplating the meaning of existence, Barbara heard of the learned Christian Origen. She managed to get in touch with him and after a time was converted to Christianity. In the tower Barbara received first of all an angel, then the Christ child and finally John the Baptist, who came to baptise her. During the building of a bathhouse she had three windows installed in honour of the Trinity instead of the two ordered by her father. This led to her having to explain to her father the significance of the three windows and to tell him about her conversion. Dioscurus was inflamed with anger. Barbara found herself in prison, but refused to renounce her faith and marry a heathen, since she had dedicated her life to her Lord, Jesus Christ. A heathen prefect tried to get her to repent by subjecting her to torture, but Barbara was miraculously protected by the angels. Dioscurus finally dragged her away to a mountain and beheaded her. However, God's punishment was not long in coming, as Dioscurus was struck dead on the spot by lightning.

Master of the Barbara Legend (Brussels, c. 1470–1500), *The baptism of Barbara by John the Baptist*, panel (detail), Koninklijke Musea voor Schone Kunsten van België, Brussels.

Most of the hagiographies have come down to us in anthologies. But even when the Barbara-legend was written up separately, it was usually still impossible to determine whether the book did in fact belong to the inventory of a nunnery or béguinage named after this saint. In accordance with medieval custom numerous miracles were added to the legend of Barbara. At least fifteen mss. are known in which these are recounted together with her history. They are written in Middle Dutch or in German frontier dialects and date from the 15th century. A number of these miracles take place in towns such as Utrecht and Brussels.[35] Just as in the Catherine-miracles, they are also grafted on the Marian miracles. An example of this is the miracle of the earthly bridegroom of Barbara, which was mentioned earlier. The motif which occurs in the majority of the stories is that of Barbara's help to the dying. Moreover, there are some miracles in which Barbara and Catherine are to be found together.[36]

One of the anthologies contains an ms. from 1448 on the life and suffering of St Barbara and her miracles. The nun Janneke Pinnox in the Lijsbetten convent in Brussels had copied it for her parents. She added a letter which gives us some insight into her spiritual state. She advises her parents to seek comfort from the Virgin Mary in difficult times: 'And from her chosen bride, the pure virgin St Barbara'. She impresses on her parents that this book, which she has specially written over for them, must never be given away but faithfully preserved in honour of Mary and Barbara.[37] How highly this ardent venerator of Barbara esteemed the power of the saint is evident from the epilogue, in which she says that apart from through 'the heavenly empress Mary', God does not allow such great miracles to occur daily through any other saint as he does through 'his faithful servant St Barbara'.[38]

In a 15th century ms., probably from Limburg, written by 'sister Aelken Yzebrants' there is a rosary for Barbara, in which Marian symbolism is transferred to this saint. The concluding prayer begins with the following lines: 'Hail. . . St Barbara, beautiful red rose of paradise and lily of purity'.

Sacred lyrics reflect the popularity of Barbara. With the exception of Mary Magdalene no other female saint has received so much attention in this sort of poetry.[40] Some of the songs recount her legend, others sing her praises in every possible way. Here too, use is made of Marian symbolism to portray the virtues of the saint. A panegyric, in which Barbara is explicitly compared with Mary, contains the following lines: 'This pure lily is almost equal to Our Lady'.

The cult of Barbara was greater in the Southern Netherlands than that of Catherine. This can be explained by the fact that since 985 her relics had reposed in the convent of St Baaf in Ghent. After that date her veneration spread rapidly, witness the innumerable churches, nunneries and béguinages which were dedicated to her. In 1390 St Barbara's day (4 December) was a day of obligation in Antwerp. Barbara was the patroness of the blessed death, the patron saint of miners, armourers and farmers, and also of married and nursing women.

Up to the end of the 15th century Barbara is portrayed in the visual arts in a long girdled gown, often covered by a mantle and with no evident influence of the prevailing fashion. At the end of the 15th and beginning of the 16th century this picture changes and we see Barbara fashionably attired as a dignified lady. Her set attribute is the tower; she often carries a chalice with a wafer (viaticum), which indicates her function as a helper in the hour of death. In a few cases she holds an ostrich feather which she is supposed to have received from the Christ child in a vision. Barbara is sometimes shown with her feet on Dioscurus, as pendant to the representation of Catherine, who tramples on Maxentius. Both pictures symbolise the victory of Christianity over paganism.

The legend of Barbara has often been reproduced in cycles. Jan van Wackerzeele's version also found its way into the visual arts. The Master of the Barbara-legend (end 15th century) used this version as his source of inspiration in depicting the life and suffering of Barbara.[41] Separate scenes from her legend have also been portrayed, but the representations where she occurs in the company of Catherine are the most numerous. Through her

Master of Antwerp (beginning 16th century), *Mary with Child and saints*, triptych, left wing *St Catherine*, right wing *St Barbara*, Museum Mayer van den Bergh, Antwerp.

patronage of the dying, Barbara is at least as important as the intercessor Catherine. Moreover, they are each other's counterpart: Barbara represents the active life, Catherine the contemplative.

In the 16th century it applied to all virgin saints, and thus also to Barbara and Catherine, that they were represented more as patron saints of founders than in the context of a *hortus conclusus*.

III. CONCLUSION

At the beginning of the 15th century the religious life received a fresh impetus which resulted in the foundation of new convents. In devotional literature there is a striving towards a more personal religious experience. At the same time we see in the visual arts a number of new themes which are closely connected with this spiritual movement: the *hortus conclusus* and the Mystic Marriage of Catherine. The motive of the 'enclosed garden' also occurs in the devotional literature for nuns and religious.

In the texts the emphasis differs from that in the visual arts, where the eternally blossoming garden is inhabited by the Virgin with Child, whether or not accompanied by virgin saints. The accent in these portrayals is on the virginity of the Mother of God; this is confirmed by the presence of the saints. In the literature the garden is compared with the soul and the flowers and herbs symbolise the virtues which man must acquire in order to give his spiritual life more depth. For religious women this meant complete communion with God in isolation from the world.

And yet we cannot simply link the popularity of these themes to the great interest shown by women in religious communities. It is true that art reflects the spiritual currents, but as a rule we do not know who commissioned the paintings nor what their motives were for the choice of a particular theme or a particular virgin saint. In the 16th century on the other hand we seldom see Catherine and Barbara depicted in the context of a *hortus conclusus* representation. The Mystic Marriage of Catherine takes place in a small circle, where Barbara is often the only virgin saint present. Catherine and Barbara appear with increasing frequency as the patron saints of founders, fashionably dressed in 'earthly' surroundings.

It has, however, become clear that the ideals to which pious women strove to attain in the 15th century, notably chastity and perserverance in faith, were embodied by virgin saints/martyrs such as Catherine and Barbara. Moreover Catherine represents the *vita contemplativa*, the contemplative life which occupies itself through meditation with the essence of belief. An institution which is withdrawn from the world is a prerequisite for this purpose, for according to late medieval notions the aim of all knowledge was to bring the individual soul into a close relation with the Son of God; in mystic terms, to become the *sponsa Christi*.

1. In the first chapter of this book this phenomenon is gone into in more depth and its development described in more detail.
2. Florence W.J. Koorn, *Begijnhoven in Holland en Zeeland gedurende de middeleeuwen*, Assen 1981, ch. VI, 78 ff.
3. R.R.Post, 'De roeping tot het kloosterleven in de 16e eeuw', in: *Mededeelingen der Koninklijke Nederlandsche Academie van Wetenschappen* (Literature section), 1950, XIII, no. 3, 31–76.
4. E.M. Vetter, 'Das Frankfurter Paradiesgärtlein', in: *Heidelberger Jahrbücher* 9 (1965), 104, 105; W. Stammler, 'Der allegorische Garten', in: *Wort und Bild, Studien zu den Wechselbeziehungen zwischen Schriftum und Bildkunst im Mittelalter*, Berlin 1972, 106–116.
5. The standard work on plant symbolism is: Lottlisa Behling, *Die Pflanze in der mittelalterlichen Tafelmalerei*, Weimar 1957.
6. D. Schmidtke, *Studien zur dingallegorischen Erbauungsliteratur des Spätmittelalters. Am Beispiel der Gartenallegorie*, Tübingen 1982, 313–353.
7. E.M. Vetter, *Maria im Rosenhag*, Düsseldorf o.J. (1956), 12, 13.
8. *Reallexikon für Antike und Christentum*, II, Stuttgart 1954, col. 528–564.
9. Jan van Ruusbroec, Werken, I, *De Gheestelike Brulocht*, adapted by J.B. Poukens s.j. and L. Reypens s.j., Malines, Amsterdam 1932.

10. Quoted from: Steph. Axters, *Mystiek Brevier*, III, 'De Nederlandsche mystieke poëzie', Antwerp 1946, 79, 80. This Sister Bertken at the age of 30 had herself immured by the Buurkerk in Utrecht, where she died in 1514 after spending 57 years there.

11. C. Poupeye, 'Les Jardins Clos et leurs rapport avec la sculpture malinoise', in: *Bulletin du circle archéologique, littéraire et artistique de Malines* 22 (1912), 50–114.

12. *Vor Stefan Lochner. Die Kölner Maler von 1300 bis 1430*, Wallraf-Richartz-Museum, Cologne 1974.

13. E.M. Vetter, *Maria im Rosenhag*, op.cit.

14. Munich, Alte Pinakothek, inv. no. 1401; cat. *Alte Pinakothek München*, Munich 1983, 342, 342.

15. Berlin, Stiftung Preussischer Kulturbesitz, Gemäldegalerie inv. no. 1238; E.M. Vetter, 'Das Frankfurter Paradiesgärtlein', op.cit., 124, 125; *Von Stefan Lochner*, op.cit., no. 27, 90, 91.

16. Richmond, Virginia Museum, The Arthur and Margaret Glasgow Foundation, inv. no. 57-39; *Primitifs Flamands Anonymes*, Groeningemuseum, Bruges 1969, no. 20, 61–63, 213–215.

17. Brussels, Koninklijke Musea voor Schone Kunsten van België, inv. no. 2576; *Primitifs Flamands Anonymes*, op. cit. no. 15, 53–54, 208–209.

18. W. Braunfels, 'Giovanni Bellinis Paradiesgärtlein', in: *Das Münster* 9 (1956), 2. The painting is in the Koninklijke Musea voor Schone Kunsten in Brussels, inv. no. 6719; *Primitifs Flamands Anonymes*, op. cit., no. 2, 37–39, 196–197.

19. *Vroomheid per dozijn*, Rijksmuseum het Catharijneconvent, Utrecht 1982, 12–21.

20. M. Glasser, *Marriage in Old and Middle English Saints' Legends*, diss. phil. (type-script), Indiana 1973, 26.

21. The first chapter of this book goes into the Church's attitude to marriage in more depth.

22. Glasser, op.cit., 79.

23. Margaret B. Freeman, 'The Legend of Saint Catherine told in Embroidery', in: *Bulletin of the Metropolitan Museum of Art* 13 (1954-55), 285.

24. L. Réau, *Iconographie de l'Art chrétien*, IIIa, Paris 1955, 263.

25. The ms. is in the Bibliothèque National in Paris. Freeman, op.cit., 289.

26. Amsterdam, Rijksmuseum; *Middeleeuwse kunst der Noordelijke Nederlanden*, Rijksmuseum, Amsterdam 1958, no. 257, 183–184.

27. W. Laureyssens, 'Een Mystiek Huwelijk van de Heilige Katharina van Marcellus Coffermans', in: *Bulletin des Musées Royaux des Beaux-Arts de Belgique* 13 (1964), 151–158.

28. P. Assion, *Die Mirakel der Hl. Katharina von Alexandrien. Untersuchungen und Texte zur Entstehung und Nachwerkung mittelalterlicher Wunderliteratur*, (diss.) Heidelerg 1969, 331, 434–439.

29. C.G.N. de Vooys, *Middelnederlandse Legenden en Exempelen*, revised and enlarged edition, Groningen/The Hague 1926, 40–44; Assion, op. cit., 262–270.

30. W. Stüwer, 'Katharinenkult und Katharinenbrauchtum in Westfalen', in *Westfalen* 20 (1935), 62–101.

31. J. Sauer, 'Das Sposalizio der hl. Katharina von Alexandrien', in: *Festschrift F. Schneider*, Freiburg 1906, 349.

32. The legend and miracles of Catherine were distributed up to about 1525 through the publication of passionals (= accounts of lives of the saints). Though a large number (9) – for that time – of biographies of Catherine were printed, in most editions the miracles are partly or completely missing. See: Fr. Falk, *Die Druckkunst im Dienste der Kirche zunächst in Deutschland bis zum Jahre* 1920, Cologne 1879, 83–85, 92–92; Assion, op.cit., 444.

33. Jacobus de Voragine, *Legenda Aurea*, ed. Th. Graesse, Osnabrück 1965³, 898 ff.

34. B. de Gaiffier, 'La Légende de sainte Barbe par Jean de Wackerzeele', in: *Analecta Bollandia* 77 (1959), 5–42.

35. W. B. Lockwood, 'Mirakelen van Sinte Barbara in Middelnederlandse handschriften', in: *Ons Geestelijk Erf* 30 (1956), 367–389.

36. De Vooys, op.cit., 110–112.

37. Lockwood, op.cit., 368.

38. De Vooys, op.cit., 43.

39. H. H. Knippenberg, 'Sint Barbara-verering', in: *Volkskunde* 58 (1957), 115.

40. J. A. N. Knuttel, *Het geestelijk lied in de Nederlanden voor de Kerkhervorming*, Rotterdam 1906, 293–296.

41. B. de Gaiffier, 'Le triptique du Maître de Légende de Sainte Barbe. Sources littéraires de l'iconographie', in: *Revue belge d'archéologie et d'histoire de l'art* 28 (1959), 3–23.

TON BRANDENBARG

St Anne and her Family

The veneration of St Anne in connection with concepts of marriage and the family in the early-modern period

I. THE EXPLOSION IN THE VENERATION OF ST ANNE AT THE END OF THE MIDDLE AGES

Introduction

A 15th century incunabulum on the life of St Anne, the mother of Mary and grandmother of Christ, begins with the following story.

The virtuous and extremely beautiful young girl Emerentiana regularly goes to Mount Carmel to visit the devout hermits there who lead a life of seclusion in imitation of the prophets Elijah and Elisha. They speak about the coming of the Messiah and about the question of which woman will be worthy enough to bring the Son of God into the world. When Emerentiana's parents want to give her in marriage she hastens to Mount Carmel for advice: should she wed or remain a virgin? The answer comes to the brothers of Carmel after three days of intense prayer. They see a beautiful tree with many branches in a vision. One branch looks more beautiful than all the others and bears an exquisite fruit on which an even more beautiful flower blooms. A voice from Heaven provides the explanation: the tree with many branches represents Emerentiana's marriage. A daughter named Anne will be born of this union and she will then bear the exquisite fruit, namely Mary. Mary, a virgin, will then give birth to the flower, that is Christ. The many branches represent Emerentiana's descendants who will fight vigorously for the Kingdom of God. After this message Emerentiana makes her way to the temple with

her parents in order to pray for a suitable suitor who will not want her for her beauty, wealth, origins or from 'desires of the flesh' but in accordance with God's plan for her. The first six candidates are killed because they approach the young girl with false intentions. The seventh, Stollanus, of the house of Judah, is evidently the true husband. St Anne, the mother of Mary and grandmother of Christ, and Hysmeria, mother of Elizabeth and grandmother of John the Baptist are born of this marriage.[1]

In the Low Countries and the Rhineland a series of texts reflecting the life of St Anne and her family were written and (in some cases published) at the end of the 15th century. They were now not only used as an aspect of the story of the birth of Mary, as had been common for a long time, for instance in apocryphal scriptures and medieval works such as *Speculum Historiale* or the *Legenda Aurea*, but as lives of the saints in their own right.[2] The attention paid to St Anne's mother, Emerentiana, is new in these late 15th century descriptions. Directly connected with this is the emphasis on the subjects of marriage, household and family. This inclination is naturally connected with Anne's important position as mother of Mary and grandmother of Christ but the various aspects had never been elaborated to such an extent. The success of texts such as *Die historie, die ghetiden ende die exemplen van Sint-Annen (1491)* and *Die historie van Sint Anna(1499)* was considerable. Seldom have any of the lives of the saints been so frequently reprinted as was the life of St Anne, with a clear peak in around 1500.[3]

Master of the family of St Anne (Ghent, end of 15th century). *The saints Stollanus and Emerentiana*, panel, Museum voor Schone Kunsten, Ghent.

This is only one indication of the explosion in the veneration of St Anne at the end of the Middle Ages. The many patronages, namings and expressions in the visual arts bear witness to an increasing veneration of St Anne during the entire 15th century at all levels of the population. In the visual arts the representations of Anne, Mary and Jesus and the Holy Kinship were particularly popular.[4] In the former, St Anne, Mary and Jesus are united in one composition; in the latter, which was widespread particularly in the Low Countries, the Rhineland and the North of France, St Anne forms the radiant centre of a sacred kindred of holy men and women.

The popularity of devotion to St Anne around 1500 was also evident in the sensational story of the plunder of the relics which is recorded in the *Chronijk der Landen van Overmaas en der aangrenzende gewesten* of the end of the 15th century.[5] A mason from Cornelimunster managed to acquire a valuable Dominican relic, namely the head of St Anne, found during restoration work at the great St Stephan's Church in Mainz. Out of deep devotion he decided to deliver the sacred object to the Franciscans in Düren, near Aachen. According to the people of Düren, this occurred as a result of 'divine inspiration', although the inhabitants of Mainz were of a rather different opinion. They believed that the mason was a cowardly thief and desecrator who deserved to be punished. There was a serious dispute between the two cities with even Emperor Maximilian becoming involved after a time. At first the Franciscans were prepared to return the relic to a delegation which had by then arrived from Mainz but after the transfer the people reacted against it. According to the story it was particularly the women of Düren who protested about the return.[6] The facts were different. Magistrates of the city seized the relic from predominantly economic motives: the St Anne relic would ensure a stream of pilgrims. In the following years thousands of pilgrims visited the small town of Düren. Mainz received compensation to salve the wound. In 1501 a Papal Bull imposed 'eternal silence' on the previous owners. The dispute between Mainz and Düren concerning the St Anne relic is an example of a combination of religious and social interests in this period.

The devotion to St Anne as socio-historical fact
In the past the devotion to St Anne was mainly only described in detail by the clergy.[7] In this article we are approaching the veneration of St Anne from a socio-historical point of view. We want to investigate the extent to which texts and pictures having the life of St Anne and her family as their subject contain ideas about marriage, household and family relationships in the period 1400–1600. With this in mind we are going to examine a number of texts and pictures related to them which were produced in the Low Countries and the Rhineland around 1500. We will look into the image the authors outline of St Anne as wife, mother, grandmother or widow and in which circles this concept was to be found. In doing so we will attempt to place the success of the devotion in the context of the religious and intellectual climate of the early modern era.

Whoever makes use of literary sources or those from art history in reconstructing ideas in the field of marriage and the family must take the complex relationships between text or picture and social reality into account.[8] Literature and art in general never reflect reality directly. This also holds for devotional literature. Although events from the life of a saint are presented as historical fact, hagiography is nevertheless intended primarily as a statement of a point of view. Content and form are subordinated to the ultimate goal: the expression and propagation of the devotion.[9] In his propaganda of the veneration the author does not usually stop at representing the 'facts'. He incorporates theological theses or insights from moral theology into his text and allows pastoral intentions which are connected with the particular public for whom the texts are intended to play a part. The veneration of a saint and his or her image can thus furnish us with information about the needs and ideals of a particular social group. The choice of subjects and motifs is thus

Master of the family of St Anne (Ghent, end of 15th century), *The saints Joachim and Anne, Mary and Child*, panel, Museum voor Schone Kunsten, Ghent.

103

Attributed to the Master of the Morrison Triptych (Antwerp, first quarter of 16th century), *Joachim and Anne at the Golden Gate*, panel, 1500, Musea voor Schone Kunsten van België, Brussels.

also dictated by the author's attitudes and the public to whom he addresses himself. The general outline of the story is well-known but the author selects, interprets and commentates on it. We also find this technique of elaboration in the story of St Anne.

The content of the legend

Although there is a total absence of information about Joachim and Anne in the Bible, Apocryphal scriptures compensate for this absence amply. By means of *Speculum Historiale*, the *Legenda Aurea* and even more by the pictorial representation of the facts the lives of Anne and Joachim enjoy widespread familiarity in Western Europe. This is the gist of the story. Joachim, a rich god-fearing man of the tribe of Judah and the royal house of David marries the devout young girl Anne from Bethlehem. They always divide their possessions into three parts: one part is for the temple and the priests, another is for widows, orphans and the poor, and the third part is for their own use. Their marriage is childless for twenty years. During the feast of the Renewal of the Temple the officiating priest, whose name was Ruben or Issaschar, rudely refuses to accept Joachim's offering because he has no descendants. Deeply humiliated, Joachim then returns to his shepherds. Meanwhile Anne mourns over the disappearance of her husband and her infertility. An angel appears suddenly in her deepest grief and explains that God has a purpose in closing her womb, namely that at a late age she will still bear a daughter who, a virgin, will bring forth the Saviour. Joachim receives a message from the angel that he should return to his wife because God is going to change his destiny. As a sign the couple will meet each other at the Golden Gate of Jerusalem. This is how it happened and Mary was born nine months later.[10]

All sorts of embellishments were added to the legend in the course of the centuries. The most important extension concerns the legend of Anne's three marriages (trinubium) which originated around 1100 or even earlier in Anglo-Norman areas.[11] After Joachim's death Anne marries the pious Cleophas, who was St Joseph's brother according to some, and Joachim's brother according to others. When Cleophas dies Anne marries Salomas. A daughter called Mary is born of each marriage. Powerful progeny grow from Anne in this way. The first Mary to be born is the mother of Jesus. Mary Cleophas marries Alpheus. They have four sons: Jacob the Younger, Simon, Joseph the Righteous and Judus. Mary Salomas marries Zebedee. Their children are Jacob the Elder and John the Evangelist.

This legend was quickly connected with St Servatius, the Bishop of Maastricht, Tongeren and Liège (4th century). His family tree was said to stem from Anne's sister, known as Esmeria or Hysmeria in these parts. In addition to a daughter Hysmeria also had a son, Eliud. As Servatius was descended from Eliud he could be counted as being a blood relation of Christ's.[12] As we have seen, at the end of the 15th century the parents of Anne and Hysmeria were also added. They were usually called Emerentia(na) and Stollanus.

We are restricting ourselves to two important propagandists of the veneration of St Anne in the Low Countries, Jan van Denemarken and Pieter Dorlant and in so doing are including a number of pictures that are connected with the texts.

II. JAN VAN DENEMARKEN AND HIS REPRESENTATION OF THE LIFE OF ST ANNE

Jan van Denemarken

We know only a little about the North Netherlandish cleric Jan van Denemarken. He was a 'doctor' or 'master' of theology and a secular priest, in other words he was not a monk from a monastery. He died in about 1545.[13] From his works he appears to have been a fervent venerator of St Anne and her kindred. He wrote two Latin tracts in which he described the life of St Anne and propagated her devotion.

In addition to St Anne, van Denemarken also took up the veneration of Joachim. For the purposes of this devotion he wrote a Leven van Sinte Joachim (Life of St Joachim) which is nevertheless to a great extent identical with that of St Anne. He wrote a biography of Joseph, Mary's husband, along with it in Dutch and wrote a pageant about the marriage of Joseph and Mary. He rebelled against the traditional representation of Joseph as a soppy henpecked husband who falls asleep at his wedding feast.[14] In the following centuries Joseph was to be represented as a young man who appreciates his responsibilities as husband and father.

The two lives of St Anne which van Denemarken wrote would never have been so widely distributed had Wouter Bor, a Carthusian monk from Monnikshuizen near Arnhem, not translated and published them. In 1491 Die historie, die ghetiden ende die exemplen vander heyligher vrouwen Sint Annen appeared in Antwerp without mention of the author or the translator. This work was reprinted five times in the period up to 1497. A few years later, in 1499, Die historie van Sint-Anna appeared in Zwolle only with mention of the name of the translator, Wouter Bor (later corrupted to Born).[16] The second edition particularly enjoyed unprecedented success. Die historie van Sint-Anna was to be reprinted until well into the 19th century, with translations appearing in German, French and Catalan. In this text the emphasis lies on the miraculous. Everything seems intended to show that Anne was just as powerful as her daughter Mary and grandson Jesus

Although Anne is central in these texts, the devotion cannot be separated from the veneration of Mary. This appears most clearly in the concluding poem of Die historie, die ghetiden ende die exemplen vander heyligher vrouwen Sint Annen:

'If you want to be Mary's friend
Be sure to be dedicated to her mother
Serve her with good faith
Jesus and Mary will not let it go unrewarded'

The life of Emerentiana: marry or remain a virgin
The story of Emerentiana is an important component in Jan van Denemarken's representation of the life of St Anne. The central element in St Anne's ancestry is the

St Anne's Family Tree and Legend, illustration in Pieter Dorlant, *Historia perpulchra de Anna sanctissima*, beginning of 16th century, manuscript Hist. Archiv, Cologne.

miraculous family tree revealed to the disciples of Elijah and Elisha on Mount Carmel in a vision (thus making them the precursors of the Carmelites). We have already commented on this in the introduction to this article.[17]

Jan van Denemarken's texts contain two alternative readings of the vision, in *Die historie, die ghetiden ende exemplen vander heyligher vrouwen Sint Annen*, Anne is born first followed by Hysmeria. This sequence is reversed in *Die historie van Sint-Anna.* The brothers also see a beautiful tree with many branches bearing fruit, which is subsequently plucked, in this version. It is the image of the birth of Hysmeria that is evoked in a natural way. Later the tree withers but a second delicious fruit is attached to the dead wood in a blinding light. A voice announces that Emerentiana will still bear a daughter at an advanced age as the result of a miracle. Only when Emerentiana is 61 and Stollanus 71 is this promise fulfilled

Both visions provide the scenario for the last phase of the holy story. Emerentiana becomes matriarch of a holy family. One branch of this family will produce Christ through Anne. Emerentiana's marriage is completely sanctioned by this prospect. Whoever might think that the marriage was solemnized as a result of more usual motives such as economic advantage (she was rich) or sexual attraction (she was beautiful) has the illusion quickly put right. Jan van Denemarken continually repeats that Emerentiana did not marry from physical desire but from chastity and virtue. To emphasize this once more the first six suitors fall to the ground dead as soon as they want to touch Emerentiana. They were moved by false motives: greed and unchastity. Only the seventh, Stollanus, approaches in the right spirit.[18]

In *Die historie, die ghetiden ende die exemplen vander heyligher vrouwen Sint Annen* van Denemarken repeats that unchastity is objectionable as a motive for marriage with each marriage Anne enters. The particular attention paid to chastity and the dangers of lust are among other things promoted by theological discussions about the correct place of Mary, her mother Anne and also her grandmother Emerentiana in the ultimate scheme of redemption.

One of the many great questions preoccupying theologians in the 15th century was the extent to which Mary as mother of the Saviour, was still tainted by original sin.[19] According to medieval attitudes original sin is passed on to the following generation via carnal lust, desire or sensuality during sexual intercourse. The immaculate conception, that is to say conception free from original sin, cannot be reconciled with sexual desire.The story in *Die historie van Sint-Anna* that Emerentiana still became a mother at an advanced age is connected with this attitude. Anne is conceived via the particular mercy of God at a time when natural fertility was out of the question.

Original sin came into the world as a result of the sin of the first people. Eve, the original mother of all human beings, brought sin into the world thereby destroying the harmony; another woman, Mary, restored the balance and the relation between God and mankind. The Saviour would be born to Mary and he would be able to overcome the curse of sin. Mary's peculiar position in the holy story raises the question at which moment she was freed from original sin: was it at the Annunciation, in her mother's womb, or before that at her conception?

In the course of the 15th century the discussion became focussed on the last two possibilities and as a result Anne's position came to take on more importance. The 'maculists', of whom the Dominicans were the most prominent representatives, held the view that Mary certainly was conceived in sin, but that she was cleansed of original sin in her mother's womb.The 'immaculists', including inter alia the Franciscans, Carmelites and Carthusians, took the contrary position and believed that Mary was unblemished from the very moment of her conception.

In addition to theological opinions with regard to the immaculate conception of Mary, attitudes to marriage and sexuality also played a part in establishing this image. The Church agreed with Paul and the Fathers of the

Master of the family of St Anne (Ghent, end 15th century) *The Holy Family with St Anne and St Joachim*, panel, Museum voor Schone Kunsten, Doornik.

Church in not permitting any doubt that the state of marriage was of a lower order of perfection than virginity. Marriage was seen more as a remedy against excessive sensuality than as an end in itself. The purpose of sexuality is to produce children who are to be brought up according to the teachings of Christ. The satisfaction of desire was regarded as a sin even within marriage. The full motivation of Emerentiana's marriage and of Anne's three marriages accorded with the Church's view of the meaning of marriage. Emerentiana and Anne chose their husbands as the result of a divine instruction. Moreover, the author makes it clear that a chaste relationship can also exist within marriage.[20] It should be noted that the Church did not only concern itself with marriage and sexuality, family and upbringing. As has been argued elsewhere in this book there was social concern about the meaning of marriage and particularly about the position of women within it.

Anne's three marriages
Van Denemarken presents the events in the life of Anne and Joachim in the same way that we can read about them in historical accounts of the birth of Mary. Van Denemarken had to consult other sources for information about Anne's other two marriages. According to him he was given information by a priest who knew the details of Anne's life. He himself offers the explanation for her following two marriages that she knew she was fertile and calculates that even after having been infertile for twenty years she was still easily able to have three children. When Anne observes she is no longer fertile she doesn't think it 'seemly', nor honest, nor godly to enter into further marriages. Afterwards she remains a widow and Jan van Denemarken emphasizes St Anne's virtues once again: she was happy alone, cared for the poor, taught children, was industrious, gentle, patient, obedient and chaste. In short, she was the opposite of all the (older) women who fill literature and drama as exponents of arrogance and sensuousness in the late Middle Ages.

Van Denemarken raises his finger as a warning to women who marry not to serve God or bear children but only from 'lusts of the flesh'. They will bitterly regret their lust in the hereafter says the writer.

The extent to which Anne's three marriages occupy a central position in *Die historie, die ghetiden ende die exemplen vander heyligher vrouwen Sint Annen* is evident from the structure of the historical section. All three of Anne's marriages are discussed, with the author continually defending Anne's decision to marry. Every argument that might place Anne in a bad light is refuted in advance.

We also find this tendency in the 'moral examples', [hereafter referred to simply as 'examples'].[21] In the first of these, 'of a devout virgin who didn't want to serve St Anne', we encounter a pious, diligent woman who refuses to venerate St Anne because of her three marriages. She sees an impressive gathering of important people in a vision in the centre of which there is an extremely distinguished woman who completely disregards her. The woman appears to be St Anne, who later visits her and explains that the holy family could never have come about had she not entered into marriage three times. From that moment the woman is convinced and venerates St Anne above all the other saints.

With an English bishop who comes to oppose the veneration of St Anne in the second example the result is considerably worse. When he sees that the people venerate St Anne with great zeal he forbids their devotion because she married three times. At the moment that he threatens the venerators of St Anne, his horse stumbles and the bishop breaks his neck. The people heave a sigh of relief and from that moment on 'serve' Anne even more zealously than before.

The legend of Anne's three marriages was accepted for centuries without many problems but it appears from the manner in which van Denemarken treats the material that he assumed that the concept had been misinterpreted by his contemporaries. It is evident that some people found the concept of Anne as an (older) woman bent on marriage less acceptable. The Church did not have a positive stance towards remarrying. The reader should

Master Johannes (ca. 1513), triptych: centre panel *Coronation of Mary in the presence of her family*, left-hand panel *Jesse's Dream*, right-hand panel *Family Tree of Hysmeria, St Anne's sister*, O.L. Vrouwe Onbevlekt Ontvangen, Brasschaat.

not draw false conclusions from the story of St Anne. Moreover, van Denemarken's contemporaries were familiar with the satirical representation of 'unequal marriage': the old man who marries a young girl or the old woman who has managed to hook yet another young man.[22] This theme was extremely popular in literature, drama and the pictorial arts. It was not inconceivable that Anne, who remarried *twice* at an older age, could be associated with the unchaste older woman who is still hunting for a husband. The defensive note in the representation of Anne's three marriages can possibly be traced back to this.

In *Die historie van Sint-Anna* far less attention is paid to the three marriages although the previously mentioned examples about it are included. In this edition, which contains an extensive collection of examples in which it is shown that Anne offered particular protection to married people, promoted fertility and growth and knew how to convert poverty into material prosperity, we also find an example about a young widow who would almost have been abducted had Anne not intervened at the very last moment. This woman has been twice widowed by her eighteenth year and decides to marry once again 'if it please God in veneration of the holy woman St Anne who also had three husbands'. She vows that were she to become a widow a third time she would remain a widow forever but her third husband also dies when she is twenty. A new suitor speedily presents himself. The young woman rejects his suit because of her vow. The suitor decides to abduct her with the help of some friends but just at the moment that he wants to lay hands on her the young woman calls on St Anne and a devout woman appears with a large crowd of followers. The attackers take flight. They are arrested and sentenced to death. Anne prevails upon the young widow to beg for mercy for them nevertheless. The attackers are pardoned and repent.[23]

This miracle illustrates once again that the example of St Anne should not lead to an unrestricted drive towards marriage. She remains an inspiring example of a Christian life of modesty and a defence of the ideal of chastity for widows.

Anne and her children's upbringing

In connection with the birth of Mary Cleophas and Mary Salomas, Jan van Denemarken discusses the tasks that parents have in bringing up their children. The aspect of upbringing could not be raised in the discussion of Mary's youth because it was unanimously accepted that she was free of personal sin: thus it was not necessary to add anything. The possibility did exist, however, in the case of Anne's other two daughters. Anne brought her children up with great honour and virtue. Jan van Denemarken addresses himself to all parents via this example:

'All good parents, both father and mother, should follow her example in bringing up their children in virtue and teaching them to believe in the holy Christ. They should also know how to experience the blessedness of their souls.' He further laments 'Where do we still find good parents who teach their children as they should?'

With reference to the birth of Mary Salomas, van Denemarken reiterates his position that parents must give their children a Christian upbringing but he adds that they must also impart manners, chastity, devotion and virtuousness. Mary Salomas and her parents continuously set the example of eschewing evil and doing good according to van Denemarken. In these passages he is particularly clear about St Anne's role in setting an example in parent-child relationships, although he does not elaborate his moral commentary further. In his view the principal duty of parents is to educate their children in Christian doctrine but he reports that qualities such as good manners and decency, modesty and devotion are directly connected with this doctrine. On the basis of these statements we cannot contend that Jan van Denemarken was explicitly concerned with young people or refers to the upbringing of young children in general. His remarks are marginalia to his story of the life of

St Anne. However, it is precisely here that van Denemarken reveals his concern for everyday life and the possible exemplary function that the story of St Anne can have for particular groups.[24]

III. PIETER DORLANT AS A PROPAGANDIST OF DEVOTION TO ST ANNE

Pieter Dorlant (1454–1507)

The Carthusian Pieter Dorlant or Petrus Dorlandus of Zelem near Diest brings us into contact with the learned world of Christian humanists at the end of the 15th century. We have little information about the man himself but there is an extensive list (from the 16th century) of his writings. He wrote most of his works in Latin. He only wrote three in the vernacular, namely the lives of St Anne, St Joseph and St Catherine.[25]

Pieter Dorlant concerned himself intensively with spreading devotion to St Anne. He wrote two lives of St Anne, one in Latin and one in the vernacular and was involved in the edition of a third work on this subject. His work *Historia perpulchra de Anna sanctissima* appeared in Antwerp in about 1490.[26] A second biography by his hand, *Historie van Sinte Anna, moeder Marie* (Antwerp, 1501), appeared some ten years later and this time in the vernacular, although it is not a translation of the first work. Considering the repeated address to 'sisters', this text must have been intended for nuns. As a result of this Middle Dutch *Historie van Sinte Anna* being translated into Latin and included in a new edition of *Vita Jhesu Christi* by Ludolph of Saxony (Paris, 1502), this text about St Anne received extremely wide distribution.

The third edition with which Dorlant was involved is the *Legendae Sanctae Annae*, which appeared in Louvain in 1497 and was a great success, particularly in Germany. Translations of this text were also made into the vernacular.[27] Nevertheless, Pieter Dorlant was not the only person behind this edition. Dominicus van Gelre from Aachen, the Dominican reformer of Dominican monasteries including those in 's-Hertogenbosch, Maastricht, Louvain and Antwerp shared responsibility for the *Legenda*. He was known to be a zealous venerator of St Anne and was in addition involved in spreading devotion to the rosary, which had been forcefully propagated from Cologne by the Dominicans since 1475. With the rosary, the faithful also literally have in their hands something by which they can practice their faith. This devotion was highly successful. Thousands of men and women were members of the Brotherhood of the Rosary.[28] A detailed description of the Brotherhood of the Rosary in Cologne is included in Dorlant's *Historia perpulchra* and the *Legenda sanctae Annae*. A powerful driving force behind this brotherhood was the Dominican Jacobus Sprenger, one of the authors of the *Malleus Maleficarum* which is dealt with in detail elsewhere in this book. In these turbulent times it is evident that it was thought desirable to motivate the masses towards a more intensive religious life and that Dorlant was also involved in these developments.

Pieter Dorlant and his depiction of the life of St Anne

The details of the life of St Anne in Dorlant's works correspond to a great extent with those in *Die historie, die ghetiden ende die exemplen van Sint-Annen* by Jan van Denemarken. We are given concise information about Anne's parents, her three marriages and her virtuous life. In addition we encounter some examples in Dorlant from van Denemarken's first work. The principal difference is nevertheless that Dorlant places the Anne, Mary and Jesus motif in a more central position. He elucidates the life of St Anne with regard to her strong ties with Mary and Christ. We also find this tendency in *Die historie van Sint Anna* in Wouter Bor's translation although in this case the biography takes on the form of an adventure story. Dorlant does not only tell St Anne's story, but also that of Mary, Joseph and the Child Jesus. In contrast to van Denemarken he represents Joseph as an impotent old 'sap'. He reports emphatically that all Joseph's desire had vanished. The wedding guests find that rather 'a pity' for such an attractive young woman. This representation fits in with the tradition perfectly.

Dorlant also begins with the description of the vision on Mount Carmel. In his Middle Dutch history we encounter a new variant. This time the tree has a particularly beautiful branch with three twigs. The beautiful branch once again symbolizes Anne while the three twigs symbolize the three daughters produced by her three marriages. In just the same way as Jan van Denemarken, Dorlant goes to great pains to defend St Anne's three marriages. Initially she wants to remain a widow he says, and that is entirely in accordance with the will of God. However, an angel proclaims that Anne should marry again. That is to say she should bear still more fruit to the glory of God. This is why she remarries even despite her advanced years according to Dorlant. He points to examples from the Old Testament such as Sarah and Rebecca. He is remorselessly critical of those people who dare to cast doubt on Anne's holiness. In his opinion this results from their own depravity. His principal argument for Anne's three marriages is that Anne belongs among the women of the Old Testament to whom other laws applied.

The choice of the moral examples concerning the three marriages does not differ from those in *Die historie, die ghetiden ende die exemplen van Sint-Annen*. Both the woman who doubts Anne's integrity but nevertheless becomes converted, as well as the headstrong bishop from England serve as examples in establishing Anne's sanctity and power and in bringing unbelievers to repentance. The extent of Anne's power is evident mainly at the end of the story. When Christ has conquered the devil and has ascended into heaven he is seated with His grandmother Anne on the throne. Joachim is seated in the background. Mary is still on earth although she desires to be in heaven. The trinity of Anne, Mary and Jesus has fallen apart but Anne begs her Grandson for a speedy reunification, which follows a short time afterwards.

Now Anne, Mary and Jesus are seated on the throne in heaven. The entire celestial population do them homage and it is obvious, according to Dorlant, that these three would stand steadfastly by any worshipper in difficulty on earth who turned to them for help. The earthly trinity has been transported to heaven. Anne still occupies a special place among this trinity which gives her almost unlimited power as a result of her alliance with Mary and Jesus. In contrast to Christ's divine lineage, which is represented patrilineally, namely from Father to Son, Anne incorporates the earthly lineage down the female line, (Emerentiana) – Anne – Mary in this representation.

Pieter Dorland and the Christian Humanists
In 1502 the humanist and printer Judocus (Josse) Badius Ascensius (1461/62-1535) from Asse (near Brussels) and his friend J. Clichtowe published a *Vita Jhesu Christi* by the 14th century Carthusian Ludolph of Saxony.[29] The life of Jesus is represented here in one story based on the four Gospels. Badius added a Latin summary of Dorlant's Middle Dutch life of Anne. As the third volume of the edition, there follows a series of odes and hymns in honour of Anne and Joachim written by humanists who occupied a prominent place in the Low Countries and the Rhineland. There are contributions by the Benedictine abbot Johannes Trithemius (1462-1516) of Sponheim, Robert Gaguin (1433-1502) General of the Trinity College of St Mathurin in Paris, the Carmelite Johannes Oudewater or Paleonydorus of Malines, who worked in Mainz and Frankfurt-am-Main, Sebastian Brant, author of the famous *Narrenschiff* (1494), Judocus Badius himself and many others.[30]

The poems originated as a result of the activities of the Ghent Carmelite Arnold Bostius or Arnold van Vaernewijck (1455-1499).[31] He occupies a key position in the network of intellectual relationships among Christian humanists in Europe. He maintained contact with Baptista of Mantua in North Italy, with Erasmus who wrote a poem on Anne at the request of Bostius, with Robert Gaguin and J. Badius in Paris and Johannes Trithemius in Germany. Bostius devoted a lot of space to study but although his work was influenced by the rediscovered principles of classical composition, the religious and moral aspects were more important than the aesthetic and literary ones. Bostius was well known as a zealous venerator of St Anne but at the same time he pleads for the veneration of her husband Joachim. In order to win supporters for the veneration of Joachim, Bostius organized a poetry competition in Windesheimer and Carthusian and Carmelite monasteries in 1497. Many learned friends of Bostius also took part in the competition. Badius included a selection of these poems and hymns in his edition and also added a rosary.

Moreover, Bostius was a defender of the view that Mary was immaculately conceived. He was supported in this by many of the friends we have already mentioned. This is particularly true of Johannes Trithemius, who had a great deal of influence on his circle of acquaintants. Trithemius enjoyed great fame as an all-round scholar. He studied Greek and Hebrew writings, was a theologian, historian and physician as well as being well up in the occult.[32] In the course of time he built up an impressive library which attracted many visitors. He was also a fervent venerator of St Anne. In this devotion he saw the means par excellence of protecting mankind in the chilly world of moral decay and moral uncertainty. He came into contact with many scholars in Western Europe through his old friend Bostius. As a result of his great authority Trithemius was consulted about the reality of the danger of witches by the Elector of Brandenburg and Emperor Maximilian.[33] In his opinions and publications he presents himself as a follower of the doctrine on the existence of modern witches. Just as they were for Sprenger, for him witches were repugnant partners of the devil, and the complete antithesis therefore of female saints, particularly of Mary and her mother Anne.

Thus we see that Pieter Dorlant's work is part of a complex whole of activities at the end of the 15th century in which piety, theological disputes, attempts at reforming the Church and monasteries and involvement in social development cannot be separated from each other.

IV. DEVOTION TO ST ANNE IN PRACTICE AND IN PICTURES

The Brotherhood of St Anne in Frankfurt

The Christian humanists were not only active in spreading the veneration of St Anne in their words and writings. They were sometimes quite directly involved in practical devotion. The Brotherhood of St Anne met in the Carmelite monastery in Frankfurt-am-Main at regular intervals.[34] Through this brotherhood we meet a number of important representatives of Christian humanism and come into contact with a specific group of venerators of St Anne.

The Carmelite monastery included various brotherhoods, but that of St Anne was the most notable. Mainly foreign merchants from countries including Switzerland, France, and the Low Countries were members of this brotherhood. They visited the famous Frankfurt Trade Fair in autumn and spring in order to forge commercial contacts. The Carmelites also frequently busied themselves with the spiritual care of foreign merchants in other cities. In Bruges, for example, Hanseatic merchants met in the Carmelite monastery for a long time.[35] The Anne brotherhood in Frankfurt was first recorded in 1479. Two years later the prior of the monastery, Rumold von Laupach, drew up a charter which was only officially ratified by the Archbishop of Mainz in 1493. Pope Innocent VIII had already given his consent in 1491.

The year 1493 was significant for this brotherhood because they also acquired a valuable relic, part of Anne's arm, which had for a long time been kept in the Benedictine monastery in Lyon. Repeated requests by Rumold von Laupach, the endeavours of friends (Trithemius?) and the city governors of Frankfurt were ultimately successful in that year. A document from 1493 provides us with further details. According to the author of this document there was nowhere that the relic could more honourably be lodged than in the Carmelite monastery. The precursors of the 'Brothers of Our Dear Lady' or Carmelites had known Anne when she was still

Anonymous master (Brussels, end of 15th century), *The legend of St Anne*, retable with sixteen pictures, Stadtgeschichtliches Museum, Frankfurt-am-Main, Inner left-hand wing, second picture: *The visit of Anne and her parents to Mount Carmel.*

alive and Anne's mother, Emerentiana, had frequently visited them on Mount Carmel. The document continues, 'We further deem that it would be of great value if the fruitful tree that has produced such abundant, beneficial fruit should be venerated on a richer, larger scale. Several things have sprouted from this tree: not only the wood of so many apostles and saints but also a branch from which the Son of Justice has sprung without the seed of a man; and it is therefore quite clear that there are no relics of a human body on earth that are closer to the body of our Saviour and His mother Mary than that of the Holy Mother Anne.'[36] It is further reported that a number of Dutch merchants, supported by Jacobus Badius Ascensius, who was known as the 'artium magister', were involved in the transfer of the relic. In this period Badius worked in J. Trechsel's printing works in Lyon. The document goes on to mention among other people Herman Bloumenberger of Antwerp, Jacobus vanden Voorde of Brussels, Herman Faber and Rumold vanden Dorpe of Malines.

A second significant event for the Brotherhood of St Anne was the publication in Mainz in 1494 of Trithemius' *Tractatus de laudibus sanctissimae Matris Annae* which he dedicated to the brotherhood in Frankfurt.[37] The tract was rather provocative as a result of the openly expressed opinion concerning the immaculate conception at a time when arguments about it were still raging. Nevertheless the work of Trithemius bears the character of pious literature rather than theological writing. We discover a tendency in the work of the abbot of Sponheim similar to that in the texts of Jan van Denemarken and Pieter Dorlant. The devotion to St Anne served as a means of deepening religious life and uplifting the masses morally. Thus Trithemius emphasizes the virtuous life of St Anne as a guideline for men and women. Day and night she reflects on God's commandments; her faith is strong and her life holy; her life is characterized by good works, she is careful in her choice of companions and humble before God.

Nevertheless she is above all an example for women. She was never seen on the streets or carrying on idle conversations with the neighbours. She never danced or went to the theatre. From her youth she had learned to stay at home and to work diligently. Just as in the texts of Jan van Denemarken and Pieter Dorlant, Anne appears as the positive antithesis of feminine anger. She brings up her daughters as an exemplary mother in the literal sense of the word. Anne's power as the mother of Mary and grandmother of Jesus is almost unlimited. Mary and Jesus would never deny her anything she asked for, says Trithemius. She protects her venerators against illness, defamation and poverty, protects a good name and snuffs out 'lust of the flesh'. (She prevents a person's blushing!)[38]

To sum up, we can say that Trithemius seized hold of the veneration of St Anne in order to inspire people to more piety, to spread his theological ideas (about the immaculate conception among other things) and to present Anne's life as a means of improving the morals of men and above all of women.

The altarpiece in the Carmelite monastery

In 1501 the Brotherhood of St Anne concluded an official agreement with the Carmelite monastery in which mutual rights and duties were formulated. In the same document reference is made to sixteen pictures which Rumold von Laupach commissioned from a master in Brussels as an altarpiece for the Brotherhood of St Anne.[39] The sixteen pictures show the story of St Anne for the most part in accordance with what we know from the works discussed here.

The retable consists of two wings each containing eight pictures, with four on the inside and four on the outside. On the inner side of the left-hand wing there are pictures of the family tree of Anne's sister Hysmeria (with St Servatius occupying a central position); Stollanus, Emerentiana, and Anne on Mount Carmel (the relationship with the Carmelites); and the engagement of Anne and Joachim and their wedding. On the inner side of the right-hand wing there are pictures of the virtuous life of Anne and Joachim and scenes of the birth and youth of Mary.

Outer right-hand wing, fourth picture: *St Bridget recording the vision she has of the angel.*

Inner left-hand wing, second picture: *The engagement of Joachim and Anne.*

When the wings are closed we can see the special position occupied by Anne in the holy story: the vision of Mount Carmel, the immaculate conception of Mary in the womb, Anne and her powerful progeny from her three marriages. Further we can see other pictures illustrating Anne's holy position and power, amongst others a number of miracles and finally a picture of St Bridget of Sweden, who has visions of St Anne and her family.

From our point of view two pictures deserve particular attention: the engagement and the wedding of Joachim and Anne. We observe that the story of Emerentiana in which suitors were selected on the grounds of chastity is now applied to the life of St Anne. In the first picture we see a diabolic figure who kills the other suitors while Anne and Joachim clasp each other's hands and while Anne's mother Emerentiana and another woman look on. In the second picture we see that the marriage between Joachim and Anne has been consummated in an 'exemplary' way from the point of view of the contemporary spectator. They marry under the law of Moses in the presence of family members and two witnesses. As is argued in the first article of this book, this form of wedding ceremony was more emphatically propagated in the 16th century.

For the members of the brotherhood the pictures could have been of social as well as of religious significance. In the picture of Anne's wedding it is possible to discern the private ideals of a civilly contracted marriage. The pictures could have been inspired by the tract Trithemius wrote for the Brotherhood of St Anne. Nevertheless we cannot point to a direct connection between the text and the pictures. Thus details of the life of St Anne are missing from Trithemius' work; he did not include any moral examples at all.[40] The master from Brussels may nevertheless have known one of the versions of the story of St Anne circulating in the Low Countries, including those by van Denemarken or Dorlant.

The pictures in Bruges and in St Goedele in Brussels

In Frankfurt we were able to determine the relationship between a series of pictures showing the life of St Anne as it were in the form of a 'cartoon strip' and the texts by associates of van Denemarken and Dorlant. However there are two other pictures in the Low Countries from the same period in which we can detect a connection between the texts and the pictures.

On a panel in the Church of St Salvador in Bruges we can discern episodes from the life of Anne and her mother Emerentiana.[41] The picture is unquestionably inspired by the story of St Anne as we know it mainly from the work of van Denemarken and Wouter Bor. In the centre of the picture we can see the birth of St Anne. Surrounding this event the story of Emerentiana and Stollanus is depicted under the name 'Sephora', Emerentiana's home. The story of Joachim and Anne is portrayed under the name 'Nazareth', their home. At the bottom on the left the wedding ceremony of Emerentiana and Stollanus is taking place, the first phase in the fulfillment of the promise that God made on Mount Carmel. We also receive a glimpse of the promise in the panel. In the centre, three midwives show the newly born Anne. Above this scene we can see the wedding ceremony of Anne and Joachim. The whole right-hand side represents the story of Joachim and Anne, including the promise of the birth of Mary, which is given an additional emphasis by the representation of the denial of Joachim's sacrifice as a result of his infertility.

The second picture in which the life of St Anne and her mother Emerentiana are depicted is a triptych by the Master of St Goedele in Brussels.[42] On the two wings we can see family trees while the central panel shows a picture of Anne's family relationships.

On the left-hand panel Emerentiana and the 'Carmelites' are kneeling on either side of a family tree which grows out of Emerentiana. The branches representing Anne and Hysmeria 'grow' on the left and right respectively. Anne and Hysmeria indicate Mary and Jesus, who are at the top of the tree, with a movement of their hands. On either

Inner left-hand wing, third picture: *The wedding of Joachim and Anne.*

117

Anonymous master (Flemish, end of 15th century), *The legend of St Anne*, panel, St-Salvator, Bruges.

Master of St Goedele (South Netherlands, end of 15th century),
The legend of St Anne, triptych, Faculté de Médecine, Paris.

side of Mary and Jesus banners with inscriptions have been unfurled, although unfortunately the text in this picture is indecipherable.

The family tree of St Servatius has been painted on the right-hand panel. At the front, probably the donor of the painting has been portrayed. Seated on the bench we can see Hysmeria with her husband Ephraim, from whom two branches grow up. On the right are Elizabeth and her son John the Baptist, on the left Eliud and his son Elimen. St Servatius is at the top.

The central panel is divided into nine equal parts. In the centre there is an image of Anne, Mary and Jesus surrounded by representations of Anne's three marriages, her children and grandchildren. In the upper left-hand corner we can see Anne and Hysmeria with their parents Emerentiana and Stollanus. Next to this is the rejection of Joachim's sacrifice by the high priest. On the far right there is the encounter of Joachim and Anne at the Golden Gate. Around the image of Anne, Mary and Jesus to the left, right, and beneath it we can see Anne's three marriages and the three Maries who are born as a result. There are respectively Anne and Joachim with Mary the mother of Jesus; Anne and Cleophas with Mary Cleophas; and Anne and Salomas with Mary Salomas. In the lower left-hand corner Alpheus and Mary Cleophas are portrayed standing with their children Jacob the younger, Joseph, Simon and Judas. Below on the right we can see Zebedee and Mary Salomas with their children Jacob the Elder and John the Evangelist.

In this picture we can make out the same subjects as in those in Bruges and Frankfurt: family trees, relationships of Christ's immediate kindred with the inhabitants of Mount Carmel and an interest in marriage. The three marriages of St Anne occupy a central position in this picture. The three marriages represent the core of the Holy Kindred which is augmented in the wings at the side with family trees. What is remarkable here is that the Holy Family is not represented as one large family portrait, but that the family relationships have been broken up into detailed representations.

Comparison between the texts and the pictures in Bruges, Frankfurt and Brussels indicates a clear thematic relationship. As far as the vision is concerned, the picture by the Master of St Goedele corresponds most closely with the family tree described in the introduction to this article. Here we see the root, Emerentiana, with the branches, Anne and Hysmeria, which finally result in the flower, Mary, and the fruit, Jesus.

A search for connections between the circle of Christian humanists who propagated devotion to St Anne and the triptych in Brussels has a surprising result. Johannes Oudewater seems to have been the canon of the church at St Goedele for which the altarpiece was made. As we have already said, Oudewater maintained close contact with Bostius, who belonged to the same order and whom we might regard as one of the great driving forces behind the veneration of St Anne. Oudewater belonged to the extensive circle of friends who were Christian humanists, of whom Badius in Paris was also a member. Thus we have been able to stress the involvement of a group of Christian humanists in the propaganda activities for devotion to St Anne in the Low Countries and the Rhineland.

Connection between images in texts and pictures and the urban middle class
Via the Brotherhood of St Anne in Frankfurt we came into contact with a specific group of venerators, namely merchants from the urban centres in the Low Countries and the Rhineland. The great value the new urban intellectual and prosperous elite placed upon marital fidelity and legally concluded marriage as pillars of social order is referred to elsewhere in this book. Literary products such as farces as well as pictorial art frequently represent the dangers of lust and unchastity via the medium of irony and satire. These show us the 'ludicrousness' of a world in which women want to be dominant and do not know their place. Moralists support this view in their tracts mainly by referring women to an ideal code of behaviour of chastity, modesty and obedience based on

Christian doctrine. Meanwhile men are reminded of their responsibility as head of the family. Anne may serve as a positive example for different groups of venerators by being the ideal model of a spouse, mother and widow fitting into the pattern of norms and values of the urban middle class.[44]

In addition to sermons in church, the ideals were propagated via social institutions such as brotherhoods, citizens' militia, chambers of rhetoric and guilds. At that time the civil authorities also considered themselves responsible for the spiritual and moral attitudes of the populace. The exemplary function of St Anne could have a favourable effect on urban morality as a whole. In many ways she reflected the ideals of the urban middle class.

An important characteristic in the development of individual morality by the prosperous middle class in the 15th century was the aspiration to imitate and adapt existing morals and customs from the world of court and clergy.[45] In the 14th century, wealthy citizens began to 'play knights' by organizing tournaments and assuming knights' names in order to distinguish themselves from the 'rabble'. In the middle of the 16th century the preference for knightly qualities disappeared, that is just at the same time as the Holy Family was fading into the background in circles of the cultural elite. The interest in family trees and representations of the Holy Kinship in the period of approximately 1400 – 1500 could have been influenced by the middle class hankering after symbols from knightly culture, in which lineage played such an important role albeit in an adapted form as regards content.

The original portrayal, which placed Christ in a central position among kings, patriarchs and prophets, corresponded more closely with a courtly monarchist attitude, which was appropriate in a feudal society, while a portrayal including Christ's closest relations corresponded more closely in the case of a bourgeois culture. The middle classes were in search of their own identity and were accordingly interested in matters affecting the home and the family. Lineage is one of the

Bernard Strigel (1460–1528), *Group portrait of Emperor Maximilian and his family*, ca. 1515/1520, panel, Kunsthistorisches Museum, Vienna.

possibilities by which one family can distinguish itself from another. In important cities such as Ulm and Nuremberg the middle classes adorned their tombs and family altars with family tree motifs. Old forms received new content in this.[46] It also occurred that royal and rich middle class families had themselves painted as the Holy Kinship. Emperor Maximilian and his family were immortalized in this way by Bernard Strigel (1515) who portrayed the emperor as Cleophas, Mary of Burgundy as Mary, Mother of Jesus, Philip the Fair as Jacob the Younger, Charles V as Simon and Ferdinand as Joseph the Righteous. After 1558, when the veneration of St Anne was losing popularity, their names were painted over with the real names of the royal family. The Holy Kinship was painted on the other side to avoid any misunderstanding.[47]

The extent of the interest in family trees at the end of the 15th century can be seen from the warning in Brant's *Narrenschiff*:

'To pride themselves on lineage and power is the prerogative of great, but foolish families' (cap. 71).

The author exhorts the reader to reject the fashion of having oneself portrayed as a 'noble' family, because true nobility lies in the heart, not in a family tree.

'Foolish are they who think themselves superior because of their lineage and nobility. What good is it if one paints or draws or sculpts one's ancestors as the family of God? Why should one say that one is descended from nobility if one lives dishonourably and corruptly before these pictures?'

Before summarizing his warnings in rhyme he repeats:

'The one who flaunts his lineage and his friends flaunts something that is not his.'[48]

These are the last growing pains of a popular subject. In the course of the 16th century the family tree for the most part disappeared and was replaced by more domestic tableaux.

Increasing criticism of the three marriages

In the texts and pictures the emphasis lies on the three marriages of St Anne. Around 1500 there was continuously increasing criticism of the three marriages by scholars. In 1517 the famous Parisian scholar Lefèvre d'Etaples attempted to prove that Anne had only been married once and had only had one daughter, Mary the mother of Christ.[49] The result was a storm of protest. Many supporters from Franciscan, Carmelite and Dominican circles defended St Anne's three marriages and in so doing stress how sensitive the subject was at this time.

Luther maintained a moderate position in the affair. He disapproved of the disputes being pursued in such detail in public. In his opinion the legend of the three marriages should not be so mercilessly denounced: the feelings of the masses who venerated Anne intensely should be taken into account. The veneration did not spring from a desire for money as was the case when it came to many other devotions according to Luther, but sprang from inner piety.[50] This remark proves once again how popular the veneration of St Anne was in this period. It certainly did not arise as a result of propaganda activities on the part of Christian humanists and others although they could indeed have strengthened the devotion.

Three causes have been cited to explain the increasing criticism of the three marriages.[51] First, the increasing critical attitude as a characteristic of the humanists has been mentioned; a better exegesis of the parts in the Bible referring to Christ's relatives may have contributed to the criticism of Anne's 'large' family. The criticism arising in Protestant circles directed at the entire question of the veneration of saints was even more vehement. The most important factor in the disappearance of the three marriages from the legend of St Anne can however be seen as the influence of the immaculate conception of Mary. The notion that Mary had two other stepsisters became more and more frequently regarded as indecent. It was not considered proper that the mother of the immaculate virgin married three times and gave birth to two daughters after Mary.

Although the last explanation may have had an influence in the course of the 16th century it does not hold for the period around 1500. Neither the opponents of the immaculate conception such as the Dominicans, nor the supporters of it challenged the three marriages considering their concerted propaganda for the veneration of St Anne and her family. They paid a great deal of attention to family trees and the Holy Family without any reservations.

V. RECAPITULATION

In the above we established that the veneration of the Holy Mother Anne flourished at the end of the 15th century. Our aim was to analyze the connection between the images in a number of contemporary texts describing the life of St Anne and her family as well as the developments in the society from which these texts arose. The images have many facets. Anne is represented as a dedicated wife and mother, as a chaste widow, and a powerful grandmother surrounded by her children and grandchildren. She is a model of chastity and virtue even though she married several times.

The period in which the devotion to Anne thrived was characterized by great social change. The nobility were losing more and more power to a new elite, the urban middle class, which had other ideas about the organization of the ideal society. Moralizing, writing which is frequently satirical and pictures accompany the process of change in the outlook of this period and in so doing stress the 'new' virtues.

The question is to what extent devotional texts could also make a contribution here. In around 1500 we can see an increase in the veneration of St Anne. This increase is directly connected with ideas about marriage, sexuality, home and family in a number of devotional writings. On the other hand this period reveals changes in marital morality. These changes were connected with new bourgeois attitudes to the value and place of marriage and the family in society. The propagandists of the veneration of St Anne included a circle of Christian humanists in the Low Countries and the Rhineland who were not only

Master of Varsseveld (ca. 1480), *Anne, Mary and Child*, oak woodcarving, Frauenhaus, Goch.

interested in theological questions such as the conception of Mary and Anne but reveal themselves to be also concerned about the social situation in religious, political and other social areas. Many of them supported movements of reform in the Church and the monasteries and regarded the veneration of St Anne as a useful means of protecting mankind against increasing corruption. Some propagandists also concerned themselves with questions in social areas, for instance Trithemius in the case of 'the danger of witches' and Sebastian Brant on moral decline in general.

By means of the material in the texts and the pictures associated with them we are brought into contact with a specific group of venerators in the urban centres in the Low Countries and the Rhineland, namely merchants who were members of the Brotherhood of St Anne in Frankfurt-am-Main. The exemplary function which St Anne represented for this group cannot be traced exactly. Merchants nevertheless represent the urban elite. Anne could have inspired them to more fervent piety but in addition other aspects of the picture could also have played a part. Anne could convert poverty into material prosperity; she enhanced one's respect and guaranteed success in business. In this regard she corresponded closely with the ideals of the urban middle classes. In addition Anne fitted in well with middle class attitudes to marriage, the family and the place of women. Anne could serve as a model for the education of young girls; she protected the chastity of widows and gave wives and mothers a model of how a woman's life should be modest and submissive.

However it was not only an intellectual and materially prosperous elite that felt attracted to the veneration of St Anne. Anne represented virtue in many areas and for the most diverse groups. Any group could find its own ideals in her depending on its particular frame of reference. Thus she could inspire monks and nuns as well as married couples, both intellectuals as well as the illiterate. Anne's power had many sides: she helped girls wanting to marry to find a husband, promoted fertility and growth, was patron of housewives, married couples, mothers, mothers-to-be and widows, although she was also the guardian of celibates, whom she supported in their attempts at sexual abstinence.

Among the masses there was a great need to venerate St Anne, as Luther remarked. This observation is supported by the many expressions in popular art. Jan van Denemarken also points to a great interest in the veneration of St Anne. In his edition of *Die historie, Die ghetiden ende die exemplen van Sint-Annen* he says that he published the book because so many people asked him for more details about the life of St Anne and because they wanted to have practical instructions for their devotion. The preference for St Anne should not surprise us. As a powerful mother she could offer relief at a time of great hardship. Her prayers had considerable influence because of her family connections. Her intercession was manifoldly augmented by Mary, Jesus and all her other children and grandchildren. Preachers such as Jacobus Sprenger, Dominicus van Gelre and Jan van Denemarken repeatedly emphasize this function of St Anne. In the course of the 16th century the devotion to St Anne became less pronounced in the cities. This depreciation was naturally accompanied by a general critical attitude with regard to the veneration of saints. Changing attitudes to marriage, family and the place of women also played a part in this. A powerful grandmother was perhaps no longer suited to a middle class ideal, in which all attention was directed at the male. The particular danger of older women is referred to elsewhere in this book. The concept of an old woman wanting to get married was regarded as unfitting. Thus the representation of St Anne shifted slowly in the direction of a loving mother instructing her daughter. Instead of the picture of the extended Holy Family with Anne as the radiant centre, attention became placed completely on the Holy Family of Mary, Joseph and the Child Jesus (or Anne, Joachim and Mary). This image corresponded particularly well with the attitudes concerning the ideal family model held by the urban upper class in this period.[52]

1. See *Die historie, die ghetiden ende die exemplen vander heyliger vrouwen sint Annen*, Antwerp 1491, 1493, 1496, 1497 (twice).
2. I refer to some editions and manuscripts from the Netherlands around 1500: a. See note 1; b. *Legenda sanctae Emerencianae* (Koninklijke Bibliotheek Brussels 4837, fol. 122r–167r); *Die historie van die heilige moeder santa anna ende van haer olders daer si van geboren is (. . .)*, hereafter referred to as *Die historie van Sint-Anna*, Zwolle 1499, translated by Wouter Bor; c. *Legende van sunte Anna moder Emerencianen ende vander heiliger vrouwen sunte Anna* (Koninklijke Bibliotheek Brussels IV 383, fol. 33r–155v) anonymous translation of b(!). *Leven van St Joachim (en Anna)*, manuscript II, Koninklijke Bibliotheek Brussels. *Historie of dat leven mit die geslechten der glorioser heiliger vrouwen Santa Anna*, manuscript, Bonnefantenmuseum, Maastricht. *Historia perpulchra de Anna sanctissima*, Petrus Dorlandus, Antwerp ca. 1500. We also find this text in the Ghent University Library, h.s. 895, fol. 60v–110r. See too my dissertation: *Sint-Anna en haar familie. Een verkennende studie naar achtergronden van de moeder- en maagschapcultus in de Lage Landen en het Rijnland in de late Middeleeuwen*, dissertation, Catholic University of Nijmegen, 1982.
3. F. Falck, *Die Druckkunst im Dienste der Kirche zunächst in Deutschland, bis zum Jahre 1520*, Cologne, 1879; see also: *Gesamtkatalog der Wiegendrücke*, Leipzig, 1925.
4. See inter alia Réau, *Iconographie de l'art chrétien*, Paris 1955–1959; J. Lafontaine-Dosogne, *Iconographie de l'enfance de la vierge dans l'empire byzantin et en occident*, Académie Royale de Belgique, classe des Beaux-Arts, I, Brussels 1964, II, Brussels 1965. 7; Mâle.E. *L'Art religieux de la fin du moyen âge en France*, Paris, 1929.
5. J. Habets 'Chronijk der Landen van Overmaas en der aangrenzende gewesten, door eenen inwoner van Beek bij Maastricht' in *Publications de la société Historique et Archéologique dans le duché de Limbourg 7* (1870), 101–108.
6. See E. Gatz 'Die Dürener Annaverehrung bis zum Ende des 18. Jahrhunderts' in *St-Anna in Düren*, Mönchengladbach 1972, 161–191.
7. *Acta Sanctorum Bollandiana Julii*, VI, Brussels 1868; E. Schaumkell *Der Kultus der H.-Anna am Ausgang des Mittelalters*, Freiburg/Leipzig 1893; P. V. Charland *Madame saincte Anne et son culte au moyen âge*, I, Paris 1911, II, Paris 1913, III, Quebec 1921; Beda Kleinschmidt *Die heilige Anna, ihre Verehrung in Geschichte, Kunst und Volkstum* Düsseldorf 1930; Lène Dresen-Coenders, 'Machtige grootmoeder, duivelse heks. Speurtocht naar de samenhang tussen heksenvervolging en de verering van de grote moeder Anna aan het begin van de moderne tijd' in *Jeugd en samenleving 3/4* (1975). Also in *Vrouw, Man, Kind, Lijnen van vroeger naar nu*, Baarn 1978.
8. See for example *Tijdschrift voor sociale geschiedenis 10* (1984) with the theme 'Literature as a source for social history'. M. Jeay, Sexuality and family in fifteenth century France, are "literary sources a mask or a mirror?" In: *Journal of family history*, 4 (1979) 328–345.
9. R. Aigrain, *L'hagiographie. Ses sources, ses méthodes, son histoire*, Paris 1953; P. Delehaye *Les Légendes hagiographiques*, Brussels 1927; B. de Gaiffier, 'Hagiographie et historiographie. Quelques aspects des problèmes' in *La storiographia altomedievale*, I. Spoleto 1970; J. le Goff, 'Les mentalités' in *Faire de l'histoire*, III, Paris 1974, 76–94; A. Vauchez, *La sainteté en Occident aux derniers siècles du Moyen Age d'après les procès de canonisation et les documents hagiographiques*, Rome 1981.
10. Gospel of the birth of Mary (in the *Legenda Aurea*); Pseudo Gospel according to Matthew; Proto Gospel according to Jacob (sequence according to the most frequently used source in the texts studied here). See for example *The apocryphal New Testament*, ed. M. R. James, Oxford 1955.
11. M. Förster 'Die Legende vom Trinubium der hl. Anna' in *Probleme der englischen Sprache und Kultur. Festschrift J. Hoops zum 60. Geburtstag*, Heidelberg 1925, 105–130; G. Albert 'La légende des trois mariages de sainte Anne' in *Etudes d'Histoire littéraire doctrinale du XIIIe siècle*, Paris 1932, 166 et seq; P. C. Boeren, *La légende de Passecrate et la Sainte Parenté*, Amsterdam 1976; B. de Gaiffier 'Le trinubium Annae' in *Analecta Bollandiana* 90 (1972), 289–298.
12. See inter alia: P. C. Boeren *Jocundus, Biographe de Saint Servais*, The Hague 1972; A. M. Koldeweij *Der gude Sente Servas*, Assen 1985.
    The family tree appears as follows:
    Stollanus X Emerentiana: 2 daughters – Anne and Hysmeria.
    Anne X Joachim: daughter – Mary.
        X Cleophas: daughter – Mary Cleophas X Alpheus: 4 sons – James the Less (Minor), Simon, Joseph the First (or Barnabas), Jude.
        X Salomas: daughter – Mary Salomas X Zebedeus: 2 sons – James the Greater (Major), John the Evangelist.
    Hysmeria X Ephraim: daughter – Elizabeth X Zachariah: son John the Baptist.
            son – Eluid X Emerentia: son Enim X Memelia: son Servatius.
13. A. Ampe is credited with having 'discovered' the author Jan van Denemarken. See his extensive studies under the title 'Philips van Meron en Jan van Denemarken' in *Ons Geestelijk Erf* (1976–1980); A. Ampe 'Jan van Denemarkens processiespel' in *Handelingen Kon. Zuidned. Maatschappij voor Taal – en Letterkunde en Geschiedenis* 32 (1978), 5–19.
14. H. Pleÿ, *Jozef als pantoffelheld* in *Symposium* III (1981).
15. For the argumentation see A. Ampe in *Ons Geestelijk Erf*, 1980, 113–157.
16. See *Ons Geestelijk Erf*, 1979, 1980 where Ampe gives a summary of the editions of this text until well into the 19th century. It is noteworthy that this text was initially popular in cultural centres and in the circle of modern devotees but 'disappeared' in the course of the next centuries to country areas and school editions. This development thus parallels that of other sorts of literature such as novels for instance, which were first popular with the urban elite and only later 'appeared' in the country. See also V. A. de la Montagne 'Schoolboeken te Antwerp, 17th century' in *Tijdschrift voor Boek en Bibliotheekwezen* 5 (1907), 23–35.
17. On family trees see inter alia A. Watson *The early Iconography of the tree of Jesse* London 1934; R. Ligtenberg 'De genealogie van

Christus. . .' in *Oudheidkundig Jaarboek* 9 (1929), 3–54; M. Lindgren-Fridell 'Der Stammbaum Maria aus Anna und Joachim' in *Marburger Jahrbuch für Kunstwissenschaft* II (1938/1939), 289–308.

18. The parallel with the Book of Tobias is clear here. Through his chastity and virtue Tobias was able to vanquish the devil. As a result he was able to marry Sarah. Previously the devil had killed seven of Sarah's suitors, all of whom were motivated by lust. Tobias began his marriage with mutual prayer and abstinence. For the relationship between Tobias' exemplary function and the danger of witches/example of a 'chaste' Christian marriage see Lène Dresen-Coenders *Het verbond van heks en duivel. Een waandenkbeeld aan het begin van de moderne tijd als symptoom van een veranderende situatie van de vrouw en als middel tot hervorming der zeden* Baarn 1983, 116, 176. (See article in this book)

19. See my dissertation (note 2) chapter 3.5; J. Gallot 'L'imaculée conception' in *Marie, études sur la Sainte Vierge 7* (1964); *Dictionnaire de Théologie Catholique* VII Paris 1922, col. 845–1218.

20. See the parallel with Tobias, note 18.

21. Cf. the discussion of [moral] examples in the article by Ellen Muller in this book.

22. Alison G. Stewart *Unequal lovers. A study of unequal couples in Northern Art*. New York, 1977.

23. The moral example probably illustrates the possibility for young widows to preserve their chastity with the help of St Anne. The example of abduction can indicate a familiar situation. References to this can for example be found in judicial archives. See also A. Weiler 'De intrede van rijke weduwen en arme meisjes in de leefgemeenschappen van de Moderne Devotie' in, *Geert Grote en de Moderne Devotie*, Nijmegen 1985 (congress anthology).

24. There has been a great deal of discussion about the historical significance of the word 'jeugd' (youth, young people). See particularly the study of Ph. Ariès *L'Enfant et la vie familiale sous l'ancien régime*, Paris 1960. English transl: *Centuries of Childhood. A social history of family life*. New York 1962, 1973.³ In the Netherlands H. F. M. Peeters *Kind en jeugdige in het begin van de moderne tijd*, Hilversum/Antwerp 1966; St Ozment, *When fathers ruled. Family life in Reformation Europe* Cambridge (Mass) 1983; L. Stone, *The family, sex and marriage in England 1500–1800*. London 1977. Jan van Denemarken pays hardly any attention at all to the child. He places Christian upbringing, modesty and honesty in the most important position.

25. Andreas Andriesz. van Amsterdam *De enormi proprietas monachorum vitio dialogus*, Louvain 1513; H. J. J. Scholtens 'De Kartuizer Petrus Dorlandus en de Elcherlycproblemen' in *Ons Geestelijk Erf* 9 (1935), 194–195.

26. See note 2.

27. See A. Ampe 'Petrus Dorlandus en Dominicus van Gelre O.P.' in *Hellinga Festschrift*, Amsterdam 1980, 29–42.

28. *500 Jahre Rosenkranz 1475. Kunst und Frömmigkeit im Spätmittelalter und ihr Weiterleben*, Erzbisschöfliches Diözesan-Museum, Cologne 1975.

29. P. Renouard, *Bibliographie d'impressions de Josse Bade Ascensius, imprimeur et humaniste (1462–1535)*, Paris 1908.

30. See A. Renaudet *Préréformé et humanisme à Paris pendant les premières guerres d'Italie (1494–1517)*, Paris 1916; J. P. Massaut *Josse Clichtove, l'Humanisme et la Réforme du clergé*, Paris 1968, 261 et seq.

31. B. Zimmerman, 'Les Carmes humanistes 1465-1525' in *Études Carmelitaines*, 1935, 19–93.

32. K. Arnold, *Joh, Trithemius (1465–1516)*, Würzburg 1971, 104 et seq.; Kleinschmidt, op. cit. 152.

33. Dresen-Coenders, *Het verbond van heks en duivel*, op. cit. 141.

34. C. Martini, *Der Deutsche Karmel*, Bamberg 1922, 143.

35. J. M. A. Beuken, *De Hanze en Vlaanderen*, Maastricht 1950, 38.

36. See H. H. Kock, *Das Karmelitenkloster zu Frankfurt am Main (13th to 16th century)*, Frankfurt-am-Main 1912.

37. Discussion of the contents of this work may be found inter alia in Schaumkell op. cit. For discussion of the immaculate conception see Arnold op. cit., 104 et seq.; P. Cl. Schmitt, 'La controverse Allemande de l'immaculée conception, l'intervention et le procès de Wigant Wirt O.P. (1494–1513) in *Archivum Franciscanum Historicum*, 1952, 379–450.

38. See Schaumkell op. cit.

39. G. de Tervarent, 'Le retable de saincte Anne au musée de Francfort' in *Les énigmes de l'art du Moyen Age*, Paris 1941, 31–46.

40. From fear of not being taken seriously in his circle of intellectual friends; see Arnold op. cit. Yet Trithemius did publish the miracles in 1512.

41. G. de Tervarent, 'Sur un tableau du musée Saint-Sauveur à Bruges' in *Revue belge d'archéologie et d'historie de l'art* 6 (1936), 301–303.

42. See Lejeune op. cit.

43. With thanks to Prof. Dr Herman Pleij who introduced me to the activities of Johannes Oudewater in Brussels, Herman Pleij is engaged on an extensive investigation of the publishers list of Thomas van der Noot. See his *De wereld volgens Thomas van der Noot*, Muiderberg 1982.

44. H. Pleij, *Het gilde van de Blauwe Schuit. Literatuur, volksfeest en burgermoraal in de late middeleeuwen*, Amsterdam 1979.

45. Idem, Afterword to the second printing, Amsterdam 1984.

46. See Lindgren-Fridell op. cit.

47. See Kleinschmidt op. cit. 158–159.

48. Ed. L. Geeraerdts, Middelburg 1981. The chapter also appears in the original edition of 1494. *The Ship of Fools* transl. Edwin H. Zeydel, New York, 1944. See chapter 76, 'Of great boasting'.

49. See Kleinschmidt op. cit. 260.

50. See Dresen-Coenders, 'Machtige grootmoeder. . .' op. cit. 44–78.

51. See Kleinschmidt op. cit. 252–260.

52. In addition to a shift of interest to the representation of the Holy Family we find an increasing preference for the veneration of St Joseph in the 16th century. Jan van Denemarken had already made a plea for the representation of a 'dignified' image of Joseph in art and literature. He himself wrote a *Leven van St Josef*. See Ampe in *Ons Geestelijk Erf*, op. cit. Bostius propagated the veneration of Anne's husband, Joachim. The developments corresponded well with the ideal representation of the man/woman relationship in this period. See Kathleen M. Davies', The sacred condition of equality. How original were puritan 'doctrines of marriage?' In: *Social History (2)* (1977) 1. 563–580.

Jan Baegert (1465–ca. 1530), *The Holy Family*, panel,
Landesmuseum fur Kunst und Kulturgeschichte, Münster.

Hans Liefrinck after Jan Swart (c. 1500–1560), *Salome's dance*,
etching on metal.

ELLEN MULLER, JEANNE MARIE NOËL

Humanist views on art and morality

Theory and image

'A white rose swiftly fades…a single breath of wind is sufficient to ruin its bloom.'
Did the 16th century artist illustrate religious and moralising themes in such a way that the viewer really understood the message? In the first section of this article it will be shown that some of the moralists had their – theoretical – doubts about this. The question is whether the practice of painting in the first half of the 16th century justified this agitation. In the second section we shall enquire into this with the aid of portrayals of three famous, exemplary women.

I. 'THE PICTURE SPEAKS ALTHOUGH IT IS MUTE'. * THEORETICIANS ON THE EXPRESSIVE POWER OF THE IMAGE

The views of a perturbed moralist

'Aristotle considers unchaste paintings and images so pernicious for morals, that he would have the legislators take measures against it in the form of public regulations, so that there should not be any pictures in the towns which could arouse dissolute thoughts. The tongue speaks to the ear, illustrations speak to the eye, and are more eloquent than language, for they often penetrate more deeply into the heart of man (. . .) What must I say of the licentiousness which we perceive (at the present time) in statues and paintings? What is portrayed and exposed for all to see is too shameful to be called by name (. .) Oh, how these matters are neglected by the legislators and their laws! Let us thank God that we have a faith which is not tainted by impurity and unchastity. All the greater is the sin of those who give a shameful content to subjects which are chaste by nature. Why is it necessary to portray every story in the churches? A young man and a girl lying in bed? David looking out of the window at Bathsheba and tempting her into adultery? The same king embracing the Shunamite woman? Or the daughter of Herodias during her dance? It is true that all these subjects are derived from the Holy Scriptures, but when they depict woman, how ingeniously do not the painters incorporate dissoluteness therein? And yet one sees paintings of this kind on altars during the celebration of the Eucharist, even though they are so unchaste that an honourable man should not tolerate them in his own home.'[1]

Desiderius Erasmus is the author of this tirade against the artistic fashion of his time, which prescribed that sensually stimulating portrayals of the lusts of the flesh should even hang in the house of God, on the pretext that they served to illustrate the stories from the Bible and to bring to mind the punishment which attended the sin depicted. The passage is to be found in the section of the *Institutio Matrimonii Christiani* (Of Christian marriage, 1526), in which Erasmus expounds the principles upon which the upbringing of young girls should be based. A genuine love of chastity should be imprinted on the young mind in all possible ways. The girl, who is weak by nature, oversensitive to impressions and influences, and moreover dependent for her future on the opinion which people have of her morals, must be protected even more than a boy against everything which can sully her soul. Unchaste portrayals of bodies and human passions already form a danger for men, but for women doubly so; thus these portrayals must be removed from public buildings and private apartments, for 'a picture speaks, albeit mute, and slowly but surely gains a hold on men's souls'.

This text about modern painting is preceded by a passage in which Erasmus sets forth his views on the notion 'immoral language' (turpiloquium).[2] This passage appears to comprise more than a short aside on colloquial language, and is placed in such a position that one is obliged to apply the ideas he has elaborated to the lines on painting. Erasmus distinguishes four types of people who are guilty of 'turpiloquium'. The first group speaks openly about matters on which a modest person should only express himself in guarded terms; these are matters which are not evil by nature, but which take on an obscene character when people talk about them in public, as for example the genitals, or the fact that one sleeps with ones lawful wife. The second group talk about unseemly matters in such a way 'that they give the impression of being advocates of vice'; thus one can use the word 'adultery' to indicate the fact, but those who clearly enjoy recounting 'the wiles employed by a woman to deceive her husband' are guilty of shameful behaviour. The third group use chaste words for improprieties, which is even worse than speaking of honourable matters in reprehensible terms. Finally there is the fourth group which talk about carnal misdeeds, 'which it is unseemly that young men and women should ever hear about, unless it is necessary' – and in that case one must clearly express ones disapproval.

Now, what does the modern painter do, who uses a medium which according to Erasmus is 'much more clearly understood than words'? He portrays unclothed bodies. He reproduces things sensual – even sinfully sensual – with a suspicious amount of interest in the subject, with an excess of detail and a degree of technical skill which show how much satisfaction he derives from dealing with this material and how little he bothers to show his abhorrence of evil. And his dangerous creations are not even kept in a private circle, but thanks to art dealers and ecclesiastical patrons are widely distributed.

Furthermore, according to another passage from the *Institutio . . .*, the modern painter adds trivial details to solemn representations: 'In the painting of Jesus, invited for a meal at the house of Mary and Martha,[3] there is a portrayal for instance of the young man John, whilst he is surreptitiously prattling in the corner with Martha; at the same time Peter is emptying a cup of wine; and all that is going on whilst Our Lord is talking to Mary. Or one sees Martha sitting behind John during the meal, with one hand on his shoulder, whilst the other is pointed mockingly at Christ, who does not appear to notice anything. Here too Peter is to be seen with a cup in his hand, flushed from the wine. And blasphemous and sacrilegious as these things may be, there are still many people who derive enjoyment from them. The same rules of propriety apply to painting sacred objects as to talking about them.'[4]

When we read the texts on painting in the *Institutio . . .*, we are bound to conclude that a man like Erasmus, who was greatly concerned about the moral and religious conduct of his contemporaries, was definitely not convinced that the art of his time had a moralising *effect* on the public – though that may perhaps have been the sincere *intention* of the patrons and artists. He even went as far as to doubt their intentions, because he considered that anyone who had his heart in edifying matters would not be capable of producing or possessing an ambiguous representation. The very fact that he would have liked to see art contributing to the atmosphere of virtuousness and piety made him take such a stern attitude towards things he saw, which led him to surmise that they might in the future result in disturbing aesthetic developments. What mattered to Erasmus was that the form in which religious and moralising subjects were presented should be suitably adapted to their edifying message. This implied that the means of expression had humbly to serve the Christian philosophy, even though they had gained strength through renewed contact with classical culture or through the originality of Northern realism.

Those who turned an evangelical scene into a genre painting, who thought they were working in the religious spirit by portraying God as Jupiter and Jesus as Apollo or the Holy Virgin as Diana,[5] who considered that they had depicted adultery in a bad light by realistically reproducing the sinners' lust, all these people had forgotten that the form should be subordinate to the message. The way in which Erasmus advocates a clear-cut division between sacred and profane, between holy and heathen, between moralising and titillating, makes us realise that at that time there was no consensus on the question of how visual amusement should serve instruction; and there is no reason to assume that his opinion was not shared by people whose taste in the realm of art was somewhat traditional.

Erasmus' point of view is in any case characteristic of strict Christian humanism. For instance, there is nothing which he finds more abhorrent than the 'humanistic snobbery from Italy, which he terms 'ciceronianism' and cruelly mocks in a long dialogue (*Dialogus Ciceronianus, 1528*). The ciceronians want to do everything 'à l'antique': they deck their houses out like Roman villas, consider that a Christian picture spoils their tasteful interior and, if they venture on an argument concerning Christian matters, they produce texts which are replicas of the speeches mady by the Roman orator Cicero (106–43 BC), but which do not fit the subject under discussion, are without any love of religion, and are ultimately unsuited to evoking pious emotions amongst the listeners.

But when Erasmus talks about art, he is not merely worried by the inadequacy of the means which are supposed to arouse pious and virtuous thoughts in the public, his principal concern is the damage which can be done to the soul. In spite of the ingenuity of today's scientists, we nevertheless still have no certainty about the effects of the stimuli to which our mind is exposed by the television set in our living room. Thus those who are concerned with our mental health have cause to talk distrustfully of the medium which is so compelling that we can hardly do without it. Comparable suspicion appears also to have existed at the time of the Renaissance with regard to the fine arts, which not only underwent a formal revolution, but also acquired wider distribution thanks to the increasing prosperity in certain circles and the technical progress, such as the invention of printing. It was a development which worried Erasmus: if we are to believe his testimony, the dubious representations were to be seen everywhere, in inns, on the market places, in churches and in dwellings.

In any period the young always occupy a central position in the arguments of those who are concerned about the effects of the media, since youth is thought to be particularly impressionable, and because the young form pre-eminently suitable material, which the architects of the future want to mould themselves. It is therefore not surprising that important remarks by Erasmus on painting are to be found in the pedagogic section of the *Institutio...*, and then, as already mentioned, in the pages on girls. The latter are not only characterised by the general susceptibility which is typical of youth, but they are also subject to the greater impressionability of the female sex.

When the Renaissance pedagogue wants to draw his reader's attention to the powerful effect of visual stimuli, and to the need to be very careful in dealing with them, he uses notions and evidence derived from the 'life sciences' of his time. The artist who makes use of the most advanced techniques in order to depict the very best and the very worst so forcefully that the viewers will be unable to forget it, proceeds from similar assumptions or knowledge about the possibility of influencing the soul. In the same way that a present day draughtsman, who uses an erotic motif in his commercial, will refer to research done by educationalists, psychologists, sociologists, media specialists and others on the 'impact' of these stimuli, but those who find the motif immoral or unsuited to the subject – and thus unenlightening – will refer to such research to demonstrate that the commercial artist is desecrating the soul, and that many people are in danger of becoming the victims of his work.

Very few texts have come down to us from the Renaissance artists themselves and those which have are mostly of a technical nature. We shall therefore have to resort to the dissertations of the worried pedagogues, if we are to understand what the rational certitudes were which formed the basis for the artist's attempt to influence the public by means of exemplary images. The concepts are derived mainly from two sciences: that of rhetoric, which embraces the tactics of pursuing an argument – and the example is an argument which reinforces the plea – and that of medicine, which provides models of the way in which the body receives impressions and passes them on to the soul.

The example in upbringing

The example makes abstract ideas tangible and is more easily remembered than subtle argumentation. From of old it was therefore regarded as an efficient means of instructing the 'simple', i.e. the common people, women and children. The medieval popular sermon, for example, was often a motley string of examples based on a central theme derived from the Bible. The Renaissance moralists attached great importance to the example. At that period, when there was particular interest in man as a concrete being and in the practical aspect of ethics, the stories – which were amassed from the writings of classical moralists, poets or historians, from the Bible, and from the texts of all the authoritative writers – represented many valuable lessons on the numerous aspects of human behaviour. The story, lengthily expounded or referred to in allusions, would be introduced into the argument in order to clarify the idea in an elegant and relaxed manner; and in the choice and variety of the examples the writer's taste and command of literature would be amply demonstrated.

The humanists, who believed that the moral and intellectual upbringing could not begin too early, recommended to those entrusted with the upbringing

South Netherlandish follower of Lucas van Leyden, *Landscape with Lot and his daughters*, second quarter 16th century, panel, Bonnefantenmuseum, Maastricht.

that they should read edifying stories to the young children. Children, who are marked by original sin and who like monkeys imitate everything they see going on around them and easily retain what they accumulate in their still pristine memory, exhibit an unmistakeable inclination to reproduce unseemly gestures, obscene words and nonsensical stories. This creates a particularly heavy responsibility on parents and pedagogues: they must see to it that their own behaviour and the environment – including the interior of the home and of public buildings – do no sully the child's soul. Indeed, they must exert their authority and prestige to imprint on the children the proper values by means of lessons suited to their youth. The humanists unanimously abhorred the gruesome fairy tales told by old women and nurses, the romantic love stories and the violent tales of chivalry. Good stories stimulate the child's moral sense, enrich its knowledge of grammar and its vocabulary and should be suitable for use in enhancing the child's exercises in composition.

Long before the child is capable of giving an ethical definition of virtue and vice, it already knows, thanks to the way in which its tutors extol pious, virtuous and learned persons and censure the godless, disorderly and worldly, that goodness is desirable and evil is repugnant. Since they will later fulfil different roles in society, boys and girls are provided with exemplary stories suited to their sex. No-one has given a more forceful description of the expectations for boys and girls than Juan Luis Vives (1492–1540), a humanist of Spanish origin living in the Low Countries. This disciple of Erasmus writes as follows in his *Institutio Foeminae Christianae* (Of the Christian woman, 1524).[6] The perfect man should be graced by various qualities and accomplishments: wisdom, insight, eloquence, knowledge of political affairs, good judgement, memory; he must do credit to his station in life or be able to practise a profession; he must be just and valiant. If he should fail in some respect, he must not be blamed, provided he possesses other good qualities. But no-one expects the woman to be eloquent or intelligent,

or to have any insight into matters which take place outside the home; or to practise a profession, concern herself with politics, pass judgement or confer benefactions. In short, only one thing is expected of her: that she is chaste and virtuous, for if she is dishonourable, that is as bad as if a man possess not a single good quality.'[7] When the examples of the classical heroines are held up to her, the reader's attention is drawn to the fact that, as a Christian, she should behave herself at least as properly as 'the heathen women, who worshipped the lustful Jupiter and the unchaste Venus, and yet valued chastity more highly than their dearest possession'. One Christian example is accorded a special place by Vives: the Holy Virgin Mary. This perfect maiden found in her spouse 'a guardian of her virginity', and later dedicated her widowhood to godliness.[8]

As long as the examples which the tutors, preachers, scholars or artists used for their edifying intentions were unmistakeably 'positive', the danger of lapsing into immorality and godlessness seemed in principle to be fairly slight. Nevertheless Erasmus considered that certain preachers related gospel events in such detail that it gave the impression that they had been present themselves. And we have already seen that he considered the portrayal of episodes from the life of Christ – example of examples – as if they could provide material for 'genre scenes', as a form of blasphemy. But matters became really complicated when temptation – either because it was succumbed to, or because it was resisted – was an important element in the exemplary story. Children and adolescents should not in any case be able to form a concrete idea of the carnal sins, and it was very much in question as to whether the grown-ups remained unaffected by an all too realistic picture of sensual evil.

There were two great dangers inherent in recounting such examples. The first was that, in order to present virtue in more relief, a detailed picture was painted of vice. In order to arouse abhorrence of adultery, female thirst for revenge and lustful pleasure, the portrayal of the sensual dance of Salomé would be particularly apposite,

DREI GŮT KRISTIN.

S. ELENA   S. BRIGITA . S. ELSBETA.

·H·B·

Hans Burgkmair (1473–1531), *Three good Christians*, 1516, woodcut.

since it is the key moment in a story, whose tragic end is familiar to everyone: the decapitation of John the Baptist. The second danger was that the edifying quality, which a certain example was supposed to have, did not always have the expected effect. Let us take a personality who for the rest forms a positive example, but who has a moral lapse: David for example, model of piety, who was incapable of controlling the sinful passion awakened in him by Bathsheba, and who let himself go to the extent of murdering her husband Uriah. This incident can be used to warn the simple soul that he must arm himself against adulterous thoughts, particularly as he is not as God-fearing as the hero. But one must be careful of this sort of 'a fortiori' argument, for as the 17th century French philosopher Pascal so aptly remarked: the example of Alexander's chastity has stimulated fewer people to practise self-control than the example of his alcoholism has encouraged people to intemperance. It is not shameful not to be as virtuous as Alexander, and it appears to be acceptable if after all one does not misbehave more than he did.'[9]

The expert reasoners realised that the use of exemplary stories could be dangerous. However, this did not alter the fact that they had no doubt whatsoever about the pedagogic value of the exemplary. The artist of that time could rely on the fact that a number of stories were well known in the milieu for which his work was intended. As long as he enabled his public to recognise the example from the motifs and the composition and to comprehend his edifying intention, he could permit himself a certain latitude in portraying the story. He could choose a certain moment in the life of a character, could emphasise a part of a story, and give visual relief to a detail of the scene. What Erasmus wanted was that the painter should be circumspect in the exercise of his free choice and his enlargement of detail. In the same way he did not want the preacher to turn his sermon into a grotesque or suggestive presentation, on the pretext that this was necessary to catch the churchgoers' attention. For in the churches, where one could gaze upon Salomé's dance during the Eucharist, one also ran the risk of hearing preachers who 'portrayed men's sins freely, not to say to their heart's content, and enumerated to a mixed congregation all the monstrous crimes which had come to their ears in the seclusion of the confessional, believing that they were providing an excellent tirade against sin if they simply exclaimed from time to time: 'Where will you end up, miserable sinners? In the devil's arse, with thirty thousand demons, in eternal fire!'

In the *Ecclesiastes*, the treatise which he devoted to preaching, Erasmus expressed himself in no uncertain terms: the portrayal of certain sexual perversities and magic practices down to the last detail amounts to propagating them. Moreover, this means that no account is taken of the children and young girls amongst the public. The preachers were also fond of ranting at the women who dressed themselves expensively and voluptuously in order to attract attention, even in church. They gave exhaustive descriptions of all the plumes, make-up, materials, pleats, trains, and embellished their tirade with all sorts of caustic remarks in order to emphasise how absurd all this is. The result? The elegant listeners, who feel flattered that so much attention is paid to them, 'recount what the preacher has said as a joke at banquets. For the sort of people who like to be portrayed in paintings, also like to be depicted in words (*lingua depingi*)'.[10]

Preachers or artists who, albeit for praiseworthy reasons, try to attract the attention of a public which is not very inclined to exert itself, did their best to portray an exciting picture of human passion and divine deeds. The danger of such a compelling course of action was that the vivid image threatened to become more important than the ideas which it was supposed to serve. Moreover, the portrayal of all kinds of vice or – in religious scenes – of irreverent details would in the long run be experienced as nothing out of the ordinary, whilst it was in fact a source of immoral thoughts. Hence the great concern of the critic Erasmus about the aesthetic development of his time, that is to say about the way in which the moralising

Hans Burgkmair (1473–1531), *Three good Jewesses*, 1516, woodcut.

135

DREI·GVT·HAIDIN

LVCRECIA · VETVRIA · VIRGINIA

Hans Burgkmair (1473-1531), *Three good heathen women*, 1516, woodcut.

and religious message took form.

The influence of the image

The moralists were all the more concerned about images, because they are visual stimuli, and from of old visual stimuli have been attributed with having special effects on man's condition.

The painter could also refer to this traditional point of view, but then for the purpose of proving the excellence of his art. Leonardo da Vinci (1452-1519), for example, writes: 'I once painted a picture with a religious subject and a man fell so deeply in love with the woman depicted that he bought the painting. He wanted to have all the religious motifs removed so that he could kiss the picture to his heart's content without being guilty of blasphemy. But respect overcame his desire and he had the picture removed from his house (...) Others paint erotic scenes with such passion, that the viewers are invited to share in the pleasure. Poetry cannot achieve such an effect.'[11]

In their plea for beginning the upbringing as early as possible and screening everything which could agitate the senses, the pedagogues based their arguments on two traditional explanatory models, which made it possible to understand human receptability to impressions. According to the first model the child's mind was compared to virgin material on which the things perceived make impressions: a waxen surface, for example, on which a seal is impressed, or a new vase which will assume the odour of the first liquid which is poured into it. According to the second model man's relation with his environment is interpreted in a less passive manner. In the corpus which is ascribed to the Greek physician Hippocrates (5th-4th century BC) and which remained authoritative into the 18th century, the individual was characterised by a specific temperament as the result of the way in which the different humors or elements were active in his body. This led to the individual being more attracted to certain representations and certain activities being more akin to him than others. The tutor must make sure that he discerns the nature of his pupil's character and submits him to a life hygiene which curbs detrimental inclinations and allows the beneficial to develop to full advantage. Woman is cold and damp, and therefore weak: she absorbs what has been observed without being able to 'combust' it. In other words, she is more inclined to imitation than men and remembers everything. That is why wrong images are so dangerous for her. Man's constitution is warm and dry, extremely inflammable in youth. Thus it is dangerous to fan the fire, as can be seen from some examples which are often quoted in arguments concerning the power of visual stimuli. Augustine (354–430) liked to refer to the anecdote which Terentius recounted in his drama *Eunuchus* (161 BC) in act III, 5: a boy was seized with great desire when he saw a picture portraying the abduction of Danaë by Jupiter. And Erasmus referred, just before his discussion of the meal at the house of Mary and Martha, to the story mentioned by Pliny the Elder (23–79 AD) in his *Historia Naturalis* (XXXVI, 20) to how a boy left 'traces of his lack of self control' on Praxiteles' Venus of Cnidos.

Just how much importance was attached to the influence of sensory impressions is apparent from the recommendations made by 16th century writers to procreators, pregnant women, nursing mothers and wet nurses. Since Antiquity both the learned and the common people were convinced that whatever occupied the mind of the father during procreation was transmitted to the sperm; that the mother's thoughts affected the foetus via the mother's blood, with which it fed itself; and that this same blood, transformed into milk after the birth, continued to permeate the extremely receptive infant with the thoughts of the nurse. Vives wrote for example: 'Because the power of the imagination is great and has a strong effect on the human body, mothers should take care during pregnancy not to allow their thoughts to wander to things which are ugly, nasty or improper. Further they must avoid places where they run the risk of seeing anything malformed or disfigured, either in its actual form or in a picture.'[12] And elsewhere, in an Italian educational tract, which was well known in Northern humanist circles, one can read the following: 'The procreators must by no means ignore the things which have been revealed and proven by authoritative physicians. The latter say that the procreators must in the first place see that their bedrooms or private chambers do not contain any painted representation of anything which is malformed or monstrous. In the ardour of procreation sight and imagination are endued with exceptional power and intensity. That is why Soranus of Ephesus,[13] a physician referred to by St Augustine, described in a book the remarkable habit of a king of Cyprus, who was totally malformed. Whenever he wanted to fulfil his conjugal duty, he saw that his wife had an elegant and pleasing picture in front of her, which portrayed a man. In this way he hoped that his wife, thanks to the pleasure derived from looking at the picture during their intercourse, would bare children who would resemble the handsome and elegant figure and not their misshapen and monstrous-looking father.'[14]

This last quotation invites us to take a look at a house which is furnished according to the requirements of a Christian humanist. Since inventories of personal art possessions are rare and incomplete, we have had recourse to an imaginary house. It is described – this is not surprising – in a pedagogic text. It is not a tract, but a textbook for young Latin scholars: *Linguae Latinae Exercitatio* ('Exercises in the Latin language, 1539), a series of dialogues by Vives.[15] Two boys are coming home from school, pass a beautiful house and ask if they may look over it. Significant detail: the house is the property of a courtier. Historians have shown that the influence of Italianism on the art of the Low Countries was principally due to the courtiers: they had often enjoyed a humanist education; they considered Southern art as the noble descendant of Greco-Roman Antiquity; they 'secured the services of humanists who were well-disposed to wards the new fashion' and who 'undoubtedly exercised influence on the choice of particular iconographic themes and on the commissioning of particular works of art'.[16]

Master of the Female Half-Figures (South Netherlands, second quarter 16th century), *Lucretia*, panel, Galleria Colonna, Rome.

That the owner of the house subjugated his love of heathen art to his piety, is already evident at the main entrance: the Ancients placed a statue of Hercules at their portal to keep off evil; he wishes to have no other janitor and guardian than Christ. Accompanied by the master builder the boys enter the great downstairs hall, which is decorated with paintings, two of which clearly have an exemplary function. First the suicide of Lucretia, a famous example of heroic female marital fidelity, which we shall come back to later on. This Roman lady committed suicide because she considered rape as a slur on her conjugal fidelity. The accompanying text draws the viewer's attention to the fact that there are few women who worry so much about their chastity as did this heroine. The second picture shows an old man who is sucking at the breast of a young woman. This picture will only evoke moral associations for those who know that it represents a famous example of a child's love. The story of the courageous daughter who daily came to nourish her father, condemned to starve to death and awaiting his sentence in prison, was told by Valerius Maximus (1st century AD) in his book about memorable facts and sayings (*Factorum et Dictorum Memorabilia, IX, 4*). In the accompanying text the father says that he is glad that he had propagated his line, whilst the girl says that she gives less than she has received.

The visitors now reach the first floor. In the dining room there are painted windows, in which three women are portrayed who were very severely tried by their husbands, bore themselves heroically in misfortune, and are thus held up as an example to all women who complain about their life companion. The first is a heroine from more recent literature: Griseldis. The last story in Boccaccio's *Decamerone* was translated into Latin in 1374 and was adapted into a Dutch version in the 15th century. It tells how the modest Griseldis patiently and submissively bore all the humiliations inflicted upon her by her royal husband to test her qualities. The second example is Christian: St Godelieve of Flanders, who was strangled in 1070 by order of her wicked husband, a nobleman. The third example is topical for that time: Catherine of Aragon (1485–1536), to whom Erasmus and Vives dedicated their respective *Institutios*. She was shamefully repudiated by her husband, Henry VIII of England, a few years before the appearance of the *Exercitatio*. The tragedy was thus still fresh in the memory.

The dining room also contains paintings. The first represents Paul, the exemplary disciple of Christ. The second portrays male courage: the Roman Mucius Scevola, who thrusts his hand into the fire in order to prove his unconditional patriotism.[17] The third picture is a clear warning against the dangers of adultery. Homer, depicted as a blind man, is pointing critically in the direction of Helen, Menelaus' adulterous wife, who was the cause of the lengthy war between the Greeks and the Trojans.

The visitors then proceed to the master bedroom. This contains no moralising exemplary portrayals. Instead the Holy Virgin and Christ. And a series of pictures which at first sight seem strange in the bedroom of a Christian married couple: classical examples of manly beauty such as Narcissus, Eurialus, Polyxenos and Adonis. Must we conclude from this that the master of the house was afraid, just as the king of Cyprus had been, about whom Soranus of Ephesus writes, that his countenance would not arouse sufficiently beautiful thoughts in his wife whilst he was fulfilling his conjugal duty?

II. VIRTUE PORTRAYED

A new imagery

From the development of painting in the Low Countries at the time of Erasmus and Vives it is apparent that – moralising – theory and practice were not entirely in keeping with one another. In the period round 1500 under the influence of the Italian Renaissance a number of important developments took place in painting in these areas, both as regards form and content. The painting became emancipated and formed an independent object, in which profane themes, classical and mytho-logical subjects, were reproduced for the first time.[18]

These innovations reached the Low Countries by various paths: the court circles round Philip of Burgundy (1465–1524) and Margaret of Austria (1480–1530) played an important part, if only on account of their international contacts. Both these princely persons had artists in their service who worked according to the new fashion. Thus Philip of Burgundy, later bishop of Utrecht, had his residences in Zeeland, the now vanished castle of Souburg and Duurstede castle in Wijk bij Duurstede, furnished entirely in the Italian style.[19] His household also numbered artists and scholars, including the Nijmegen humanist Gerrit Geldenhouwer and the painter Jan Gossaert of Mabuse.[20] Both travelled in Philip's retinue to Italy. The influence of the Italian masters is clearly visible in Gossaert's work.[21] There were also other artists who made this 'pilgrimage' to Italy; those who stayed at home were able to learn about the innovations from the prints and drawings which the travellers brought back with them.

The nobility and the rich upper middle class, which emulated the taste and status of the nobles, were also at that period beginning to orientate themselves to the newest trends and thus helping to disseminate these ideas. The result was that, in contrast to the medieval tradition, as well as the moralising message a more important place was accorded to aspects which were (sensually) pleasing to the eye. It would appear that in some cases the edifying content was even pushed entirely into the background.

The same phenomenon also occurred in the 'genre' paintings, which often developed from religious representations, whereby the trivial details apparently become the main subject and monopolise the entire surface. Examples of this are themes such as 'Christ's visit to Mary and Martha' and 'The prodigal son with the harlots'. In the first example the religious theme 'disappears' into the background in the kitchen scenes of painters such as Pieter Aertsen (1508–1575) and Joachim Bueckelaer (c. 1530–1573). Opinions are still divided on

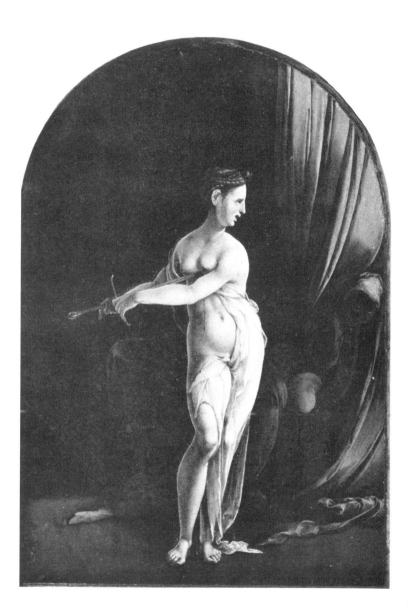

Jan van Scorel (1495-1562), *Lucretia*, panel, Staatliche Museen Preussischer Kulturbesitz, Berlin-Dahlem.

whether this sort of composition was an excuse to depict a profusion of food in an ingenious manner, or whether as an entity it did indeed have a cautionary function. Probably both aspects are present in the paintings, but the interpretation was determined by the buyer.[22] The theme of the 'The prodigal son with the harlots' developed from being part of a cycle, which illustrated the whole parable, into the principal subject, whereby it is not immediately clear to us whether it treats the biblical theme or a random inn or brothel scene.[23]

But if we return to our subject 'the portrayal of virtue', then it appears that in the depiction of exemplary women, we most frequently come across the first mentioned development: the increasing influence of the Italian Renaissance. For a painter who kept abreast of the times this meant learning to reproduce the beauty of the body according to the ideas of the classical artists and after the example of Roman statues excavated at that time. If the expression of this aesthetic ideal made Erasmus question the good intentions of the artist, as far as theory of art was concerned the painter was praised for his very command of form.

The painting by Jan van Scorel (1492-1562) of Lucretia, an outstanding example of chastity, is a good illustration.[24] Here we have a classical subject depicted in Renaissance style by a painter who had worked for some years in Rome. Lucretia is standing naked beside a bed, on the point of stabbing herself. Without any previous knowledge of the history of the Roman lady we, as 20th century viewers, only see a naked, voluptuous woman who is about to commit suicide. In the first instance the scene will certainly not evoke associations with chastity. For the contemporary who knew the story, this representation did indeed have a moralising content. But Erasmus would, as has become apparent earlier on, certainly have condemned such a portrayal of this exemplary woman, whom he highly esteemed. After all, she is standing here with 'naked parts, which you yourself [= reader/viewer] would cover up for the sake of chastity'.[25] And what is even worse, the painter has done this with great skill and attention to detail – as we have seen earlier, also a thorn in the flesh of the moralist Erasmus. In other words, the subject is right, but the portrayal is wrong; Lucretia's nakedness could after all induce in the observer less edifying thoughts and titillate his senses.

Yet here we have an example of the pre-eminent female virtue, *Castitas*, chastity. In their tracts Erasmus and Vives mention many women who are exemplary in this respect. Three of them, who judging by the number of portrayals which have been preserved, must have been very popular, have been chosen for closer examination: the heathen Lucretia, the Old Testament figure of Judith and Mary Magdalene from the New Testament: a married woman, a widow and an unmarried woman.

Lucretia

Both in the official teachings of the Church and also in Christian humanism the notion of chastity occupied an important place. All things considered, female virtues such as moderation, patience and humility all serve to preserve chastity; not for nothing were Lucretia's last words according to Vives: 'What is there left for a woman who has lost her chastity?'[26]

In a long literary tradition, which begins with the Roman authors Livy and Ovid,[27] she is the personification of this so highly esteemed virtue. Lucretia, a scion of a Roman patrician family, is visited in her husband's absence by Sextus Tarquinius, the son of the king. When she refuses to allow him to seduce her and does not yield to his threats, he rapes her. Although Lucretia is not to blame and her family forgive her, she feels that suicide is the only honourable solution.

Lorenzo Lotto's 1553 portrait of a lady makes Lucretia's exemplary function evident in an inventive manner: in her left hand a richly dressed woman holds a drawing depicting Lucretia's suicide. On the table there is a paper with the text: *Nec ulla impudica lucretiae exemplo vivet* (So that through the example of Lucretia not a single immoral woman shall remain in existence).[28]

Over the centuries the reactions to this story have not

Lorenzo Lotto (c. 1480–1554), *Portrait of a lady as Lucretia*, c. 1528, canvas, National Gallery, London.

been exclusively positive. The influential Church Father Augustine (354–430), in his famous book *De civitate Dei* (I, 19), declares himself against suicide; there is after all nothing in the Bible which says that a man may take his own God-given life. The deed is not compatible with the fifth commandment 'Thou shalt not kill', and that is all the plainer, since there is no addition, as there is in the ninth and tenth commandment, of 'thy neighbour'.[29] According to Augustine admiration of Lucretia is out of place, all the more so since he had his doubts about the true motive of her deed.[30] Under such circumstances a clear conscience in God's sight should be sufficient for a Christian woman. Augustine was certainly not the only opponent of suicide, his contemporary Prudentius (348–410) shared his opinion. In his allegorical poem *Psychomachia* (the battle between virtues and vices) he condemned suicide in the struggle between Patience and Anger.[31]

Only in the Renaissance, when the notion of personal honour became a socially accepted norm, could Lucretia serve as a purely positive example. In the developing urban society the notion of honour acquired new significance by emphasising the obligations which were attached to it with regard to society. Boccaccio's book *De casibus virorum illustrium* (Of the vicissitudes of famous men, c. 1360) contributed in particular to the restoration of the classical ideal; certainly not least because the book was soon translated into French and English. In a French version made in about 1415 for Duke John the Fearless the miniatures depict suicides for the first time, including that of Lucretia. Many authors have used the story of Lucretia as a positive example of chastity, also in marriage, including Christine de Pisan in her book *Livre de la cité des dames* (1405), known in the Low Countries in a West Flemish translation of 1475 as *Die lof der vrouwen* (The praise of women).[32] In her refutation of the proposition that women want to be raped, a point of view taken by men, Lucretia is the first who must serve to prove the contrary.[33]

In Italy we come across the theme sporadically, depicted in several scenes on 15th century dowry chests. In the 16th century Lucretia was portrayed with increasing frequency. This popularity is partly to be explained by the interest in the classics, which had been set in train by the humanists, partly by the ideas which were developing about female decorum, in which chastity played a central role. Even the name Lucretia was extremely popular in Italy, with Lucrezia Borgia and Lucrezia d'Este as the best known examples.

In the Netherlands the earliest representations of Lucretia date from the first half of the 16th century, when the theme began to attract interest. Thus the landvogt Margaret of Austria possessed three Lucretias: a statuette made by Conrad Meit, a panel and a relief in wood.[34] The representations of this exemplary woman by Dutch painters show a great resemblance to one another: a half figure against a dark background.[35] Lucretia, shown frontally, is sumptuously attired, with the upper part of the body wholly or partly bare. The differences occur mainly in the facial expression. The moment which the painters and engravers most frequently portray is that at which Lucretia plunges the sword into her breast. The story is condensed into this one moment, in which the essential point, the chastity of Lucretia, is proved by her heroic deed. In this way Lucretia is not only a symbol of, but also a martyr for chastity. She is as it were represented as a secularised saint, without a narrative context, her only distinguishing mark being her attribute, the sword. Captions such as *Lucretia Romana* and the phrase *satius est mori quam indecore vivere* (it is better to die than to live in dishonour) reaffirm the moralistic message of the representation.

Although the theme came from Italy, notably Florence, few Dutch artists of the first half of the 16th century appear to have imitated the Italian manner of portrayal – a standing, usually naked figure with loosely fluttering veil – in contrast to German artists such as Dürer and Cranach.[36] Amongst those who did do this in the Low Countries were Jan Gossaert and Jan van Scorel. The painting by Van Scorel discussed above is interesting for various reasons; it was painted on the back of a panel with the portrait of a man. Taking into account the use of such paintings as an engagement or wedding present, the man depicted is probably expressing himself pictorially on the qualities of the woman whom he desires to marry.

As far as prints are concerned, the Lucretia of Israhel van Meckenem (died 1503) is one of the earliest examples. Lucas van Leyden followed the Italian example by depicting Lucretia standing and entirely naked.[37] We scarcely come across any narrative series of this theme in prints. Lucretia does, however, form part of a series of 'the nine Worthy Women' in a late Christian version. The theme dates from the 13th century and shows nine men, or, from the 14th century onwards, as a pendant, nine women who personify the medieval chivalric ideal. The series with Lucretia, which Hans Burgkmair was the first to depict in 1516, shows three heathen women, Lucretia, Veturia and Virginia, three Jewish women, Esther, Judith and Jael, and three Christian women, the saints Helen, Bridget and Elizabeth of Hungary. These women together personify the ideals of upbringing as expressed by the Christian humanists, namely: *Castitas* (chastity), *Virtus* (virtuousness) and *Sanctitas* (sanctity).[38]

Judith

As simple as is the iconography of Lucretia, so complex is that of the chaste and virtuous widow Judith, the principal character in the apocryphal book of the Bible named after her. Not until the Council of Trent (1545-1564) was the book declared canonical. Luther included the apocryphal books Tobias and Judith in his Bible translation of 1534, with the comment that though these books do not possess the value of the Holy Books, they are very useful to read.

Judith is a rich and beautiful widow, who lives a retired life in the city of Bethulia. During the siege of this city by the Assyrian army under the command of Holofernes she went to the enemy camp where, on the pretext of being a defector, she was admitted to Holofernes. The latter, impressed by her wisdom and beauty, allows her to stay in

Master of the Holy Blood (Bruges, first quarter 16th century), *Lucretia*, panel, Szépmüvészeti Múzeum, Budapest.

143

Jan Massys (Antwerp, c. 1531–1575), *Judith with the head of Holofernes*, panel, Museum of Fine Arts, Boston.

the camp. Some days later he gives a banquet to which he also invites Judith. After the festive meal is over she remains behind alone with a drunken Holofernes. She takes his sword and beheads him. When she is back in the city, Judith shows the people the head of Holofernes with the words: 'The Lord our God has killed him by the hand of a woman.'[39] The Assyrian army, now without its captain, was put to flight and defeated.

Of the many virtues which Judith possesses, there are two which are to the fore: humility (Humilitas), with which she sees herself as the instrument of God's hand, and her retired, irreproachable life as a chaste widow (Castitas, Continentia). Both in the sacredly tinted and also in the profane literature of the period before the 16th century the figure of Judith is frequently to be found. This is due in the first place to medieval typology. Judith's victory over Holofernes is seen as a prefiguration in the Old Testament of Mary's victory over the devil. Thus Judith, just as Esther and Jael, is associated with Mary, based on the idea that a concordance exists between the Old and New Testament. From the 13th century onwards the figure of Judith gained ever greater significance through the flourishing veneration of the Virgin Mary. Sermons and statues in churches also made the necessary contribution.

Another reason for her popularity was the frequent occurrence of her story in moralising literature. The moralising import of these texts was illustrated with examples. Thus Judith was represented in religious works as one of the examples of Christian piety, patience, devotion to duty and courage. Writings of a more profane nature present Judith as an example of a virtuous and chaste way of life. She also serves as an example in the 'battle between virtues and vices', the *Psychomachia* of Prudentius; the struggle between Humilitas (humility) and Superbia (presumptuousness) is illustrated by a portrayal of a scene from the story of Judith and Holofernes.[40] A passage from Christine de Pisan's *Die lof der vrouwen*, in which she speaks of the good which women have brought to the world, although men always maintain the contrary, also fits in with this tradition of allegorical use of the Bible. In that connection the history of Judith is recounted in detail.[41]

But how did people view Judith in the 16th century? It appears that in poetry the theme was still used in the traditional manner, as for instance by Anna Bijns, as an example in a refrein. In the dramatic performances of the chambers of rhetoric, however, the story of Judith was turned into an independent play, whilst of course maintaining its moralising character.[42] The Christian humanists, in particular Erasmus, saw Judith as a widow living in perfect chastity. For Erasmus the chaste Judith represented the realisation of the highest to which a woman could attain. In his book *De vidua christiana* (Of Christian widows) of 1529, dedicated to Mary of Hungary, he used Judith as an example of resolve, chastity and humility.[43] Vives also passed a positive judgment on Judith, but he found it difficult to reconcile her enterprising, martial behaviour with what he considered fitting for a woman.[44]

Up to the end of the 15th century the Judith theme is only to be found in the Low Countries in miniatures in mss. and in woodcuts in books. From the 16th century, representations have survived which formed part of individual series of prints. These series are of a narrative nature and indirectly moralising, through the choice of theme. Where present, captions only refer to the relevant passage from the Bible. There are also separate prints in existence, the production of which got underway at the end of the 15th century. One of the essential scenes from the story is usually depicted: the beheading of Holofernes or Judith with the head of Holofernes, standing victorious on his body at the entrance to the tent. A third possibility is the moment at which she puts the head into the sack which her maid servant holds in readiness. The engraving by Israhel van Meckenhem is an early example of this. On closer inspection we also see in the background a scene depicting the defeat of the Assyrians. This is a common – in effect medieval – practice, to present several scenes on one plane. The crucial moment is given relief by

the addition of the foregoing, in this case the corpse of Holofernes, and by the outcome.

Judith is used not only as an example of virtuousness and chastity, but also as a warning about the power of woman.[45] The moral interpretation can equally well be negative: the seductive woman who fells the man. Although women's wiles, which illustrate the pernicious power of the weaker sex, were fashionable in the 15th and 16th century, we find comparatively few representations of this 'evil' Judith. The virtuous character of the story evidently predominates, which is emphasised by her inclusion in the series of the nine Worthies.[46]

Paintings of Judith are to be found principally in Italy. In the Low Countries she first occurs in the first half of the 16th century in the oeuvres of masters such as Vincent Sellaer, Jan Massys, the Master of the Mansi-Magdalene and Jan Sanders van Hemessen. This was partly due to the renewed interest in the Old Testament in this period.[47] This part of the Bible was also receiving increasing attention as a guideline for everyday life, and was no longer regarded simply as a foreshadowing of the story of Salvation. The Italian influence is clearly evident in the portrayals of Judith, for even though the story, just as with Lucretia, does not in any way call for it, she is usually portrayed naked or near-naked at the moment at which she emerges from the tent with the head. The Master of the Mansi-Magdalene even painted her entirely nude, with the head of Holofernes in one hand and her sword in the other. Next to Judith stands a naked boy with a snake, the youthful Hercules. The significance of Hercules, who usually symbolises the male virtue *Virtus*, is still obscure in this context.[48]

Mary Magdalene

The story of Mary Magdalene has been recorded in a number of medieval anthologies, the best known of which is Jacobus de Voragine's *Legenda Aurea*. This story of a saint is a compilation of biblical data and later additions. The biblical figure of Mary Magdalene, the unspecified sinner in the gospel according to St. Luke, and Mary of

Israhel van Meckenem (died 1503), *Judith & Holofernes*, engraving.

Bethany, the sister of Lazarus, have become one person in the legend: Mary Magdalene. The Western church tradition has always proceeded on this assumption.[49]

Mary, the daughter of rich parents, inherits on her father's death Fort Magdala, from which the name Magdalene is probably derived. Whilst Mary Magdalene abandons herself to the pleasures of life, her sister Martha looks after the family property. As a result of her way of life Mary Magdalene is looked upon by the townspeople as a sinner. When she hears that Jesus is at the house of Simon the Pharisee, she makes her way there. She washes His feet with her tears, dries them with her hair and anoints them with costly ointment. Christ forgives her all her sins, drives seven devils out of her and allows her to stay in His vicinity. When He visits her and her sister Martha at their house, He defends Mary Magdalene to her sister, who reproaches her for laziness, with the words 'Martha, Martha, how thou worriest and art concerned about many things. Only one thing is needful. Mary hath chosen that good part, which shall not be taken away from her.'[50] At the crucifixion Mary Magdalene is also present; together with the two other Maries she anoints Jesus' body and keeps watch by the tomb. After His resurrection Christ appears first, as a gardener, to Mary Magdalene. Thereafter she preached the gospel in Provence, near Marseille, for a number of years; she then withdrew to a grotto near Sainte-Baume, where she lived for thirty years without food and water. But God looked after her; every day angels came and lifted her into the air to hear their music, after which she returned to her cave entirely refreshed and without the slightest need of food.[51]

Mary Magdalene was one of the best loved saints of the Middle Ages and later centuries for people from every station of life. Various reasons are to be adduced for this. Every human being can turn to her, the patron saint of sinners and example for penitents, for she is after all the intercessor with God for all who have sinned and who show remorse. The dramatic nature of her legend also contributed to her popularity. She is described as a beautiful, emotional woman with an adventurous life:

Master of the Mansi-Magdalen (Antwerp, c.1510–1530), *Judith & Hercules*, panel, National Gallery, London.

Ascribed to the Master of the Mansi-Magdalen, *Mary Magdalene*, panel, Anhaltische Gemäldegalerie, Dessau.

from sinner to saint.[52] The importance of the position which Mary Magdalene occupied in medieval life can hardly be overestimated; the enormous amount of written material alone is proof of this. Further confirmation of her popularity is to be found in the foundation of the Order of Magdalen, the Magdalen houses and the many churches and convents which were named after this holy woman.[53]

If we restrict the veneration of Mary Magdalene to the area of the Low Countries and neighbouring areas of Germany, then we see that here her conversion receives the most attention. In the 14th century this part of her life was elaborated into an independent legend, written in Latin, which must have been widely read in view of the numerous 15th century translations into Middle Dutch and Lower Rhenish with titles such as *Van sunte maria magdalena bekeringhe* (Of saint mary magdalene's conversion) and *Van maria magdalenen bekeringhe ende hoe is ghescide* (Of mary magdalene's conversion and how it happened). There is even a 16th century printed version of this legend which has been handed down.[54]

In 1517 the French humanist Lefèvre d'Étaples (c. 1455–1536) wrote a tract on Mary Magdalene in which the question of the three persons came under discussion. Lefèvre maintained that the Mary Magdalene who was venerated by the Church could never have been a sinner and possessed by devils in her earlier life. He urged a splitting up, so that only the pious and chaste Mary Magdalene could be venerated. Since this made an unambiguous interpretation of Mary Magdalene possible, Erasmus was one of his supporters. The tract caused a considerable stir in the ecclesiastical world, the principal effect of which was to give the interest in Mary Magdalene a fresh impetus.[55]

In contrast to Lucretia and Judith, Mary Magdalene does have a long tradition of visual illustration. Her legend provides the explanation: she figures in the life of Christ. It is true that in the Middle Ages there was a certain amount of reserve in depicting scenes which did not occur in the Bible, and certainly where the worldly life of the saint was concerned. She is usually portrayed in scenes from the passion cycle. We also see her as the patron saint of donors and in the Marian context, that is to say with other female saints in a group round the Virgin and Child. In the art of the Low Countries we usually find her as a sumptuously dressed lady with her attribute, a jar of ointment, as her identification. The book which she is sometimes holding is a reference to her contemplative life, 'the good' which she has chosen and which cannot be taken away from her, even by death.

As far as 16th century art is concerned, it is striking that almost exclusively Netherlandish artists, and then not even a great many, took the secular life as their subject. An explanation of this could be the popularity of the said legend about her conversion and the passion plays which were based on it.[56] The best known work of art is Lucas van Leyden's engraving of 1519, entitled 'The dance of Mary Magdalene'. She is to be seen three times in this print: in the foreground with her escort, in the middle distance participating in the hunt, and in the background to the right of the rocks we see her assumption. The latter scene points to her unworldly, contemplative life. It is misleading to think that sinfulness occupies the central place: the fool, far left, appreciates the foolishness of these activities and warns the couple standing next to him, and also those who contemplate this print.[57]

Artists often portrayed Mary Magdalene living a life of contemplation in the grotto in Sainte-Baume. A good example of this traditional representation is the painting by Adriaen Ysenbrant. We see Mary Magdalene in the foreground, demurely dressed, kneeling in prayer, whilst an angel holds a crucifix aloft.[58]

Apart from the representations mentioned above there is also a large group of portrayals of Mary Magdalene, which stand on their own without any narrative context. These panels have in common that the saint is portrayed as a half figure, is dressed according to the fashion of the time and carries her attribute, a jar of ointment. These paintings can be roughly subdivided into two categories: religiously or profanely orientated. In the former group

Lucas van Leyden (1489/94–1533), *The dance of Mary Magdalene*, 1519, engraving.

Mary Magdalene is standing or sitting with her jar of ointment against a mountainous background, which refers to Ste.-Baume. There is also a large group of panels, on which Mary Magdalene is depicted against a dark background and where it appears to be a question of the portrayal of individual persons. It was fashionable at that time for princesses and women of noble birth to have their portraits painted as Mary Magdalene. Unfortunately in most cases we do not know who the ladies are. A well known example is the (supposed) portrait of Isabella of Austria, ascribed to Jan Gossaert.[59] Philip of Burgundy is known to have possessed a painting which represented *'Sinte Marien Magdalena nae een ander vrouken van Mechelen'* (Saint Mary Magdalene after another woman of Malines). It is assumed that it was the portrait of one of his common law wives.[60]

In the profane version Mary Magdalene is seated playing a lute or a clavichord, writing a letter or reading. These paintings give rise to certain questions: do they represent the elegant and transient worldly life of Mary Magdalene, with the jar of ointment as a vague reference to her further life, or do they not represent the saint at all, but are simply 'vanitas' pictures. After all, the jar of ointment is not only the attribute of Mary Magdalene, but also the personification of Luxuria (voluptuousness), where it serves as the symbol of female vanity. And though it is known that the clavichord was very fashionable in court circles in about 1530, musical instruments can also be symbols of frivolity. The lute in particular denotes the much used theme of music as a temptation to love. The texts on the music sheets, in so far as they are decipherable, also point to a 'vanitas' interpretation.[61]

We have seen that both in 16th century literature and also in the visual arts a great deal of attention was paid to a woman's chaste attitude to life. Chastity is the common virtue of Lucretia, Judith and the Magdalen, and representations of these three women thus have a didactic role: their example shows that this is the most important virtue for a woman at all stages of her life. Lucretia, the

Adriaen Ysenbrant (Bruges, c. 1510–1551), *Mary Magdalene*, panel, National Gallery, London.

16th century prototype of the chaste wife, drew far-reaching conclusion from the fact that she had lost her chastity on account of rape. The rich and beautiful Judith, widowed at an early age, did not remarry and led a retired and sober life. Without abandoning her chastity she used her femininity as a weapon in God's hand to save her people. Mary Magdalene's life shows that even after a sinful life it is possible to better ones ways and return to the straight and narrow path. Her chastity gains as it were an extra significance on account of the licentiousness which preceded it.

To what extent the chastity of these women finds expression in the visual arts appears to be a question of interpretation. In this context we must not forget that via Italy not only new themes, but also ideas on the classical ideal of beauty, were adopted and integrated into the existing traditions. The moralistic message was not lost, however, in spite of the often sensual appearance of the images. But seen through the eyes of Erasmus and the like-minded we should regard the paintings in question as an expression of moral deterioration. Anna Bijns also had scruples about likenesses of Lucretia or Venus 'puer moeder naeckt' (absolutely stark naked). It evidently did not occur to the owners that these pictures could influence other people in the wrong way: 'Hoe sÿn sy misraeckt!' (how they have gone astray!)[62]

Judith and in particular Mary Magdalene have an old tradition in the visual arts in which a change takes place in about the 16th century. Both develop from a narrative context into an independent female character with more emphasis on their chastity. In the medieval art of the Low Countries Lucretia was almost unknown. It was not until the 16th century that she became a popular example of chastity there. But she is not the only figure from classical Antiquity who was introduced into the repertoire of images with an updated significance. A host of mythological and other classical figures make their appearance in Netherlandish painting. These 'heathen' figures are legitimised by providing their story with a moralistic interpretation; a tradition which already existed in the Middle Ages.[63] Because these figures are often extremely

Jan Gossaert (?) (1478/-1532), *Mary Magdalene*, panel, Koninklijke Musea voor Schone Kunsten van België, Brussels.

sensually portrayed – according to Renaissance ideals of beauty – it is often difficult for us to recognise the moralistic message, unless our attention is specifically drawn to it by means of the explanatory captions. Thus the distich on the frame of Gossaert's *Venus and Cupid*, painted for Philip of Burgundy, clarifies the 16th century moral for us: 'Shameless son, thou who art wont to titillate men and gods, you who do not spare your mother, cease all this or you will be ruined'.[64] The Roman goddess, portrayed in the nude, keeps her similarly naked son Cupid in check: she is the ideal of pure love which can be sullied by Cupido (Latin for lust).

III. CONCLUSION

About 1525, the same period in which scholars and moralists were urging that religious and classical sources should be treated with respect, there were artists who were allowing their sensual imagination free rein when they portrayed the content of edifying texts which are extremely discreet over physical and erotic details. To us, who are interested in the Renaissance, this situation seems paradoxical, and we can therefore imagine – albeit that we are moved more by ironic amazement than by ethical motives – that the moralist Erasmus cast doubts on the artistic developments of his time. As far as he was concerned, however, there was no question of amused amazement, but of genuine indignation. Painting the chaste Lucretia with bare breasts, presenting the worthy Judith as a half naked woman, portraying a woman who is certainly not yet planning to renounce her frivolous and sinful life and yet has herself depicted as Mary Magdalene: these were all symptoms of an unbridled spirit, of moral hypocrisy with which Erasmus, as an intellectual and moralist, would have had no patience. After all, the examples of Lucretia, Judith or Mary Magdalene were intended to direct women along the chaste path, not to

Master of the Female Half-Figures (South Netherlands, second quarter 16th century), *Mary Magdalene*, panel, Koninklijke Musea voor Schone Kunsten van België, Brussels.

Jan Gossaert (1478/88–1532), *Venus & Cupid*, 1521, panel, Koninklijke Musea voor Schone Kunsten van België, Brussels.

attract their attention to the dangerous enticements of life. 'A white rose swiftly fades. . . a single breath of wind is sufficient to ruin its bloom.'[65]

However, the artists took little notice of the moralists' criticism of their 'unedifying' practices. They were concerned in the first place with the wishes of their patrons and – as professionals – were interested in aesthetic innovations. The case of Albrecht Dürer (1471–1528) is particularly instructive in this respect. As a follower of Luther he had for long been hoping that the great Erasmus would come to the aid of the German reformer in his difficulties. Dürer corresponded with the Rotterdammer, painted his portrait and was praised by Erasmus as a new Apelles.[66] In spite of the respect which Dürer exhibited for the moral and religious struggle which Erasmus and Luther were waging, he could defend other points of view than his masters if it were something concerning his profession. For instance, on the question of whether it was permissable to depict biblical and Christian characters as though they were mythological figures. Disguising holy figures as classical gods was contrary to Erasmus' principle that the form should be subservient to the content: things sacred and things profane, things holy and things heathen, things moralising and things titillating were all mixed up together. Luther bluntly termed the disguise 'prostitution'.[67] And on that particular point the official Catholic philosophers were in agreement with the suspect Erasmus and Luther. But listen to the opinion of the artist Dürer: 'Just as they [the Greek and Roman artists] gave the most beautiful human form to their false god Apollo, we shall use the same proportions to portray our Lord Christ, who was the most handsome man in the world. And just as they used Venus as the most beautiful woman, we shall represent in a chaste manner the same lovely figure as the most pure Virgin Mary, Mother of God. We shall make a Samson of Hercules, and so on with all the other figures.'[68]

In this context we must remember that the copious attention which the artist paid to aesthetics did not necessarily exclude a religious intention, and could even be a means of expressing this intention. In the same way the sensual compositions, to which themes such as the suicide of Lucretia, the beheading of Holofernes by Judith and the life of Mary Magdalene gave rise, could form part of a moralising message. Continuing in the medieval tradition, so too in the 16th century every picture served as instruction and entertainment, albeit the moral aspect was becoming increasingly secularised. The 16th century representations of the theme of 'Lot and his daughters' are a good illustration of this. For though in the foreground the temptation scene is sometimes depicted in an extremely debauched manner, in the background the sinful city of Sodom is always to be seen in flames, serving both as factual detail and also as a warning.[69]

The artistic products which Erasmus condemned did not, however, form the entire artistic output of his time. Certainly in a city such as Antwerp the artistic market offered something for everyone, provided one had enough money to spend. By no means every artist immediately oriented himself to the new influences, or incorporated the new fashions into his style. In short, it was possible to order a traditional altarpiece, with a Holy Kinship or a biblical scene as the subject, painted entirely in the 'old-fashioned' style. The traditional patrons, such as churches, monasteries or brotherhoods were not all eager to have a dancing Salomé or a bathing Bathsheba in their chapels. But then who bought or ordered the works of art which so upset Erasmus? The devotees will often have been people who had been influenced by humanism: nobles, prelates with taste and well-to-do burghers. Thus the humanist Hieronymus Busleyden (1470–1517), councillor of the Great Council of Malines, had his town house decorated with paintings, tapestries and stained glass windows, whose subjects were mainly taken from classical Antiquity.[70]

About 1520 the very prosperous city of Antwerp was the most important mercantile centre of Europe on account of the new route round the Cape and the trade with North and South America. Many artists, including a number from the Northern Netherlands, flocked to the town to study or to establish themselves there. From Antwerp and also from Bruges a great deal of art was exported to other parts of Europe, such as Spain, Portugal and the Baltic countries. Though prosperous, Antwerp was becoming increasingly acquainted with political and religious disturbances, which naturally had repercussions on the artistic climate and the life led by the artists, some of whom left the town as a precaution or under duress. Furthermore, those who believed that they alone had found the true faith, sought all possible points of criticism of their opponents. Not only religious practices and everyday behaviour, but also artistic preferences could be a reason for condemnation.

Erasmus' criticism of the art of his time was by no means an isolated phenomenon in the 16th century. In a sense it may be said that he heralded the various expressions of severe censure, which became manifest when Renaissance art blossomed forth in Europe. The Protestants were convinced that the Catholics were guilty of idolatry, that they worshipped 'rude blocks and dead stones',[71] to which they ascribed quasi-magic powers. They considered that the papist clergy wasted fortunes – which they sometimes amassed in a scandalous manner, such as the sale of indulgences – on the embellishment of ecclesiastical buildings, whilst the offerings of the faithful could be better spent on poor relief and on education.[72] And finally they regarded the paintings in the churches, which in their eyes certainly violated biblical exactitude if they did not actually arouse lust, as irrefutable proof of the depravity into which the Roman Catholic Church had sunk. In 1566 this Protestant condemnation assumed violent form: the Iconoclasm. An incalculable number of works of art were destroyed in the churches and monasteries of the Low Countries.

Erasmus himself was not in agreement with the iconoclasts of his time.[73] He did, on the other hand, express himself very critically about all sorts of abuses in the Church, so critically in fact that the Catholic authorities asked themselves whose side he was really on. He condemned the superstitious folly of the Christians who sought their salvation more in stammering formulas before the belovèd image of a saint, than in praying to Our Lord.[74] He was very much against the luxury which was displayed in Certosa di Pavia, where people went not so much to address themselves to God, as to gaze at a mountain of marble.[75] He also agitated against the unchaste and blasphemous representations which hung in the churches. And yet Erasmus remained faithful to the principles of the Catholic theologians, who, relying on the authority of Gregory the Great, Thomas Aquinas or Bonaventura, justified the use of religious images. As a book for the 'simple', images have an instructive function and stimulate worship. Thus the faithful must have seemly representations put before them, and must learn that images do not possess any magic power, but should be honoured on account of what they represent.

The Protestant action compelled the Roman Catholic Church to react, both against the dissident views, and against the abuses within the Church, which represented a perversion of Catholic principles and played into the hands of their opponents. The Catholic counter-offensive also found support through literature, as for example through Anna Bijns, who advised the Protestants to put their own house in order instead of desecrating the churches:

'That they want to cast the images out of the churches,
That comes from the love of God; it is clearly to be seen
From the images which they place in their rooms,
That is all vileness, with which they strengthen the flesh,
To desire the unchaste works even more,
As if the devil could not tempt them enough.'[76]

The principles of the Counter Reformation were drawn up during the Council of Trent. The prelates who ordered the introduction of censorship of texts and images were principally concerned with stopping the spread of heretical ideas. They therefore expressed themselves in forceful, but succinct terms against the immoral representations which violated the religious sphere.[77] The Iconoclasm, which erupted three years after the conclusion of the Council, rudely drew the attention of Catholic thinkers once again to the problem of images. It is not surprising that the first book in the post-Tridentine spirit which provides an in-depth discussion of the question, *De Picturis et Imaginibus Sacris* (Of Sacred Paintings and Images, 1570), was the work of a Netherlander: Johannes Molanus (or Vermeulen), a theologian of Louvain (1533–1585). In the chapter 'In picturis cavendum esse quidquid ad libidinem provocat' (In paintings one must be careful that there is nothing to arouse lust), Molanus elaborates the brief remarks of the prelates of Trent on the immoral aspect in religious art into an argument against all dissolute portrayals. Since visual impressions have more effect than auditive, as had already been suggested by Horace in his *Ars Poetica*,[78] and since debauchery poisons the Christian conscience, immoral representations are not to be tolerated anywhere and must be forbidden by law. A scholar like Molanus could not pretend that he did not know that at the beginning of the century another author had forcibly expressed this opinion: his fellow countryman Erasmus. And although the Council of Trent had just placed the work of the Rotterdammer on the Index of forbidden literature, Molanus – in order to clarify his own views – quoted the two passages on painting from the *Institutio* to which we referred at the beginning of this article. The theologian does, however, mention that in every other respect the book has rightly been placed on the Index.

*   *Institutio Christiani Matrimonii*, in: *Desiderii Erasmi Opera Omnia*, published by Jean Leclerc (abbr. LB), V, Leiden 1706, col. 716D.

1.   LB, V, col. 719 C.E. References: Aristotle, *Politics*, VII, 17; David and Bathsheba: II Samuel 11, 12; David and the Shunamite woman: I Kings 1, 1–4; Salomé, the daughter of Herodias: Matthew 14, 1–12 and Mark 6, 14–29.

2.   LB, V, col. 718C – 719A.

3.   Luke 10, 38–42.

4.   LB, V, c. 696E.F. It is not clear whether Erasmus had an existing picture in mind. There is, however, a painting by Pieter Aertsen from 1553 to which Erasmus' text could be applicable. See: P.K.F. Moxey, 'Erasmus and the iconography of Pieter Aertsen's Christ in the house of Martha & Mary', in the Boymans-van Beuningen Museum, Rotterdam, in: *Journal of the Warburg and Courtauld Institutes* 34 (1971), 335 ff.

5.   *Dialogus Ciceronianus*, LB, I, col. 991F.

6.   Several French translations of this book already existed when in 1579, on the recommendation of two Antwerp schoolmasters who wanted their confidants to read it, Christophe Plantin put a new edition on the market: *L'Institution de la Femme Chrestienne*. A Netherlandish translation had already appeared in 1554, based on a very unreliable French translation. See further the thesis to be published by J.M. Noël on the schoolmaster Gabriel Meurier (ch. 2). In this article use has been made of the French edition of Plantin (abbr. Vives, *Inst.* Plantin 1579), Museum Plantin-Moretus, Antwerp, no. A 158, and – in order to check the accuracy thereof – the Latin edition of the works of Vives, Basle 1555 (II, 650–756, UB. Utrecht B.fol. 18).

7.   Vives, *Inst.*, Plantin 1579, I, 55–56; on the upbringing of girls: ch. 'De la Virginité' (Of virginity).

8.   Vives, *Inst.*, 1579, I, ch. 'Des vertus de la femme; et des exemples qu'elle devra suivre' (On the virtues of woman; and the examples which she should follow).

9.   Blaise Pascal, *Pensées*, bibliothèque de la Pléiade, 182 (227), 870.

10.   See: *Ecclesiastes*, LB, V, col. 890A – 892A.

11.   *Trattato della pittura*, Codex Urbinas Latinus 1270, Vatican, fol. 13v–14r.

12.   Vives, *Inst.*, Plantin 1579, II, on the married woman; ch. 'De la cure & soin qu'elle doibt avoir de ses enfants' (on the care which she should have for her children), 139.

13.   Author of *Gynaicologia*, 2nd century AD.

14.   Maffeo Vegio, *De Educatione liberorum*, I, ch.2.

15.   Basle edition of 1555, I: *Linguae Latinae Exercitatio, Domus*, 30–31. The authors of this article are preparing a critical edition of the dialogue *Domus*, with an integral translation.

16.   See: D. Roggen, E. Dhanens, 'De humanist Busleyden en de oorsprong van het Italianisme in de Nederlandse kunst', in: *Gentse Bijdragen tot de Kunstgeschiedenis* 13 (1951), 127.

17.   Titus Livius, *Ab urbe condita*, II, ch. 12,13.

18.   W. Krönig, *Der italienische Einfluss in der flämischen Malerei im ersten Drittel des 16.Jahrhunderts. Beiträge zum Beginn der Renaissance in der Malerei der Niederlande*, Würzburg 1936, 4 ff.

19. J.J.B.M.M. Sterk, *Philips van Bourgondië (1465-1524). Bisschop van Utrecht als protagonist van de Renaissance. Zijn leven en maecenaat,* Zutphen 1980, 27, 39.

20. Geldenhouwer wrote of this: 'Philip conferred exceptional favours on outstanding artists, in whatever art you choose, and provided for them in his own residence in a most liberal manner. . .Moreover, he was particularly attached to the tutors of good literature. From amongst their number he had become friendly with Mr Erasmus of Rotterdam, on account of his excellent scholarly works which are well known, and with Joannes Paludanus, tutor of oratory at the University of Louvain.' See: J. Prinsen Lz., *Collectanea van Gerardus Geldenhauer Noviomagus gevolgd door den herdruk van eenige zijner werken,* Amsterdam 1901, 235, 236; quoted in: Sterk, op. cit., 27.

21. *Jan Gossaert genaamd Mabuse,* Rotterdam/Bruges 1965, 15; G. Glück, 'Mabuse and the Development of the Flemish Renaissance', in: *Art Quarterly* 8 (1945), 116-138.

22. H. Buijs, *Voorstellingen van Christus bij Martha en Maria in het 16e-eeuwse keukenstuk,* Master's thesis University of Utrecht, 1984, 78, 79.

23. See: E. Vetter, *Der verlorene Sohn,* Düsseldorf 1955.

24. Berlin, Staatliche Museen Preussischer Kulturbesitz, *Katalog der ausgestellten Gemälde des 13.-18. Jahrhunderts,* Berlin-Dahlem 1975, 397, 398; no. 644B painted about 1530-1535.

25. LB, V, col. 718C-719A.

26. Vives, *Inst.,* Plantin 1579, I, 56-57; Ilja M. Veldman, 'Lessen voor vrouwen. Thema's uit de oudheid in de 16de en 17de eeuwse propaganda voor de christelijke huwelijks-moraal', in: *Kunstlicht,* no. 15 (1985), 4-6.

27. Livius, *Ab urbe condita,* I, 57-58; Ovidius, *Fastii,* II, 761-852; see for the literary tradition: H. Galinsky, *Der Lucretia-Stoff in der Weltliteratur,* Breslau 1932.

28. C. Gould, *The sixteenth-century Italian schools,* London 1975, 137-138, no. 4256 (National Gallery Catalogues). The woman is probably Lucrezia Valier; she married in 1533. To judge by her clothes the picture could have been painted just before or just after her marriage. The text is a quotation from Livy (op.cit., I, 58, 10): 'Nec ulla deinde impudica lucretiae exemplo vivet', or from Boccacio, *De mulieribus claris* (XLVIII,7): 'Nec ulla deinceps impudica, Lucretie vivet exemplo'.

29. For the ten commandments see: Exodus 20, 1-17; Donat de Chapcaurouge, 'Selbstmorddarstellungen des Mittelalters', in: *Zeitschrift für Kunstwissenschaft,* 1960, 135.

30. Augustine suggests that the most important motive for Lucretia was her typically Roman sense of honour, as expressed in her concern for her posthumous reputation.

31. Prudentius, *Psychomachia,* verses 142-161; De Chapeaurouge, op.cit., 136 ff.

32. This 'city' was inhabited by personfications of three virtues, namely, Reason, Sincerity and Justice, and links up as far as the theme is concerned with earlier work of Christine de Pisan, in

which she also joins issue with the anti-feminist tenor of the *Roman de la Rose.*

33. Christine de Pisan, *Livre de la cité des dames,* II, 44,I.

34. Conrad Meit was a German sculptor from Worms, who worked for many years at the court in Malines for Margaret of Austria; see also Glück, op.cit., 134.

35. This type of depiction is very seldom to be found in the Italian and German paintings of the first half of the 16th century; see D. Schubert, Halbfigurige Lucretia-Tafeln der I. Hälfte des 16. Jahrhunderts in den Niederländen, in: *Jahrbuch des kunsthistorischen Institutes der Universität Graz* 6 (1971), 100.

36. A known example was the famous engraving (B.192) after a drawing of Raphael's by Marcantonio Raimondi (c.1480-c.1536) in which Lucretia is portrayed standing, wearing a loose robe which leaves her left shoulder uncovered. See: W. Stechow, 'Lucretiae Statua', in: *Beiträge für G. Swarzenski,* Berlin 1951, 118-119.

37. Engraving by Israhel van Meckenhem (died 1503), (Lehrs IX,8; B.4); engraving by Lucas van Leyden, c. 1519 (B.134).

38. Horst Schroeder, *Der Topos der Nine Worthies im Literatur und bildender Kunst,* Göttingen 1971, ch.4: 'Der Kanon der Nine Worthy Women', 168-174. These women are not 'prudes', but 'three good heathens, three good Jewesses, three good Christians', as stated on the prints.

39. Judith, 16,7.

40. Hans Martin von Erffa, 'Judith-Virtus Virtutum-Maria', in: *Mitteilungen des kunsthistorischen Institutes in Florenz* 14 (1969-70), 460-465.

41. De Pisan, *Livre de la cité des dames,* II,30. I & II,31.1.

42. Anne Marie Musschoot, *Het Judith-thema in de Nederlandse letterkunde,* Ghent 1972, 66-114.

43. Erasmus was in complete agreement with the views of the apostle Paul that a loosely living widow is 'dead while she liveth' (I Tim. 5,6); see also: Elisabeth Schneider, *Das Bild der Frau im Werk des Erasmus von Rotterdam,* Basle 1955, 72,73.

44. Vives, *Inst.,* Plantin 1579,289, ch. 'De se trouver és lieux publiques' (on behaviour in public places). It is noticeable that Vives does not mention Judith in the third part of the *Institutio,* which deals with widows.

45. Susan L. Smith, *'To women's wiles I fell'. The power of women topos and the development of medieval secular art,* Diss.phil. Pennsylvania 1978 (type-script), 15-16 and 354 note 6,7.

46. Representations of Judith and Holofernes as women's wiles are to be found in the decorative arts in particular: love caskets, textiles etc. For Judith as one of 'the three good Jewesses', see: Schroeder, op.cit., 168-174; Adelheid Straten, *Das Judith-Thema in Deutschland im 16. Jahrhundert. Studien zur Ikonographie: Materialien u. Beitr.,* Munich 1983, 46-50.

47. Gina Strumwasser, *Heroes, Heroines and Heroic Tales from the Old Testament. An Iconografic Analysis of the Most Frequently Represented Old Testament Subjects in Netherlandish Painting, c.1430-1570.* Diss. phil. Los Angeles 1979 (type-script), 137-145.

48. M. Davies, *Early Netherlandish School*, London 1968³, 120, no. 4891. (National Gallery Catalogues).

49. Mary Magdalene: Luke 8,2; John 20, 11–18; the sinner: Luke 7, 36–50; Mary, the sister of Martha and Lazarus: John 11, 19 and 12,1–8. See: H. Hansel, *Die Maria-Magdalena-Legende:eine Quellenuntersuchung*, Bottrop i/W 1937, 23–52.

50. Luke 10, 41–42.

51. Jacobus de Voragine, Legenda Aurea, ed. Th. Graesse, Osnabrück 1965³, ch. 90, 407–417.

52. Helen M. Garth, *Saint Mary Magdalene in Medieval Literature*, Baltimore 1950, 98–107.

53. This order was established in Germany in the 13th century. In the Netherlands, for example Amsterdam, there were also institutions of this order for women, wrested from Babylonian slavery, i.e. repentant sinners. About 1500 most of the convents abandoned their original objective and concentrated amongst other things on the education of girls.

54. According to this legend Martha has converted her sister; see: C.G.N. de Vooys, 'De legende "Van Sunte Maria Magdalena Bekeringhe"', in: *Tijdschrift voor Nederlandsche Taal- en Letterkunde*, dl.24, no.16 (1905), 16–44; Hansel, op.cit., 114–127.

55. A. Hufstader, 'Lefèvre d'Etaples and the Magdalen', in: *Studies in the Renaissance* 16 (1969), 31–61.

56. Hansel op.cit., 127.

57. Thea Vignau Wilberg-Schuurman, *Hoofse minne en burgerlijke liefde in de prentkunst rond 1500*, Leiden 1983, 25–26.

58. National Gallery London no. 2585; see: Davies op.cit., 177–178. Robert A. Koch, 'La Sainte-Baume in Flemish landscape painting of the sixteenth century,' *Gazette des Beaux-Arts*, 1965, 273–282.

59. Koninklijke Musea voor Schone Kunsten van België. *Inventariscatalogus van de oude schilderkunst*, Brussels 1984, 123, inv. no. 4341, ascribed to Gossaert. The crowned Y leads to the assumption that this could be a portrait of an Isabella (Ysabeau) of princely blood. The question is whether it portrays Isabella of Austria (1501–1526) or Isabella of Portugal (1503–1539).

60. Sterk, op.cit., 227, 285.

61. C. Harbison, 'Lucas van Leyden, the Magdalen and the Problem of Secularization in early Sixteenth Century Art', in: *Oud Holland* 98 (1984) 124; see also: Marga Janssen, *Maria Magdalena in der abendländischen Kunst. Ikonographie der Heiligen von den Anfängen bis ins 16. Jahrhunderts*, diss. (type-script) Freiburg i/B, 349.

62. 'But that they portray Cupid, with his arrows/Lucretia, Venus or one of her relations/ stark naked in their rooms/ which can easily lead to unchastity/even if every body should be offended/ they take no notice; how they have gone astray.'
from: *Refereinen van Anna Bijns*, ed. W.L. van Helten, Rotterdam 1875, 106.

63. See: J. Seznec, *La Survivance des dieux antiques*, London 1940.

64. 'Nate effrons homines superos que lacessere suet(us) non matri parcis: parcito, ne pereas.' Brussels, Koninklijke Musea voor Schone Kunsten van België. This painting could be exhibited 'speaking' and

'silent', since the outer frame with the text could be removed. Sterk, op.cit., 133–136.

65. Erasmus, *Institutio*, LB, V, col.716D.

66. The Greek artist Apelles was the court painter of Alexander the Great (356–323 BC). During the Renaissance reference was often made to the stories in Pliny's *Naturalis Historia* (Pliny 23–79 AD) about this painter and his patron in order to demonstrate the dignity of painting. Erasmus greatly esteemed Dürer as an artist, witness the fact that he referred to him as 'our Apelles'. Moreover, Dürer is the only artist about whom Erasmus has written. In the well known passage in the *Dialogus de recta latini graecique sermonis pronunciatione* (Dialogue over the correct pronunciation of Latin and Greek, 1528), Erasmus characterises Dürer's mastery, based on the great qualities of Apelles. LB,I, col. 909, special col.928; quoted in: E. Panofsky, 'Erasmus and the visual arts', in: *Journal of the Warburg and Courtauld Institutes* 32 (1969), 220–227.

67. *Luthers Werke, Kritische Gesamtausgabe*, XLIII, Weimar 1912, 668; quoted in: Panofsky, op.cit., 212 note 33.

68. Quotation taken from: K. Lange and F. Fuhse, *Dürers schriftlicher Nachlass*, Halle a.S. 1893, 316, 11.9–17; quoted in: Panofsky, op.cit., 213–214 note 36.

69. Lot and daughters: Genesis 19, 30–38. The story can be interpreted in different ways: as a warning against drunkenness, against women's wiles and against incest. In his *Encomium Matrimonii* (1518) – in praise of marriage – Erasmus uses this incident in the positive sense in order to show how important it is that a good family, which is dying out, should be carried on. See: *Opera Omnia Desiderii Erasmi Roterodami*, 1,5, Amsterdam/Oxford 1975, 416, II. 412–413. The story of Lot and his daughters was seldom depicted in the Middle Ages. In the second quarter of the 16th century it became quite a popular theme for paintings and engravings in the Low Countries. The erotic aspect of the subject may partly explain this. See: Strumwasser, op.cit., 124–129.

70. We can form a picture of the art treasures and the furnishings of Busleyden's house with the aid of his own writings, published and edited by H.De Vocht, *Jerôme De Busleyden, Founder of the Louvain Collegium Trilingue, his life and writings*, Turnhout 1950; quoted in: Roggen, Dhanens, op.cit., 128. This article gives a reconstruction of the interior. A poem of Thomas More's, who was a guest of Busleyden in 1515, is the only one known devoted to this house. Erasmus gives a description of the interior of the house of Canon Johannes Botzheim at Constance. Erasmus finishes his enthusiastic letter with a moralising remark, namely that the owner is much more to be admired than his beautiful house, that the nine Muses and three Graces live more in his heart than in the paintings, more in his character than on the walls. See: Letter to Marcus Laurinus, 1 February 1523; quoted in: Panofsky, op.cit., 206, note 20.

71. 'P. Marnixii, Lord of St Aldegonde, answered the assertion of a Martinist by saying that no one except the high authorities is permitted to cast down images'; in: *Philips van Marnix, Godsdienstige*

en Kerkelijke Geschriften, ed. J.J. van Toorenenberghen, I, The Hague 1871, 27; quoted in: D. Freedberg, 'The Hidden God: image and interdiction in the Netherlands in the sixteenth century', in: *Art History* 5 (1982), 149 note 55.

72. See for instance Luther's sermon on indulgences in *Luthers Werke, Kritische Gesamt Ausgabe*, 1, Weimar 1883, 236, 556, 598; 32 (sermon of 12 March 1522: 'We do God no service, nor is it pleasing to Him if we make an image of Him, and it would be better to give a poor person a guilder than to give God a golden image'; quoted in: Freedberg, op.cit., 150 note 56.

73. He expressed himself very critically over the Iconoclasm in Basle, February 1529. See: Panofsky, op.cit. 207 note 21.

74. Erasmus, *Lof der Zotheid (Praise of Folly)*, Utrecht/Antwerp 1969, 71–73 note 40: 'And they all trust in miracles', and 74–75 note 41: 'A sea of superstition'.

75. *Colloquia (Convivium religiosum)* LB,1,col.685A; see: Panofsky, op.cit., 211 note 31.

76. *Refereinen van Anna Bijns,* op.cit.,118. The same sounds are to be heard in: M. Duncanus (=Donk), *Een Cort Onderscheyt tusschen Godlijcke en Afgodische Beelden*, Antwerp 1579, B iv (r/v): (Why do we not first cleanse our own houses, of which we are the master, of such idols before we sully and desecrate the churches); quoted in: Freedberg, op.cit. 146 note 18.

77. Session XXV, *Decretum De invocatione, veneratione et reliquiis sanctorum et sacris imaginibus, Concilium Generalium Ecclesiae Catholicae Tomus Quartus Pauli V Pont. Max. Auctoritate Editus*, Rome 1612, 284; quoted in: D. Freedberg, 'Johannes Molanus on provocative paintings, De Historia Sanctarum Imaginum et Picturarum, Book II, chapter 42', in: *Journal of the Warburg and Courtauld Institutes* 34 (1971) 238 note 1. We have used the chapter from Molanus' book which was critically edited by Freedberg in the article mentioned, based on the 1594 edition and the subsequent edition.

78. Horace, *Ars Poetica*, II, 180–182.